AF531531

# SIX HUNDRED THOUSAND VILLAGES
## Policy, Planning and Praxis of Rural Development

# SIX HUNDRED THOUSAND VILLAGES

## Policy, Planning and Praxis of Rural Development

A.K. Jain

DISCOVERY PUBLISHING HOUSE PVT. LTD.
NEW DELHI-110 002

*Published by:*
**Tilak Wasan**
**DISCOVERY PUBLISHING HOUSE PVT. LTD.**
4831/24, Prahlad Street, Ansari Road
Darya Ganj, New Delhi-110002 (India)
Phone: +91-11-23279245, 43764432
Fax: +91-11-23253475
E-mail: parul.wasan@gmail.com
info@discoverypublishinggroup.com
web: www.discoverypublishinggroup.com

***First Edition:* 2011**
**ISBN: 978-81-8356-920-0**

***Six Hundred Thousand Villages***
***Policy, Planning and Praxis of Rural Development***



***Printed at:***
Shree Balaji Art Press
Delhi

# Preface

*'One half of our society guzzles aerated beverages while the other has to make do with palm full of muddied water. Our three-way fast-lane of liberalization, privatization and globalization must provide safe pedestrian crossing for the unempowered India.*

***—K.R. Narayanan***

India is an agrarian country with about 72 per cent (about 80 crore) of its population in about 5,75,936 villages, which are largely inhabited by the poor with agriculture as their predominant occupation. Most of them are small and marginal farmers, agricultural labourers, artisans and scheduled castes and scheduled tribes. During 1901 to 2001, the total population of India grew by 431 per cent while the number of people in the urban and rural regions increased by 1106 per cent and 349 per cent respectively. The rural population always outweighed the urban growth but notes a gradual drop as percentage of the total population. A large number of rural people (about 30 crore) are still living below the poverty line and often face the basic problems of survival, viz., job, poverty, hunger, shelter, ill-health and disease. The increasing unemployment in the rural sector and its distress migration are likely to have serious ramifications on India's socio-economic and political balance. Today, we often witness serious contradictions-an aeroplane, a sign of progress and power and a bullock cart dragging in a slushy and deeply rutted kaccha road. We cannot afford to lose the focus of rural areas and make them subservient to the urban life. The major challenges of rural areas today are the eradication of poverty, disease, inequality and providing basic human needs such as, water, roads, medical care, shelter and literacy.

The contribution of rural areas/agriculture in proportion to the urban areas (predominantly secondary and tertiary sectors of economy) had been continually declining. The agricultural methods by and large continue to be traditional with huge inefficiecies in the land resource, fertilisers, water and energy. The most striking paradox in Indian agriculture is that of productivity. India has one the largest cultivable landmass on the planet. Although productivity gains were sustained in the 1990s after the liberalization process began, the yield rates for most crops in India are far below the comparable rates in several other countries. One of the major reasons for the poor yields is inefficient fertilizer and water use and poor cultivation practices, which lead to deficient production. The agriculture sector in India use 85% of the country's available freshwater. However, irrigation efficiency is only 20-25%. In other words, Indian agriculture wastes up to half of the country's fresh water supply. Although from a basin perspective, much of the wasted water is reused, still significant amount of water is wasted primarily due to irrigation inefficiencies. Agriculture accounts for about 27% of the total electricity consumption in India. The consumption is somewhat higher in states like Andhra Pradesh, Gujarat, Madhya Pradesh, Uttar Pradesh, Karanataka and Haryana where agricultural electricity use is between 35-45%. However, sale of this electricity amounts to not more than 5-10% of the state electricity boards' revenues.

The Seventy-third Constitutional Amendment Act has recognized panchyats as institutions of self-government and expanded the jurisdiction of panchayats. Eleventh Schedule of the Constitution of India contains a long list of subjects on which panchayats have jurisdiction. The list has 29 subjects. However, power of panchayats are basically executive in nature and include planning function as well. District Planning Committees in each district and Metropolitan Planning Committees in each metropolitan area have to prepare draft development plans for the area under their jurisdiction by putting together the plans prepared by municipalities and panchayats in the district, and will forward such plans to the state government. They have no control over police and no juidicial role under the new law. Thus, in spite of widening of their jurisdiction in terms of subjects and the recognition as institutions of self-government, panchayats continue to have only developmental functions. Article 243G of the 73$^{rd}$ CAA envisages that PRIs should be developed into institutions of self government. States were expected to take forward the process of democratic decentralization by making suitable provisions followed by further devolution.

In spite of numerous laudable programmes and huge investments, the reality of rural livelihood is rather dismal. There is a continuous distress migration to the cities and most of the villages lack the basic amenities and services, like pucca road, transport, communications, drinking water supply, power, sanitation, healthcare, irrigation facility and jobs for survival and sustenance. The power is concentrated in the hands of few and the village administration is by and large urban-controlled. The concepts of citizen empowerment, participatory governance and decentralization are confined to the seminars and papers. The decision making is often piecemeal disjointed, ad-hoc, motivated and lacks an overall perspective. A lion's share of subsidies is eaten up by the administration/establishment structure and their salaries. The programmers are too many, so are the departments involved in each one of them. There is often overlapping and lack of clarity about the organizations and their accountability. The programmes too often exceed the time and financial allocations and the facilities, including housing, built up by the government bodies have sometimes remain unoccupied.

The rural schemes often suffer from lack of linkages with livelihood, health, amenities and well being needs, ecological orientation and poverty alleviation programmes. The spatial dimension of the program is usually missing. The projects and plans are prepared and implemented by the technical professionals and officials with urban mindset and do not belong to the people. The convergence among Central, State and annual plans/budgets and among regional, district and local/village governance is often missing.

Participatory learning with the target groups provides useful clues towards adopting a 'needs based approach'. The needs of the rural population can be categorized in the following priorities:

1. Survival: Freedom from hunger and malnutrition, food security, agriculture and employment, credit facility.

2. Supportive: Shelter, drinking water supply, power, transport, sanitation, etc.
3. Transformation: Education, literacy, skill development, environment upgradation and access to information.
4. Empowerment: Access to human rights (jobs, food, education, security, equality, etc.), Equal access to resources (including land, finance and services), justice, people's participation in decision making, security, gender equality and freedom from oppressions, etc.

With a little external support the rural poor are often capable of meeting their survival needs. The organized sector has a vital role in helping the rural poor in meeting these needs. The experience indicates that the supportive needs really help the rural poor in climbing up the economic ladder.

The provision of basic services and facilities in the rural context is a major concern. Accordingly the rural amenities and services and the priorities of planning, development and investments should be worked out. Based on participator learning, a network of rural amenities and facilities can be provided keeping in mind the public transport facility, topography and characteristics of potential areas. A system of clustering of the facilities will lead to conceptual hierarchy of rural settlements, such as 'ciies in green field' PURA centres, growth centres, etc. The plans of rural development need to be based upon the critical aspects of community development, funding, administrative reality, equity principle, employment creation, integrated development, poverty alleviation and basic needs provisions. This would lead to the plans which are pro-poor participatory and meaningful for the local rural population and are implementable.

Amartya Sen's seminal ideas on 'Development as Freedom', focus on the increasingly important topic of how development policy can address cultural needs and values in the context of rural deprivation and social exclusion. It provides a practical review of the range of multi-demensional approaches to poverty reduction for rural development. He mentions that 5 freedoms, viz., Political, Economic, Social, Transparency and Security are simultaneously necessary for integrated development.

No plan or program can be successful unless it is tied up with community empowerment and address to the operessive traditions, customs and practices. This means evolving a tactical strategy based of economic inclusion, spatial enablement, social empowerment and technological innovation. The governance system needs to change towards an effective decentralization, devolution and deregulation. The plans and programs should enable the rural people towards transformation of the prevailing image of backwardness, inferiority, oppressions, depressions and that of a poverty stricken, devoid of electricity, water and sanitation and basic amenities.

The book 'Six Hundred Thousand Villages-Policy, Planning and Praxis of Rural Development' looks at these critical issues. It establishes a link between the rural development, policy and programs in a socio-cultural context. It identifies spatial integration and enablement, transparency and an inclusive, sustainable praxis as the crucial elements in the success of policies and programs of rural development. The central theme is that it cannot be imposed on people but must be a common journey led by the people themselves.

As an Eminent Citizen, MG NREGA, Ministry of Rural Development, I had the opportunity to capture first hand knowledge of the rural poverty, policies and implementation of various programs.

The book reflects participatory learning and focuses on the critical issues. It is not a text book but a sharing of learning with the practitioners, policy makers and young learners who are passionate about India's inclusive growth and its unique rural landscape.

While teaching planning and business administration to the younger generation, I realized that they want to change the world, but grope in the dark when it comes to application of knowledge. This has been the main reason of writing this book, which has been an exciting journey of discovery. It presents a sort of roadmap which the students can explore for a fascinating and complex area of enquiry. I have tried to keep the text as flowing as possible and to draw out key threads of concerns of rural development. The text is organized and illustrated for easy understanding of the subject. A wide range of the concepts have been explained in a simple language and with graphics, which should provoke the readers into new ways of thinking and the way rural growth should be planned and managed. The structure of the book is easily understandable and allows ample opportunity for discussion of the processes and the ways the systems work. The examples provide reference points for application of the ideas and understanding of the nuts and bolts of rural development system and how they fit together.

Although my name appears on the cover of this book, behind the scene many people have contributed a great deal to make it possible. Saying thank you to them seems a poor reward for their support and help. The inspiration for the book came from many persons dedicated towards scripting a success story of India's inclusive growth. This list is topped by the young and compassionate Rahul Gandhi and Union Minister for Rural Development Vilasrao Deshmukh who has a passion to implement Mahatma Gandhi's vision of Rural India.

I have enjoyed a happy relationship with the Discovery Publishers and am grateful to Mr Tilak Wasan who is always patient and encouraging. He has converted an unwieldy manuscript into this compact, beautiful book. The people I relied most heavily and persistently have been my wife. While writing the book, the following quote of Swami Vivekanand was visible on my desk :

*"Let new India arise-out of the peasants' cottage, grasping the plough, out of the huts of fisherman, the cobbler and the sweeper. Let her emanate from the factory, from the marts and from the markets. Let her emerge from groves and forests, from hills and mountains."*

**A.K. Jain**

# Contents

Chapter **1**

# Rural Development—An Overview

> *"The true India is to be found not in its few cities, but in its seven hundred thousand villages. If the villages perish, India will perish too."*
>
> ***—Mahatma Gandhi***

India is an agrarian country having 72 per cent (about 80 crores) of its population in about 5,75,936 villages, mostly inhabited by the poor with agriculture as their predominant occupation. They are largely small and marginal farmers, agricultural labourers, artisans and scheduled castes and scheduled tribes. A large number of rural people (about 30 crore) are still living below the povertyline and often face the basic problem of survival, viz., jobs, poverty, hunger, shelter, ill-health and disease.

The increasing unemployment in the rural sector is likely to have serious ramifications on India's socio-economic and political balance. Today, we often witness serious contradictions—an aeroplane, a sign of progress and power and a bullock cart dragging in a slushy and deeply rutted kaccha road. We can not afford to lose the focus of rural areas and make them subservient to the urban life. Since the pre-independence era of Mahatma Gandhi, every government has committed itself to rural development. However, the results are often tardy and partial.

During 1901 to 2001, the total population of India grew by 431 percent while the number of people in the urban and rural regions grew by 1106 percent and 349 percent respectively. Fig. 1.1 illustrates that the rural population has always outweighed the urban growth but notes a gradual drop as a percentage of the total population.

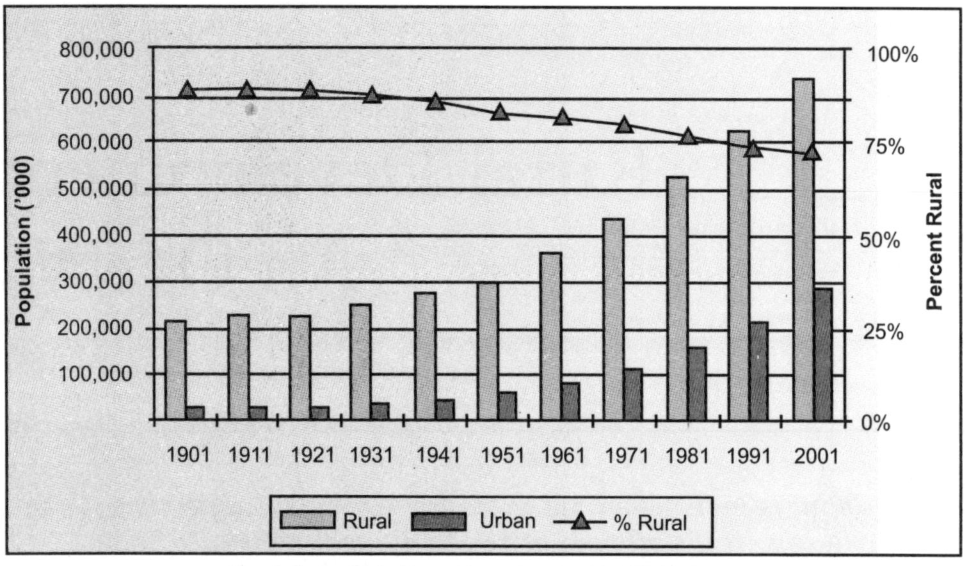


**Fig. 1.1 : India's Demography during 1901-2001**

**Table 1.1 : Rural share of India's GDP**

| | |
|---|---|
| 1950-51 | 73% |
| 1980-81 | 53% |
| 2007 | 37% |

**Source:** Planning Commission, 2002

The contribution of rural areas (agriculture) in proportion to the urban areas (predominantly secondary and tertiary sector of economy) had been continually declining (Table 1.1) The agricultural methods by and large continue to be traditional with huge inefficiencies in the use of land resource, fertilisers, water and energy.

The most striking paradox in Indian agriculture is that of productivity. We have one of the largest cultivable land mass on the planet. Although productivity gains were sustained in the 1990s after the liberalization process began, the yield rates for most crops in India are far below the comparable rates in several other countries. The major reasons for the poor yields is inefficient fertilizer use and poor cultivation practices which lead to imbalanced nutrition.

India is at a point where productivity levels are declining and the land area under cultivation is falling, while demands from a young population are growing and escalating. Increase in

**Fig. 1.2 : India is a paradox of contradictions. We see a bullock cast dragging and shrieking leisurely in a slushy and deeply rutted kuchha road and an aeroplane zooming in the sky. It is not a question of improving the bullock cart or the road, but to bridge the wide gulf between rural areas and urban centres by economic inclusion, social empowerment spatial establishment and technological innovation. The image of the village that it is something backward, oppressive and poverty stricken, devoid of electricity, water, sanitation and other services has to change**

farm productivity becomes vitally important and advocating balanced nutrition, reducing rainfall-dependence by using micro-irrigation, and increase in use of high-yielding seeds seem promising. SOM (soil organic matter) is often viewed as the thread that links biological, chemical, and physical properties of the soil. It has been associated with numerous soil functions and also provides sites for microbes to colonize and decompose organic pollutants. Cover crops are those crops planted after the main crop is harvested. Cover crops are usually killed the following spring, prior to planting the next season's cash crop. Planting cover crops of green manures build the SOM in several ways. Both protect the topsoil and greatly decrease soil erosion by reducing raindrop impact.

The agriculture sector in India uses 85 per cent of the country's available freshwater. However, irrigation efficiency is only 20-50 per cent. In other words, Indian agriculture wastes up to half of the country's fresh water supply. Although from a basin perspective, much of the wasted water is reused, significant amount of water is wasted primarily due to irrigation inefficiencies. There are inefficiencies on the energy front as well. Agriculture accounts for about 27 per cent of the total electricity consumption in India. The consumption is somewhat higher in states like Andhra Pradesh, Gujarat, Madhya Pradesh, Uttar Pradesh, Karanatka, and Haryana where agricultural electricity use is between 35-45 per cent. However, sale rural electricity amounts to not more than 5-10 per cent of the state electricity revenues.

Apart from agricultural shortcomings and stagnation, the rural habitations and livelihoods too present a depressing picture.

## Various Programmes of Rural Development

The governments (Central and States) have taken up numerous programmes of rural development, which cover almost every aspect of rural livelihoods. These cover economic, agricultural productivity, infrastructure, social (education, healthcare, women, etc.), shelter, communications, governance (Panchayati Raj), etc.

**Table 1.2 : Some Major Programmes of Rural Development**

| Rural Livelihood/Rights | Policy/Programmes |
|---|---|
| – Employment | Mahatma Gandhi National Rural Employment Guarantee Act (MG NREGA) |
| – Agriculture Productivity | Bharat Nirman, various programmes of Govt. of |
| Marketing, storage, etc. | India/State Govt., 20 point programme |
| – Irrigation | National/State Irrigation, Canals, Water Supply Projects |
| – Education | Sarva Siksha Abhiyan, |
| | Right to Education Act |
| | Mid-day Meal Scheme |
| – Communications, Infrastructure & Roads | Bharat Nirman |
| | Pime Minister Gramin Sadak Yojana |
| | PURA (Provision of Urban Amenites in Rural Areas) |
| – Water and Sanitation | Drinking Water and Sanitation Programme |
| – Energy/Power | Rural Electrification Programme |
| – Healthcare | National Rural Health Mission |
| | Integrated Child Development Programme |
| | Polio Eradication Programme |
| – Empowerment | Panchayati Raj, Women's reservation, |
| – Social Inclusion/Equity | 73rd Consitution Amendment Act |
| | Child and Mother Programmes, Creche, Anangwadi, Adult Literacy, etc. |
| – Land | Computerisation of land records |
| – Shelter | Indira Awas Yojana |
| – Miscellaneous | New 20 point programme (2004) |

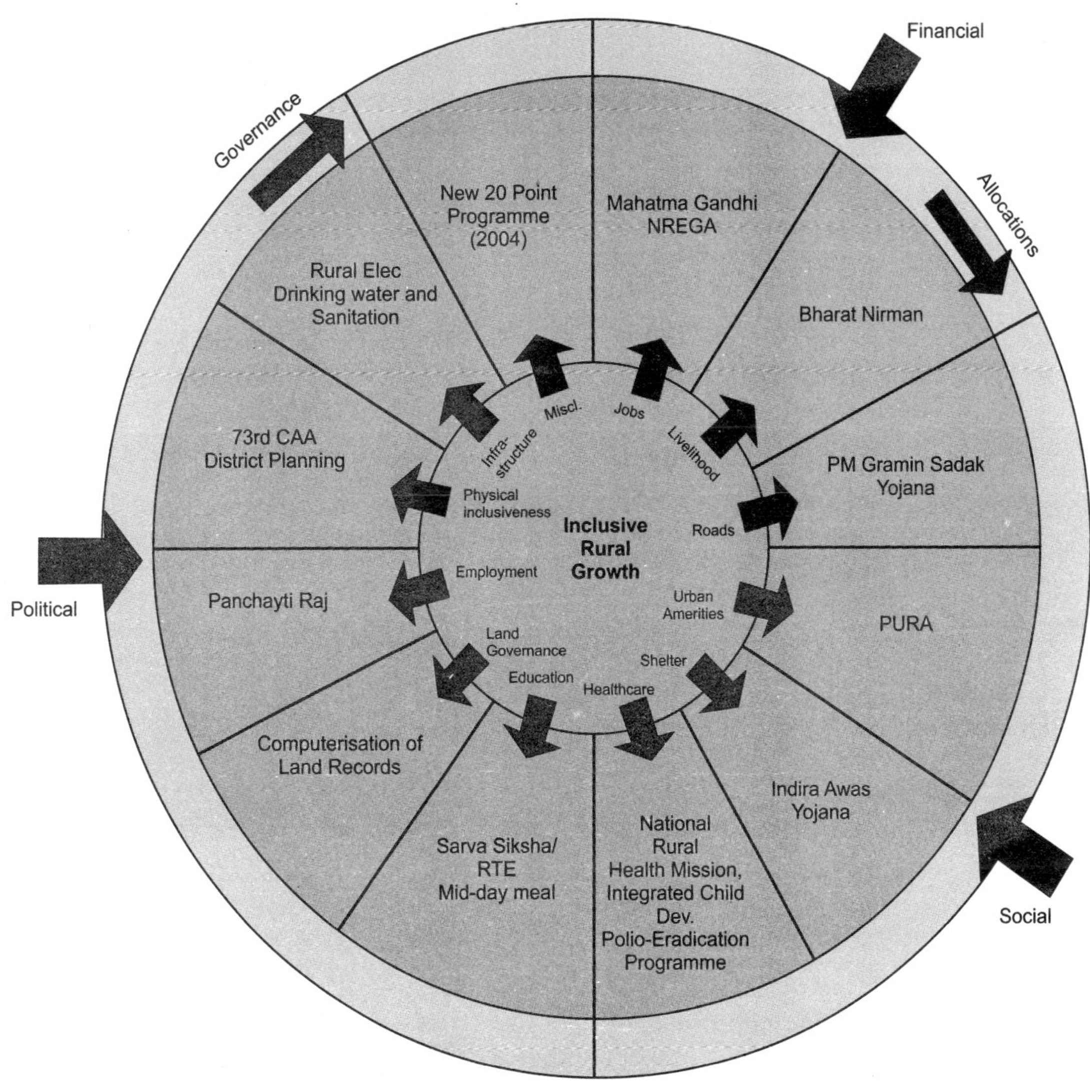


**Fig. 1.3 : Policies and Programmes of Inclusive Rural Growth**

Some of the salient features of the current programmes are explained below :

## National Rural Employment Guarantee Act (NREGA)

The Prime Minister (2006) announced the National Rural Employment Guarantee Act (NREGA) for creating new rural infrastructure, improving road connectivity, school buildings and water supply to villages.

**Fig. 1.4 : Village Pond desilting and improvement under MG-NREGA**

Source: Ministry of Rural Development

The NREGA confers upon the rural households various rights such as :

- The right to demand employment
- The right to get employment within 15 days of their demand.
- The right to get unemployment allowance if the employment is not given within 15 days.
- The right to be paid statutory wages prevalent in a State.
- The right to work site facilities like drinking water, sheds for children and first aid.

The application of employment may be given to the gram panchayat or to the programme officer at the Block level. The NREGA programme was launched on 2nd February 2006. The Prime Minister described the event as a landmark in the history in removing poverty from the face of the nation. The Act guarantees 100 days of wage employment in a year to every rural household in 285 districts across the country. During 2009-10,253 crore households were provided employment generating 87.01 crore person days of work. The participation of SC/ST was 55 per cent, women participation was 52 per cent (2009-10). MGNREGA facilitated financial inclusion of over 7.33 crore rural people, who opened the individual bank accounts.

Over Rs. 44,480 crore were spent till end of 2009. Implementation had been highly uneven across states. The share of registered households given work varies from as high as 73 per cent in Rajasthan, 68 per cent in Chattisgarh and 63 per cent in Assam to a low 13 per cent in Mahrashtra. 30 per cent in Gujarat and 31 per cent in Orissa. The average number of days of work given also varies from 79 in Rajasthan and 63 in MP, to 22 in Bengal, 28 in Bihar and 33 in Gujarat. NREGA has given on an average 48 days of work to about 50 per cent of the 1000 million registered job card holders.

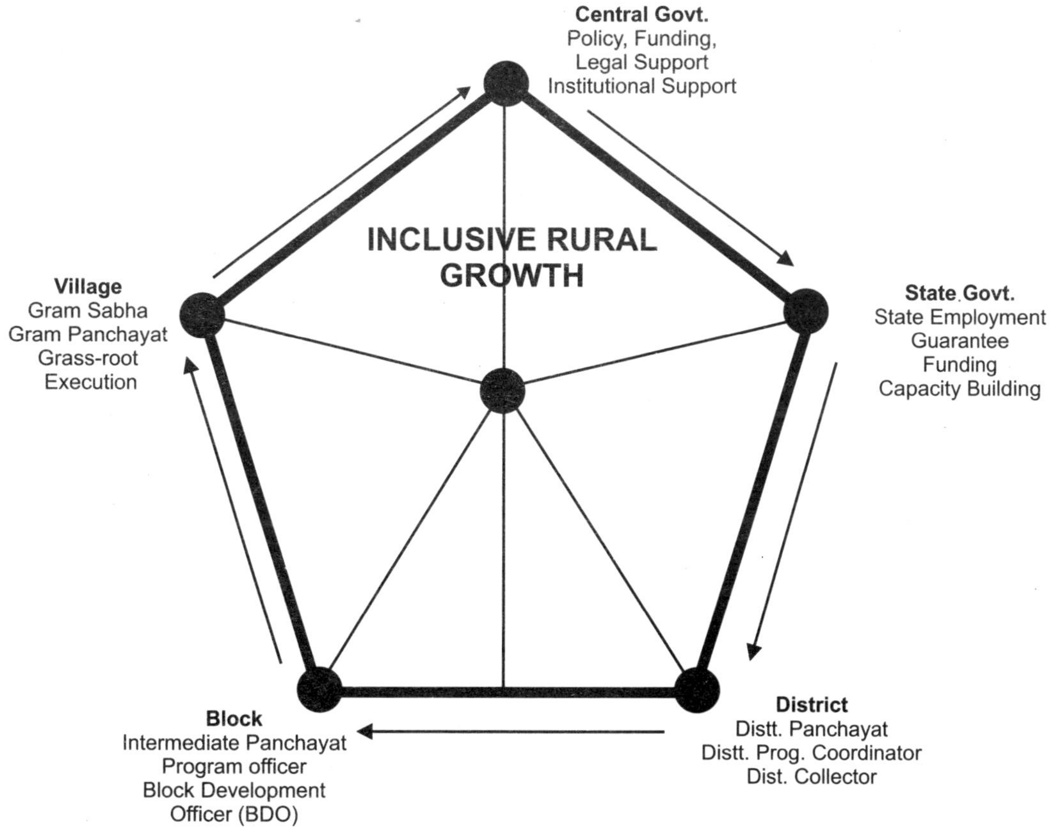


**Fig. 1.5 : Key Actors in MG-NREGA Scheme**

The 5 key actors in NREGA programmes (Fig 1.5) are the following :

1. Central Government (Ministry of Rural Development): Policy, funding, legal and institutional supports, operational guidelines, monitoring, auditing, etc.
2. State Governments: State share of funding, selection of districts and schemes, capacity building, monitoring, etc.
3. District: administration, district development, mapping, programme coordination and monitoring.
4. Block/Taluk: Programme/project implementation, planning, accounting, community mobilization and participation, supervision.
5. Village Gram Sabha/Panchayati Raj Institution (PRI): local level implementation, grassroot participation, community mobilization, servicing and maintenance.

## Spreading Out Inclusive Growth

The NREGA schemes intend to spread out inclusive growth to India's 6 lakh odd villages. The Act recognizes employment as a basic right that is essential to livelihood in rural areas. It also intends to curb migration of rural youngmen and women to urban areas in search of jobs. The 5 levels of stakeholders are interlinked for a smooth transition of policies, programmes, plans and projects to ground level development, participation and employment generation (Fig. 1.6).

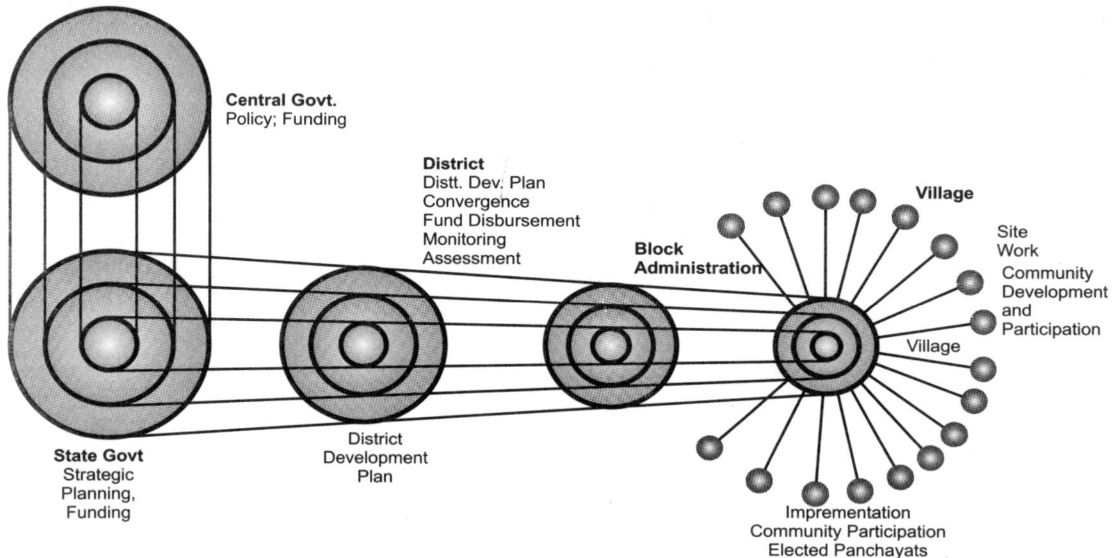


**Fig. 1.6 MG-NREGA-Spreading out Inclusive Growth**

## Provision of Urban Amenities in Rural Areas (PURA)

With a view to bridge wide gap in the availability of physical and social infrastructure, between rural and urban areas, then President of India Dr. A.P.J. Abdul Kalam gave the vision of Provision of Urban Amenities in Rural Areas (PURA). During his address on eve of Republic Day 2003, Dr. Kalam visualized providing physical connectivity, electronic connectivity, knowledge connectivity and economic connectivity of rural areas. PURA was envisaged as a self-sustainable and viable model of service delivery through local people, public authorities and the private sector. The scheme envisaged the following conectivities to the village clusters:

(*i*) Physical Connectivity (road transport facilities, etc.)

(*ii*) Economic Connectivity (Banks, markets, industry, etc.)

(*iii*) Knowledge Connectivity (School, colleges, vocational education, etc.)

(*iv*) Social Connectivity (Hospitals, recreational facility, religious - cultural facilities, etc.).

(*v*) Electronic Connectivity (Phone, internet, cable, etc.)

PURA provides four types of amenities to households—potable water, smokeless fuel, modern sanitation, and internet, plus others at the community level, transport, education, healthcare, and economic services like banks, warehousing and the like. PURA aims to raise rural prosperity to urban levels and halt rural-urban migration. As PURA provides urban amenities without sacrificing rural ambience, it is described as a *rurban* habitat.

**Table 1.3 : Rural and Urban Ambience**

| Item | Urban Ambience | Rural Ambience |
|---|---|---|
| Water | Import | Self reliant |
| Waste | Export | Local recycling |
| Housing | High-rise apartments | Low-rise houses |
| Daily commuting | Long hours | Little or none |
| Neighbourhood | Isolated; dormitory | Close companionship |
| Open fields | Far away | Walking distance |

According to P. Indrisen, one of the authors of the scheme, PURA is planned as a habitation of about 1 km in width, restricted to a walking distance of about 500 m on either side of a ring road some 30-40 km in circumference. This configuration minimizes the length of all infrastructure and hence, capital costs of development.

**Fig. 1.7 : The Concept of PURA (Providing Urban Amenities in Rural Areas)**

The mission of PURA Scheme is accelerated development of compact areas around a potential growth centre in a Gram Panchayat (or a group of Gram Panchayats) through Public Private Partnership (PPP) framework. It aims providing livelihood opportunities and urban amenities to improve the quality of life in rural areas. The primary objective of scheme is to bridge the rural urban divide.

The objectives of PURA are proposed to be achieved under the framework of PPP between Gram Panchayats and private sector partner. Core funding shall be sourced from the Central Sector scheme of PURA and complemented by additional support through convergence of different Central Government schemes. The private sector shall also bring on board it's share of investment besides operational expertise. The scheme would be implemented and managed by the private sector on considerations of economic viability but designed in a manner whereby it is fully aligned with the overall objective of rural development. To attract the private sector, there is a need to design the scheme that would be 'project based' with well defined risks, identified measures for risk mitigation and risk sharing among the sponsoring authority (Gram Panchayat), Government of India, State Government and the private partner.

Through the impelementation of proposed pilot projects, the scheme would be tested on the ground that will provide lessons for upscaling in the future. This will help strengthen the institutional ability of a Gram Panchayat to undertake PPP and help pilot-test the viability of rural infrastructure development. Based on the experience of the pilots, the scheme would be suitably modified for scaling up.

PURA projects cover a Gram Panchayat/a cluster of geographically contiguous Gram Panchayats for a population of about 25,000—40,000. Whereas, the cluster would be the project area, there may be sub-projects to cover each of the Panchayats within the cluster. Alternatively, a large single Panchayat could individually provide critical mass to make the project viable. An illustrative list of infrastructure, urban amenities and economic activities to be provided under PURA are as follows:

**Table 1.4 : An Illustrative List of Urban Amenities for Rural Areas**

| (*a*) Amenities/Activities to be provided under MoRD Scheme (Mandatory) | (*b*) Amenities to be provided under Schemes of other Ministries (non-MoRD Schemes)-illustrative list | (*c*) Add-on Projects (Revenue earning, people centric projects)-illustrative list |
|---|---|---|
| 1. Water and Sewerage<br>2. Construction and maintenance of Village Streets<br>3. Drainage<br>4. Solid Waste Management<br>5. Skill Development<br>6. Development of Economic Activities | 7. Village Street Lighting<br>8. Telecom<br>9. Electricity generation, etc. | 10. Village linked tourism<br>11. Integrated Rural Hub, Rural Market.<br>12. Agro-common Services Centre and Warehousing<br>13. Any other rural-economy based project |

**Source:** Ministry of Rural Development, GOI, 2010

The type of infrastructure envisaged under PURA along with their funding sources and implementation modality is given in Table 1.5.

A necessary element for PURA projects is the availability of land. For the public amenities, land will be made available free of cost by Gram Panchayat/State Government. For add-on facilities, if land is provided by Gram Panchayat/State Government, the revenue will be appropriately shared between Gram Panchayat and private partner through mutual agreement and such add-on facilities shall revert back to Gram Panchayat/State Government at the end of the concession period. If land is not provided by Gram Panchayat/State Government, it will be purchased by the Private Developer

**Table 1.5 : Urban Amenities, Funding and Implementation Agency**

| Type of Infrastructure | Funding | Implementing Agency |
|---|---|---|
| **Core Facilities/External infrastructure** linkages to the PURA area (road to the village, electricity to the village, bulk water supply etc). | Under existing schemes of Government of India/State Government | Government of India/State Government or their agencies |
| **Urban Amenities** | | |
| A. MoRD Schemes (drinking water supply and sewerage, construction & maintenance of village streets, drainage, solid waste management, skill development, and development of economic activity) | Existing MoRD schemes and funding by Private Developer | Private Developer—Build Operate and Transfer (BOT) model |
| B. Schemes of other Ministries (telecom, street lighting, electricity, etc.) | Existing schemes of non-MoRD Ministries and funding by Private Developer | Private Developer—Build Operate and Transfer (BOT) model |
| **Add-on Facilities:** village linked tourism, rural marketing centre, agriculture common services centre, industrial estate for village industries, technical/vocational training institutions, etc. | Private Developer | Private Developer |

**Source:** MORD, GOI, 2010

from the open market, but its cost will not be included in the project costing. As PURA envisages creation of livelihood opportunities, while approving the DPRs it will be ensured that the transfer of common lands for PURA projects from Gram Panchayat/State Government does not affect livelihoods security of local poor. PURA is an attempt to kickstart a process of creation of livelihoods and urban amenities in potential growth centre in rural areas. Hence, PURA project will not be allowed to become an instrumentality for undertaking Rehabilitation and Resettlement (R&R) of Project Affected Persons (PAPs) in and around an ongoing/proposed economic project.

The initial version of the PURA scheme proposed the constitution of Pura Development Authority (PDA) in each district and the PDA was to prepare Economic Plan, Structure Plan and Implementation Plan for the projects :

- Economic Plan :

  Identification of local resources and skills, key investors as anchors, ascertain industry ancilliarization/outsourcing, etc.

- Structure Plan:
  * Utility Infrastructure: Water Supply, Sewerage, Drainage, Low Cost Sanitation, Power, Transport, Solid Waste Management, etc.
  * Social Infrastructure:

    Health, Education, Community Halls, Parks, Play grounds, etc.
  * Commercial Infrastructure: Shopping Centre, Markets, Theaters, Trade Centre, etc.
- Implementation Plan: PDA would prepare implementation plan to execute various provisions of PURA. The Chief Executive of PDA would be a professional on 5-year contract to supervise the works.

The broad specifications of a District Plan under PURA are envisaged as given below :

**Table 1.6 : Broad Specifications for PURA**

| Item | Specification |
|---|---|
| Ring Road | 30-40 km long; 50 meter reserved width. |
| Maximum Time | No two points more than half an hour apart. |
| Bus service | Minimum 15 minute service |
| Developed space | About 500 metres on either side. |
| Zoning | 20% roads, 20% open space; 10% commercial |
| Water | Water harvesting, recycling; min 100 lpcd |
| Waste disposal | Biodigesters |
| Electronic Connectivity | As demanded |
| Starting population | Minimum 30,000 |
| Maximum Pop. | 300,000 |
| Starting trigger | 1000 jobs in production; 2000 in services |

## Bharat Nirman

The Bharat Nirman programme targets to bring one crore hectares of land under assured irrigation, road connectivity to all villages with a population of 1000 and construction of addition 60 lakhs houses for the poor in rural areas. The government decided to provide a corpus of Rs. 8,000 crore to the Rural Infrastructure Development Fund. The World Bank agreed to provide a $ 3 billion loan for the Rs. 1,74,000 crore Bharat Nirman programme to develop rural infrastructure.

**Table 1.7 : Targets under Bharat Nirman**

| Component | Targets (2009) |
|---|---|
| Irrigation | To create 10 million ha of additional irrigation capacity. |
| Roads | To provide all-weather roads to every habitation over a 1000 population and above (500 in hilly and tribal areas); remaining 66802 habitations to be covered. |
| Electricity | To provide electricity to remaining 125000 villages and to 23 milliion households. |
| Housing | To construct 60 lakh houses. |
| Drinking water | To provide drinking water to 55067 uncovered habitations. All habitations failed sources and water quality problems will be addressed. |
| Telephone connectivity | To connect remaining 66822 villages with telephone. |

**Table 1.8 : Bharat Nirman Progress**

| Component | Financial status Expendiutre (Rs. Crore) | Physical Status | | | |
|---|---|---|---|---|---|
| | | | Target | achieved | % Achieved |
| Rural Roads | 30,737 | New road length (km)<br>Upgraded Road Length (km)<br>Habitations (no.) | 146,185<br>194,132<br>50,948 | 72,185<br>106,284<br>25,068 | 49<br>55<br>49 |
| Electrification | 11,275 | Villages (no.) | 470,039 | 128,072 | 27 |
| Telephones | 137 | Villages (no.) | 66,822 | 56,030 | 84 |
| Irrigation | 29,349 | Area ('000 hectares) | 10,000 | 5,583 | 56 |
| Drinking Water | 20,588 | Villages (no.) | 603,639 | 479,898 | 80 |
| Rural Housing | 22,172 | Houses (lakh) | 60 | 61 | 102 |
| **Total** | **1,14,257** | | | | |

Source: MORD/Nodal Ministries, 2009

## Pradhan Mantri Gram Sadak Yojana (PMGSY)

The Government of India launched the Pradhan Mantri Gram Sadak Yojana (PMGSY) with a view to connect rural regions and to reduce poverty in the nation's outbacks. The steady progress of PMGSY is a testament to meeting the objective of improving the rural infrastructure. The first phase of this programme addressed the regions with population of 1000 (500 in the case of hill States, tribal and desert areas) and above. During the second phase, the regions with population of 500 (250 in the case of hill States, tribal and desert areas) have been covered. About 3,68,000 km of new road construction and 3,70,000 km of upgradation or renewal have been targeted.

**Table 1.9 : Connectivity of Villages with Roads**

| Population category | Total No. of villages | Number of Villages Connected (2000) |
|---|---|---|
| 1500 and above | 71623 | 71000 (99%) |
| 1000-1500 | 58229 | 52000 (89%) |
| Less than 1000 | 45465 | 200000 (43%) |
| **Total** | **589317** | **323000 (55%)** |

**Source:** Planning Commission, Vision 2020.

## SOME OPTIONS OF RESOURCE MOBILIZATION FOR RURAL ROADS

**Independent Road Fund :** There is practically no scope for private sector financing of rural roads since they carry very low volumes of traffic. Creation of an independent road fund in various States, as has been done by a few States such as Uttar Pradesh and Karnataka for maintenance, needs to be explored.

**Market Committee Funds :** Extension of the scheme of levying marketing fee and rural development cess on agriculture produce to all States with the support of the farmers' community could be explored.

**Vehicle Fees :** In addition to taxes on fuels, additional funds should be generated through special purchase tax on two wheelers, cars, and agricultural tractors. Part or whole of such funds so collected may be allocated for rural roads and provision of road transport services in rural areas.

**Domestic Borrowings :** Recently, NABARD in India has come up in significant way to provide loan assistance for construction of rural roads in several States under RIDF programme. As the financial institution like NABARD may not have the requisite technical expertise, it may be worthwhile to consider providing NABARD loans with technical and management inputs of NRRDA. This would enhance the financial and technical discipline, as well as help in adoption of uniform standards for these roads, on the lines of the PMGSY. This can be channelized by transferring the total loan amount to a pool to be availed of by the States under guidelines similar to that of PMGSY.

**Source:** Planning Commission, 2007, 11th V Year Plan, Govt. of India, New Delhi.

## Drinking Water Supply

The sources of drinking water in rural India are quite diverse ranging from dug wells to hand pumps. There are the multi-village schemes that bring water over long distances in villages. Hand pumps continue to be the largest source of public drinking water, followed by single village schemes and open dug wells, as given below :

**Table 1.10 : Access to Water Services (2002)**

| Water Service | Population (in lakh) | % share |
|---|---|---|
| Unserved Population | 560 | 8 |
| Hand Pump | 3350 | 44.6 |
| Open dug wells | 1290 | 17 |
| Mini water schemes for Group of households | 470 | 6 |
| Single village schemes | 1650 | 22 |
| Multi-village schemes | 180 | 2.4 |
| **Total Rural** | **7500** | **100** |

**Source :** The World Bank (2006)

In India's 6 lakh odd villages, drinking water is hardly available through the municipal system. By and large hey depend upon multiple sources, even if municipal water system is available, as it is usually inadequate for the needs :

**Table 1.11 : Sources of Drinking Water in Inhabited Villages in India**

| Source Village | Percent |
|---|---|
| Well | 69.8 |
| Hand pump | 55.9 |
| Tubewell | 21.1 |
| Tap | 18.2 |
| Tank | 14.3 |
| River | 10.0 |
| Nala | 3.6 |
| Canal | 3.5 |
| Fountain | 2.6 |
| Spring | 1.7 |
| Lake | 0.1 |
| Others | 4.5 |

**Source :** Ministry of Rural Development, Government of India.

The Government of India initiated water services first through the Minimum Needs Programme, and then through the Accelerated Rural Water Supply Programme (ARWSP). Initially, rural water supply in India followed a supply-led approach where water access was a deemed social good. Financial and operational failures in the ARWSP led to a fundamental shift in the sector towards demand-driven approaches, which the GOI brought about a significant shift by integrating the concept of beneficiary cost-sharing at 10 per cent of the capital cost and the entire O&M cost.

The strategies of Rural Water Supply Programme revolve around the basic premise that provision of safe drinking water is the responsibility of the government. Increased outlay by the government, particularly in the last one decade and, a change in technology focus to handpumps fitted on tube wells and bore wells, had resulted in an impressive increase in the total rural water supply coverage. However, the availability of potable drinking water in rural areas, especially during the summer months is still not satisfactory. Even though about 1 lakh habitations are covered every year, the number of problem habitations has not declined proportionately. The reasons identified for uncovered villages were:

- Fast depletion of ground water level, which also increases incidences of Arsenic and Fluoride contamination.
- Water source go dry and defunct due to deforestation with consequent reduced recharge.
- Heavy emphasis on new construction and poor attention to maintenance.
- Non-involvement of people in operations an maintenance.
- Neglect of traditional water management practices/systems.

The revised guidelines envisaged to energise the system towards overcoming the above problems and to achieve the goal of providing safe and sustainable drinking water to all rural habitations of the country by exercising over the following:

- Control on over-extraction of groundwater,
- More funds for repairs and rehabilitation,
- Increasing people's participation,
- Reserve 20 per cent funds for States promoting sector reforms,
- Water to be treated as a socio-economic good,
- Stronger links with watershed development programmes.

Hence, the prime objectives of the guidelines are as under;

- To ensure coverage of all rural habitations especially to reach the unreached with access to safe drinking water.
- To ensure sustainability of the systems and sources.

- To preserve quality of water by institutionalizing water quality monitoring and surveillance through a Catchement Area approach.

## Rajiv Gandhi National Drinking Water Mission

Funds are provided to the States by the Rajiv Gandhi National Drinking Water Mission under the following programmes:

(*a*) **Accelerated Rural Water Supply Programme (ARWSP):** To supplement the efforts of the State Governments is providing access to safe drinking water to all rural habitations of the country.

(*b*) **Sector reform programme:** Funds would be provided for institutionalizing community participation in capital cost sharing, Operation and Maintenance and Water Quality Monitoring & Surveillance in identified pilot districts.

(*c*) **Sub Missions:** Five Sub Missions on problems of water quality and sources drying up needing construction of water conservation and recharge structures and other measures with the States planning and approving them on their own.

(*d*) Human Resources Development (HRD).

(*e*) Research and Development (R&D).

(*f*) Information, Education and Communication (IEC).

(*g*) Management Information System (MIS).

(*h*) Provision of water supply in rural schools.

(*i*) Monitoring and Investigation Units, Purchase of Rigs, Water Quality Monitoring and Surveillance, Monitoring and Evaluation, Solar Voltaic Pumps and other innovative projects.

## Accelerated Rural Water Supply Programme (ARWSP)

The Accelerated Rural Water Supply Programme (ARWSP) alms at providing safe and adequate drinking water facilities to the rural population by supplementing the efforts made by the State Governments/UTs under the State Sector Minimum Needs Programme (MNP).

The following norms are being adopted for providing safe drinking water to rural population :

- 40 litres of drinking water per capita per day (lpcd) for human beings.
- 30 lpcd additionally for cattle in the Desert Development Programme (DDP) areas.
- One handpump or standpost for every 250 persons.

- The water source should exist within the habitation/within 1.6 km in the plains and within 100 metres elevation in the hilly areas.

Water is defined as safe if it is free from biological contamination (guineaworm, cholera, typhoid, etc.) and chemical contamination (excess fluoride, brackishness, excess iron, arsenic, nitrates, etc.). The priorities of is rural drinking water supply are the following :

- To cover not covered (NC) habitations and to fully cover partially covered (PC) habitations getting less than 10 lpcd. Among them, priority may be given to the ones inhabited exclusively by SC/ST or having larger SC/ST population.
- Coverage of quality affected habitations with acute toxicity first and the others, larger.
- Upgradation of source level of safe source habitations which get less than 40 lpcd water to the level of 40 lpcd.
- Coverage of schools and anganwadis where safe drinking water sources could not be provided under the outlays allocated by the Tenth Finance Commission.

Once the task of providing every habitation with safe drinking water source is completed as per the norms and priorities indicated above, in the entire State, the State Government may consider relaxation of norms with the prior approval of the Government of India, subject to the condition that beneficiaries of the relaxed norms are willing to share a part (which should not be less than 20%) of the capital cost and shoulder full responsibilities of subsequent O & M and replacement so as to meet their service expectations.

Under the Accelerated Rural Water Supply Programme (ARWSP), being implemented since 1972-73 with an investment of over Rs. 50,000 crore (up to March 31, 2005), more than 3.7 million hand pumps and 1.73 lakh piped water scheme have been installed in the rural areas. As on April 1, 2005, 96.1 per cent of rural habitations were fully covered, and 3.6 per cent were partially covered, leaving 0.3 per cent not covered with drinking water facilities.

## Rural Water Supply & Sanitation Programme (RWSS)

Under rural water supply and sanitation component of Bharat Nirman, till year 2009 the following habitations were covered :

- 3,052 Not Covered (NC) habitations;
- 38,894 Partially Covered (PC) habitations;
- 2,52,060 slipped-back habitations; and
- 1,47,576 quality-affected.

A budgetary provision of Rs. 7,300 crore was made during the 2008-09 out of which Rs. 4,912.16 crore had been utilized. An additional Rs. 100 crore for stand alone system in rural schools for safe drinking water had been provided. Of the targeted 2,18,286 habitations, till October, 2008 nearly 79 thousand had been covered and about 90 lakh quality-affected habitations were addressed.

In the case of Accelerated Rural Water Supply Programme (ARWSP) a comprehensive scheme incorporating all aspects of availability, sustainability and quality to be introduced, allocation criteria for states has been revised to encourage decentralization and handing over assets to PRIs for management and O&M. To enable the NE States and Jammu & Kashmir to utilize full central share, funding pattern is on 90:10 basis. Under *Swajaldhara* the integrated approach to ensure sustainable drinking water supply-priority to water conservation and RWH leading to in-situ remediation of water quality problems has been initiated.

The Total Sanitation Campaign (TSC) is being implemented in 590 districts of the country. The project outlay for 590 TSC projects sanctioned is Rs. 14,014.61 crore. The Central government's contribution is Rs. 8,823.54 crore. Till December 2009, 51.96 lakh IHHL for BPL, 57.26 lakh IHHL for APL, 2,830 sanitary complexes, 2.36 lakh school toilets, 0.69 lakh *Balwadi* toilets and 507 RSP/PC were constructed. 12,130 Gram Panchayats, 105 blocks, 8 districts and one State (SIkkim) were awarded the Nirmal Gram Puraskar (NGP).

## OORANIS—THE LIFELINE OF RURAL TAMIL NADU

For the people of Tamil Nadu the traditional ooranis or ponds have proved to be a blessing. The oorains were developed as the main supply systems in Tamil Nadu centuries back. These earthen bunded ponds were constructed by the collective efforts of the people over the ages and have been designed hydrologically to have adequate and assured inflow of surface runoffs. Almost all oorains are well connected with irrigation tanks called Kanmoi.

In recent years however the ooranis were neglected and dilapidated due to implementation of new water supply facilities such as hand pumps, deep borewell, and Combined Water Supply Schemes. Initiatives were taken therefore improve and strengthen them under the Ministry of Rural Development's RGNDWM, *Pradhan Mantri Grameen Yojana,* programmes. These included measures like desilting the pond, treatment of catchment areas, clearing of the supply channels provision of filter media, and providing draw well arrangements and fencing of the oorani. 360 ooranis have revived in several districts with the combined efforts of the government, the community technical expertise form the University and NGO participation. With the rainwater flowing into the ooranis, a sustainable water supply system has become a reality.

**Source:** Planning Commission, 2007, Eleventh V Year Plan, Govt. of India, New Delhi.

### HOW SURAVADI PANCHAYAT IN PHATAN BLOCK IN SATARA DISTRICT (MAHARASTRA) WON THE NIRMAL GRAM PURASKAR (NGP)

This Panchayat has a population of 2891 people and 412 households out of which 112 are BPL households. The Panchayat has a village primary school, an anganwadi centre, and a Primary Health Centre five km away. There was no community toilet facility in the village. Men, women, and children used to defecate in the open. Out of 47 individual toilets 34 were not in use (used only for other purposes). Village was always highly stinking, no drainage, many ill with diseases like jaundice, flu, cholera, etc. Several village meeting were held for stoppage of open defecation. It looked like a Herculean task in the begining, as people were not coming forward for construction of toilets.

Things began to change when Sant Gadge Bada Gram Swachhata Abhiyan started in year 2000 and motivational campaign and meetings were organized by Panchayat. The school teachers and students were involved in this campaign. Sanitation campaign started with making a 28-seater complex and few individual units. Persons still going for open defecation were penalized with no distribution of wheat and kerosene from FPS. It was also decided to give Rs. 500 to very poor family to construct its own latrine. Construction of toilets geared up slowly but taken up in later stages by community participation. The Gram Panchayat and youth group of the same village monitored the sanitation programme.

Everybody is using toilets in the village today. Recognition of community is shown by painting all houses using toilets in pink colour. With the campaign, people also gained knowledge on bio-gas plants and about conservation of sources. The scheme was also linked with and benefited through other rural developmental schemes like Yaswant Gram Samruddhi Yojana.

To sustain the programme women and children get regular knowledge on cleanliness through school. Extra classes have been organized for students on promotion of sanitation and hygiene activities in the schools. The village now has a better school facility and the Panchayat is fully involved, as it had initiated this campaign. There is a feeling of pride with their becoming the first village in the entire State to get the NGP award.

**Source:** Planning Commission, 2007, Eleventh V Year Plan, Govt. of India, New Delhi

## Rural Housing-Indira Awas Yojana

Rural housing is not only a key component of development but also an important ingredient in ensuring sustainable poverty reduction. The proper development of infrastructure and housing in rural areas improves rural economy and quality of life. It promotes better productivity, increased agricultural incomes, adequate employment, etc. According to the assessment by the Registrar General of India (RGI) out of every 100 households in rural areas, 36 live in pucca houses, 43 live in semi-pucca houses and the rest live in kutcha houses. On the other hand, out of every 100 households in urban area 77% live in pucca structure, 20% in semi-pucca houses and 3% in kutcha houses. Pucca houses mean both roof as well as walls are made of building materials like cement, bricks, stone, metal sheets, asbestos, etc. Kutcha houses mean, where both roof and walls are made of kutcha materials/non-pucca materials. Semi-pucca houses means a roof or wall (but not both) made of pucca materials.

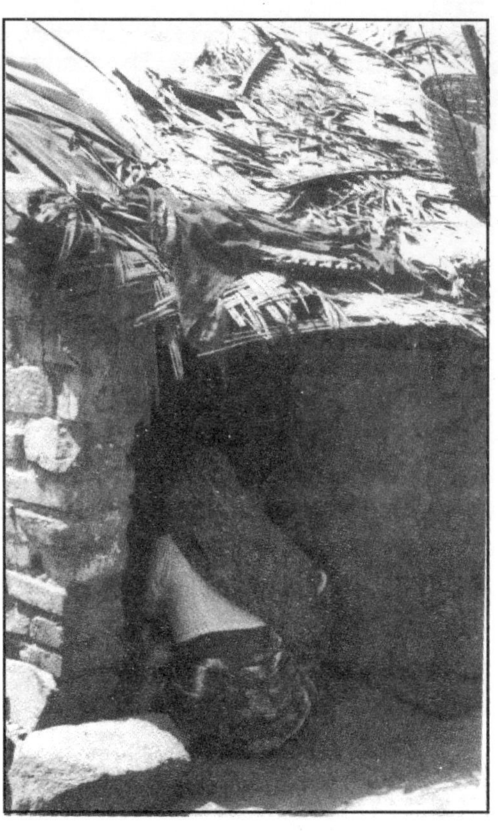

**A rural hut-dark, dingy and devoid of services and sanitation**

As per the Census of India, the percentage of coverage of rural water supply was 73.2 percent in the year 2001 and only 21.9 percent of rural population have access to toilet facilities or sanitation as compared to national figure of 36.4 percent. As regards the rural electrification the situation has become better in last decade. According to the census of 1991 only 30.54 percent of rural households had electricity which increased to 43.5 in 2001.

Village roads are narrow and kutcha alongwith open drainage, the breeding place for mosquitoes, flies and insects cattle are usually tied adjacent to the houses on narrow roads. In all, environmental conditions in the village are not conducive to healthy living and are out of control of individual household.

Human beings and animals live together in close proximity thereby impairing health of these people. Despite the increasing prosperity, growing education and spread of knowledge, housing condition continued to be unsatisfactory in large number of cases in the countryside. A considerable proportion of the rural houses are made of mud of combination of wood, bamboo, and thatched roofs. Village house are usually dark, damp, ill-ventilated and insanitary. Windows are conspicuous by their absence. The waste water is allowed to accumulate near the house. The problem of open air defection in the rural areas is the most serious and challenging one about two thirds rural households are not having sanitary latrines and one fourth respondents were using veranda and living room for bathing purpose. Lack of proper sanitation facilities is one of the major factor affecting adversely the quality of life of the rural people.

**Fig. 1.8 : Rural houses reflect local livelihoods**

**The Rural Housing Policy aims at:**

- Upgradation, repair and renewal of serviceable kutcha houses
- New rural houses in replacement of unserviceable houses.
- Retrofitting of existing rural houses to provide resistance to natural calamities like, earthquakes, cyclones, etc.
- Improving villages abadis.
- The optimum use of local materials and appropriate housing technology.
- Introducing appropriate technology for building with local materials, conventional traditional practices.
- Improving rural housing finance.
- Grassroot level technology transfer through Building Centres and skill upgradation of villagers.

Indira Awaas Yojana (IAY) is a flagship scheme of the Ministry of Rural Development to provide financial assistance to the BPL households in rural areas for construction of a dwelling unit. The funding of the IAY is shared between the Centre and State in the ratio of 75:25 and in the case of UTs, 100% funding is done by the Government of India. In the case of NE States the funding is shared in the ratio of 90:10. The unit assistance for an IAY house is Rs. 35,000/- per house for plain areas and Rs. 38.500/- for hilly areas. Rs. 15,000/- is provided for upgradation of the house. Under Differential Rate of Interest (DRI) Scheme, an IAY beneficiary can borrow up to Rs. 20,000/- from any Nationalized Bank at 4% interest per annum to top up the assistance under IAY.

For those rural BPL householders who do not have house sites, the provision is made to provide house-sites under the Indira Awaas Yojana. This funding is to be shared between Centre and State is the ratio of 50:50.

Rural housing is also one of the six components of Bharat Nirman Programme. Under the first phase of Bharat Nirman (2005-06 to 2008-09) 60 lakh houses were envisaged to be constructed. As against this target, 71.76 lakh houses were constructed thereby exceeding the target. The target for the year 2009-10 had been fixed at 210.52 lakh houses. It is proposed to double the target of Bharat Nirman and to construct 120 lakh houses during the Phase II Bharat Nirman (2009-10 to 2014-15).

Efforts are being made to ensure that Indira Awaas Yoajana beneficiary gets access to benefits available under other schemes meant for rural BPL households by convergence of various Centrally Sponsored Schemes (CSS) with IAY. IAY beneficiaries can avail benefits available under Rajiv Gandhi Grameen Vidyutikaran Yojana (RGGVY). Total Sanitation Campaign (TSC), Janshree and Aam Aadmi Bima Yojana and Differential Rate of Interest (DRI) Scheme and Health Insurance Scheme. NHB has also been providing refinance support to banks and other housing finance institutions at concessional rates to encourage lending in rural areas. Nearly 50% of NHB's total refinance was for housing in rural areas under the Golden Jubilee Rural Housing Finance Scheme (GJRHFS) which is provided to banks, HFCs and cooperative institutions. Refinance under the scheme is provided at concessional rate of interest of 25 bps less than applicable rates.

## National Rural Health Mission

The National Rural Health Mission (NRHM) was launched by the Government of India (GOI) in April 2005. It seeks to provide effective healthcare to the rural population throughout the country with special focus on eighteen states, which have weak public health indicators and/or weak infrastructure. These states are Arunachal Pradesh, Assam, Bihar, Chhattisgarh, Himachal Pradesh, Jharkhand, Jammu and Kashmir, Manipur, Mizoram, Meghalaya, Madhya Pradesh, Nagaland, Orissa, Rajasthan, Sikkim, Tripura, Uttranchal, and Uttar Pradesh. The GOI will provide funding for key components in these eighteen high focus states.

The NRHM covers all the village in these eighteen states through approximately 2.5 lakh village based 'Accredited Social Health Activities' (ASHA) who act as a link between the health centres and the villagers. One ASHA will be raised from every village or a cluster of villages, across these

States. The ASHA is trained to advise village population about sanitation, hygiene, contraceptives, immunization and to provide primary medical care for diarrhea, minor injuries and fevers, and to escort patients to medical centers. They would also be expected to deliver direct observed short course therapy for tuberulosis and oral rehydration, to give folic acid tablets and chloroquine to patients, and to alert authorities of unusual outbreaks of disease. ASHA will receive performance-based compensation for promoting universal immunization, referral and escort services for RCH, construction of household toilets, and other healthcare delivery programmes.

The goals of the NRHM include:

1. Reduction in Infant Mortality Rate (IMR) and Maternal Mortality Rate (MMR);
2. Universal access to integrated comprehensive public health services;
3. Child health, Water, Sanitation and Hygiene;
4. Prevention and control of communicable and non-communicable diseases, including locally endemic diseases;
5. Population stabilization, gender, and demographic balance;
6. Revitalization of local health traditions and mainstream Ayurvedic, Yoga, Unani, Siddha, and Homeopathy Systems of Health (AYUSH);
7. Promotion of healthy lifestyles.

The strategies to achieve the goals include:

1. Train and enhance capacity of Panchayati Raj Institutions (PRIs) to own, control and manage public health services;
2. Health plan for each village through Village Health Committee of the Panchayat;
3. Strengthening sub-centre through an untied fund to enable local planning and action (each sub-centre will have an Untied Fund for local action at Rs. 10,000 per annum). This Fund is deposited in a joint Bank Account of the ANM and Sarpanch and operated by the ANM, in consultation with the Village Health Committee, and Multi Purpose Workers (MPWs);
4. Provision of 24 hour service in 50 per cent PHCs by addressing shortage of doctors, especially in high focus states, through mainstreaming AYUSH manpower;
5. Preparation and implementation of an intersectoral District Health Plan prepared by the District Health Mission, including drinking water, sanitation, and hygiene and nutrition;
6. Integrating vertical Health and Family Welfare programs at National, State, Block, and District levels.

The duration of NHRM is from 2005 to 2012. The total allocation for the Department of Health and Family Welfare was hiked from Rs. 8420 crore to Rs. 10,820 crore in the year 2005-06.

During 2006-10 nearly 6.47 lakh ASHAs had been appointed, but only about 40% were trained to level 2, while only 1% completed all 5 levels. Drug kits were given to only 64%. Infrastructure had been built up and facilities are improving, but trained staff is still lacking. Through about Rs. 31,000 crore had been given by the Central government, the state governments have been unable to spend about one third of this.

## Polio Eradication

Launched in 1999, Polio Eradication Programme drastically reduced polio cases by 2000 and India is on the verge of becoming polio-free. However, a few pockets are showing resistance to immunization and it is feared that, if not controlled, polio may again become rampant. Nearly Rs. 9,000 crore was spent on polio immunization in the 5 years, while confirmed cases were counted to 559 in 2008. The government is planning to introduce the injectible vaccine which costs 20 times more than the oral version. There had been a neglect of the routine immunization programme, which protects against many other deadly diseases, which had got Rs. 5,000 crores covering 44% of children.

**Fig. 1.9 : "Give the villagers village arithmetic, village geography, village history and the literary knowledge that they must use daily, i.e. reading and writing letters, etc." — Mahatma Gandhi**

## Sarva Shiksha Abhiyan (SSA)

The Constitution of India in 1950 directed that within 10 years all children should be in school, now 60 years later India is on the verge of achieving this. Launched in 2001, SSA could not meet its earlier target of getting allchildren in school by 2003. Increased allocations in recent years have led to over 100% gross enrollment ratio in the primary sections. The number of out-of-school children have dropped from 3.2 crore in 2001 to 76 lakh in 2008. Over Rs. 60,000 crore had been spent on SSA between 2001 and 2008. About 50% of enrolled children drop out by class 8, especially among vulnerable sections like landless labourers and members of scheduled castes and tribes. The SSA has been extended to secondary level and seeks effective implementation of Right to Education Act.

## Integrated Child Development Services (ICDS)

This scheme provides nutritional supplements, health check-ups and immunization coverage to children up to the age of 6 years to reduce mortality and disease. It also provides nutritional supplements to pregnant and lactating mothers. These services are delivered through a vast network of 12.43 lakh anganwadi centers. Of the estimated 20 crore children in the 0-6 years age group, over 7 crore (35%) are officially benefiting from ICDS. Running since 1975, ICDS has been restructured in recent years with NGOs being given an increasing share of work. Over Rs. 32,000 crore had been spent on the scheme since 2001, mainly on food.

## Mid-Day Meal Scheme (MDMS)

Initiated in the 1990s, MDMS got on track after a direction from the Supreme Court in 2001 making it mandatory for schools to provide cooked meals. Since then, over Rs. 33,000 crore have been spent on implementing the program. As of 2009, about 11.74 crore children studying in classes 1 to 8 were getting mid-day meals, making it the largest school meals programme in the world. Of these, 8.24 crore students are in primary sections (class 1 to 5). The scheme is a key factor for growth in enrollment in the primary sections.

## Rural Electrification

The Rajiv Gandhi Grameen Vidhyutikaran Yoajan (RGGVY) was launched in April 2005 to complete household electrification within next five years' time and modernizing the rural electricity infrastructure. The scheme also lays special emphasis on sustainability of rural supply through collection of the cost of electricity from the beneficiaries. To achieve this objective, it is proposed that franchises like NGOs and consumer associations be deployed with appropriate involvement of

Panchayati Raj institutions. The State Governments are free to provide appropriate subsidy to poor households. The Ministry of Power has chalked out a blue print 'Mission 2012' which sets out milestones to be crossed during the 5 years. This exercise entails additional electrification of 62,000 villages by 2007, 18,000 remove villages by 2012, and complete electrification of all households by 2012.

Pradhan Mantri Gramodaya Yojana (PMGY) encourage pooling resources from other schemes under Minimum Needs Programme (MNP) and Rural Infrastructure Development Fund (RIDF) to meet the objective of 100% electrification. A new scheme called Accelerated Rural Electrification Programme (AREP) has been launched. The participation of Decentralized Power Producers, PRIs, Rural Co-operatives, NGO, etc. is encouraged. The Ministry of Power is pushing the concept of Rural Electricity Supply Companies (RESCOs) involving the private sector players by leasing out solar panel based light systems to village homes.

## Bio-fuels

The Government is targeting fallow land as well as barren/unused land belonging to farmers for the plantation of TBOs so that the set objectives are achieved in the minimum possible time. The various policy initiative taken by the state government included supply of Jatropha saplings to farmers, land allotment policy for investors and support price for purchase of Tree Borne Oilseeds (TBOs). To ensure that the farmer planting Jatropha on fallow and get proper price for their TBO produce, the state government has declared a support price for procurement of the same. The support prices are fixed for Jatropha seed (Rs. 550 per quintal), *karanja* seed (Rs. 450 per quintal) and *Jatrophalkaranja* oil (Rs. 18 per kilo).

In line with the National Mission on Bio-diesel the Chhattisgarh state government took up an exhaustive programme for planting Jatropha on almost one million hectares of fallow land available in the state by 2012. This includes the land unused for want of desired soil character or irrigation. To start with, the Government of Chhattisgarh set up a Chhattisgarh Bio-fuels Development Authority, in January 2005 for the promotion of biofuels programme in the state.

The State has about 44 per cent forest cover, which produces numerous types of underutilized TBOs (Tree Borne Oilseeds) such as Jatropha, *karanja, mabua* and *kusum* in abundant quantities. This provides ample opportunities for the promotion of the bio-fuels programme. It is projected that by undertaking the plantation of Jatroph a *karanja* on one million hectares of fallow land in Chhattisgarh, the following production will accrue :

1. Jatropha seed: 10 million tonnes
2. Bio-diesel: 3 million tonnes
3. De-oiled cake (bio-manure): 7 million tonnes

4. Glycerol: 0.5 million tonnes
5. Bio-gas: 3500 million cubic metres
6. Electricity: 700 MW (megawatt)

The estimated figures reflect the huge potential available for setting up biofuel projects through private investments. However, as Jatropla is a crop, failure can have a devastating effect and there is a need is provide risk cover and insurance to the farmers.

## Computerization of Land Records (CLR)

The Union Ministry of Rural Development took the initiative to identify the deficiencies in the systems of revenue administration and land records came out to be the most important obstruction in proper governance of revenue policies and rural development. Started in 1988-89, CLR project (Computerization of Land Records) started with the intention to remove the problems inherent in the manual system of maintenance and updating of land records to meet the requirements of the users. It was decided that efforts should be made to computerize core data contained in land records, so as to assist development planning and to make records accessible to people/planners/administrators. Its objectives are the following :

- To employ state of art information technology to transform the existing land record system of the country.
- To ensure efficient, accurate, transparent delivery mechanism and conflict resolution in ownership.
- To provide electronic record of rights (ROR) to land owners at nominal rates.
- Information empowerment of land owners.
- Low cost and easily reproducable data for reliable and durable preservation.
- Value addition and modernization in land administration.
- Integration with other data sets towards comprehensive Land Information Systems (LIS).

### Advantages

- Provides a transparent method of property valuation and calculation of stamp duties.
- Simplifies registration procedures.
- Enhances speed, reliability and consistency of the system. Cuts delays by replacing the manual systems of copying, indexing and accounting.
- Introduces state-of-the-art document management system, Scanning of documents replaces manual copying, Images of documents are preserved on CD's in four copies.
- Retrieval of the documents and obtaining copies is made instantaneous.

The overall effect is a smooth public interface.

## Status of Implementation

CLR project is being implemented in 569 districts out of about 619 districts in the country. The States of Karnataka, Tamil Nadu, Goa and Gujarat are fully operational and have banned the manual distribution of Records of Rights where online system is available. The States of Madhya Pradesh, West Bengal, Rajasthan, Maharashtra, Orissa, Uttar Pradesh, Sikkim, Andhra Pradesh, Pondicherry and NCT of Delhi are already in an advanced stage of computerization of land records. Various kinds of land records software operational in different States include Bhoomi (Karnataka), Tamil Nadu (Tamil Nadu) e-Dharni (Goa), Bhuyan (Chhattisgarh), Apna Khata (Rajasthan), e-Dhara (Gujarat), Bhumi (West Bengal), Himbhoomi (Himanchal Pradesh) etc. Statewise dtails of this project are as follows:

**Table 1.12 : Status of Computerisation of Land Records (CLR)**

| State | Status: No. of Taluks out of total where ROR completed/completion stage | Status: No Taluks out of total where CLR process is at advanced stage |
|---|---|---|
| Goa | having 100 percent computerization of land records. ROR* is being issued in all 11 taluks. | |
| Karnataka | 130/177 | |
| West Bengal | 257/- | |
| Rajasthan | 18 | 140/241 |
| Gujarat | 3 | 52 |
| Tamil Nadu | 7 | 50 |
| Sikkim | 1 District | 4 Districts |
| Orissa | Tehsil level computerization in progress. | |
| Andhra Pradesh | Data Entry completed in all 23 districts | |
| Haryana | Data entry work completed for 19 districts of the State. | |
| Madhya Pradesh | Tehsil level computer centers ready in 136 out of 256 taluks. | |
| Uttar Pradesh | Data entry for Khatiyan (ROR) completed for 84857 out of 98449 villages of the State. Data validation and verification work in progress. | |
| In all other states data entry, verification and validation are at various stages. | | |
| ROR* Record of Right. | | |

Various government and external agencies have been monitoring this project and their common view is that CLR project is of great significance for public as well as planners, policy makers and business leaders of the country. In order to potentially utilize the information resource thus generated, it is very important to create IT awareness among grass root functionaries and establish an integrated network for district and tehsil level users. Further, there is a need for formulating standards and guidelines for security, legal sanctity and routine facility management. However, ultimate goals of CLR operations would stand accomplished only when title related litigation across the country reduces, process of property registration completes on click of a mouse and property documents are available to everybody.

## Implementation Gap

The experience indicates that in spite of elaborate policies and programmes there are serious gaps in the implementation. This is largely due to administrative and governance bottlenecks, vested interests, lack of macro-economic orientation and lack of planning.

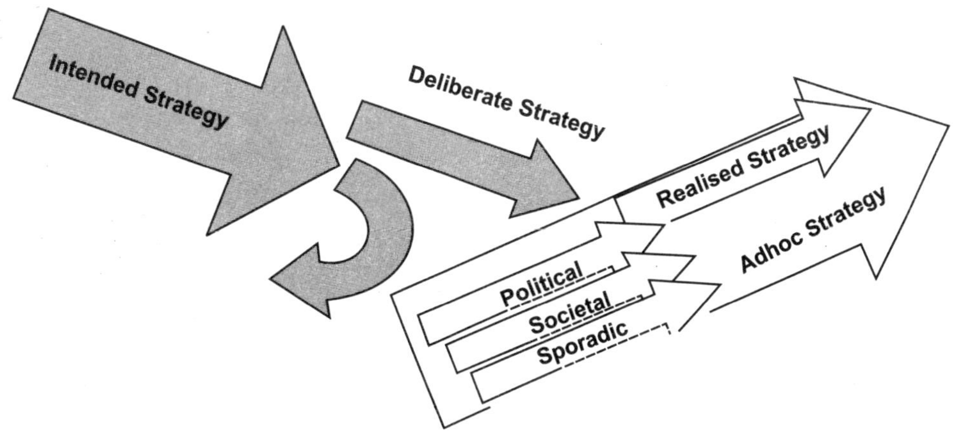


**Fig. 1.10 : Wide Gap between Intended and Realised Strategy**

As it happens, every policy, programme and project has certain strengths and weaknesses. It also provides certain opportunities and faces threats. In case of rural development programmes, a generalised SWOT analysis gives a picture of weaknesses and threats which need to be addressed so as to bridge the gap between intended and realized strategy. (Fig. 1.11)

The various programmes can be analysed and evaluated on the basis of 5 critical factors which any policy/programme should contain, viz., Efficiency, Simplicity, Flexibility, Suitainability and Delivery. The scheme/services can be be rated as Excellent, Good, Fair and Poor (Fig. 1.12) This provides clues towards improving the schemes for better end result, that is, delivery.

An evaluation of the rural schemes, such as MG-NREGA, PURA, SSA, Bharat Nirman (BN), PMGSY, IAY, NRHM, CLR, Rural Electrification, Drinking Water and Sanitation, etc. can be done on the basis of these 5 factors, viz. Simplicity, Efficiency, Delivery, Sustainability and Flexibility/ Adaptability.

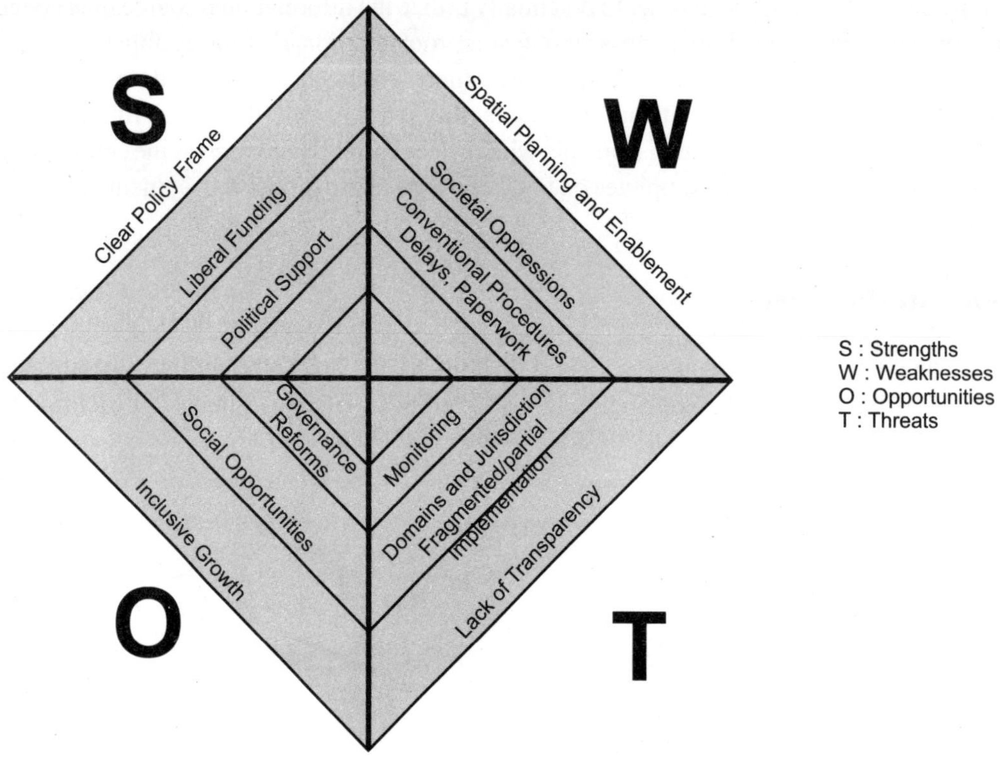


**Fig. 1.11 : Generalised Swot Analysis of Rural Development Programs**

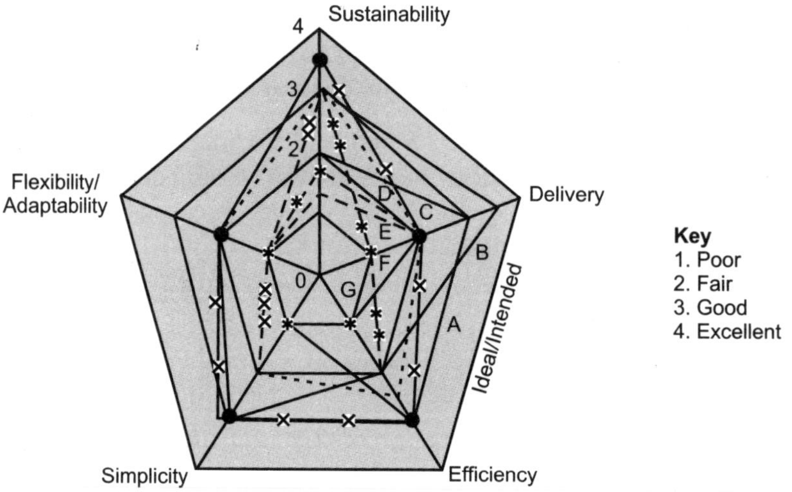


**Fig. 1.12 : Rating System and key components in delivery of Rural Development**

## Rural Development as Freedom

With a view to capture the socio-economic dimension of rural development, Amartya Sen evolved the concept of 'development as freedom'. This is an essential ingredient of inclusive development. Amartya Sen's seminal ideas on 'Development as Freedom' focus on the increasingly important topic of how development policy can address cultural needs and values in the context of rural deprivation and social exclusion. It provides a practical review of the range of multi-dimensional approaches to poverty reduction by linking rural development with the 5 freedoms, viz., political, economic, social, transparency and security.

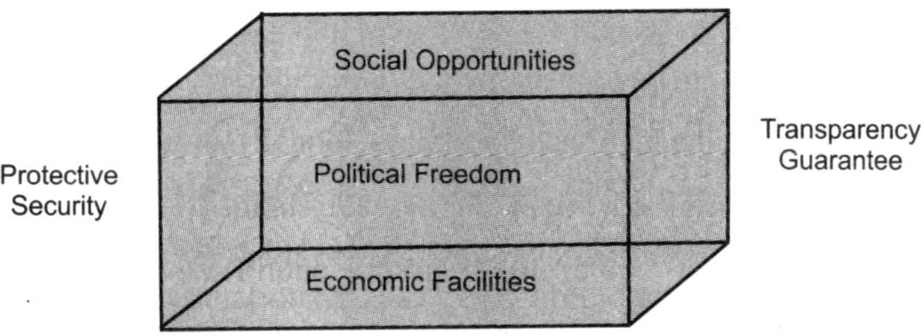


**Fig. 1.13 : The five freedoms interconnect like five sides of a box**

### A Partial Listing of the Five Freedoms

**Political freedom**

- Access to voting
- Access to law and order services
- Access to telecommunications
- Access to adequate housing
- Protection against evictions and demolitions
- Access to choose cultural/festivals/religious expressions
- Forum for free debate

**Economic facilities**

- For consumption, production, trade and exchange
- Access to economic resources
- Access to finance potential opportunities
- Access to self-help solutions

**Social opportunities**

- Access to education, healthcare and other facilities to live a better life.
- Expression of cultural activities, including daily, seasonal
- Celebrations and rituals, including open space for festivals

**Transparency guarantee**

- Guarantees for openness to accurate information and disclosures.
- Evidence of trust
- Social contacts between city administrators and the citizens
- Social contacts between city administrators and the citizens
- Social contacts defined and enacted between the police, politicians, health authorities, developers and industry.

**Protective security**

- Access to protection of social security-net that prevents the spread of poverty
- Natural disasters
- Epidemics
- War

Amartya Sen reminds how the first time the Indian electorate showed that it had any muscle at all, the government was thrown out of office nor on the issue of hunger but on the issue of civil rights, suppression of fundamental rights, including habeas corpus. He emphasized how the first democratic government of India lost power on account of a poor civil rights record and it has happened many times since then. Sen believes that despite being poor, the Indian electorate was not saying that one can prioritize in such a way that political freedom does not matter until one becomes richer. On the contrary it is a question of how to interprete the circumstances :

*"priorities will take the form of the relative way we attach the different concerns of the people which become known through public discussions. It is often not recognized just how much the absence of basic civil rights affects the lives of the most deprived."*

In Sen's analysis, this illustrates how in many ways civil rights are less important for wealthier, educated people than for the slum dwellers, as they were the only ones subjected to such a violent response:

*"To say that for the slum dweller what really matters is food and not civil rights is a mistake. One cannot make a priority like that. We can never get into a formula. We will have to look at the circumstance, produce the kind of appropriate analysis and then see which is the aspect we ought to emphasize now. It is a question of emphasis and the question of relative weights."*

This provides clues to the way rural development should be planned and implemented. It also points towards the alien 'urban' thinking, which has been the main reason for serious backlogs in rural development in India.

The rural economy may constitute only 30 per cent of India's GDP, but it still holds over 70 per cent of the population and remains a crucial determinant of overall growth. A rural economy with urban priorities and pretensions leads to skewed development and a great waste of national rural resources and manpower. Our rural society today is a deadly mix of illiteracy, unemployment and stifling governance and controls that have led to a vicious cycle of dependency and demoralization. With the rural-urban linkage being extremely uneasy and artificial, rural-to-urban migration is becoming a sociological and economic problem. This is the reason why so many cities are becoming shanty towns if not outright slums. The rural economy needs urgent re-conceptualization and integration within the mainstream. This is especially important if we want to achieve over seven per cent growth.

Chapter **2**

# Rural Poverty and Social Oppressions

> *"The service of India means....the ending of poverty and ignorance and disease and inequality of opportunity."*
>
> ***—Jawaharlal Nehru 14 August 1947***
>
> *"....the task that Nehru identified remains, alas, largely unaccomplished"*
>
> ***—Jean Dreze and Amartya Sen, 1996***

Taking off from Amartya Sen's idea of 'Development as Freedom', it is necessary to refocus the issues of rural development in the following inter-connected areas:

1. Socio-cultural context and widespread oppresive social practices
2. Transparancy guarantee in rural governance
3. Spatial integration of socio-economic development.
4. Water, Sanitation and Environment.
5. Praxis for Inclusive and Sustainable Development

Understanding these frameworks provides the clues to the gaps between the rural policies, plans, programmes and their implementation on the ground. It is also necessary to understand why in spite of all the skills, hardwork, new systems of management, innovative technology and allocation of the resources (especially finance), the delivery on the ground is lacking or it is only partial. It is necessary to understand the socio-cultural, political and oppressive traditions which come in the way.

## India's Poverty vis-à-vis World Economy

The World Bank divides the countries into four economic classes by per capita annual incomes :

- Rich Countries $ 9361 and above
- Upper middle class $ 3031—$ 9360
- Lower middle class $ 761—$ 3030
- Poor countries $ 760 or less

India falls in the last category of poor countries. The surveys reveal that 50 percent of the people in the least developed countries (LDCs) live on less than US$ 1 a day. In 2000, this group totalled 334 million. By 2015, they could be 471 million. The countries of the South have 75 percent of the world's people but only:

- 15 percent of the world's energy consumption.
- 30 percent of the world's foodgrain.
- 18 percent of the world's export earnings.
- 11 percent of the world's spending on education.
- 6 percent of the world's spending on health.
- 8 percent of the world's industry.
- 5 percent of the world's science and technology.
- Of the approximately 1.3 billion people living in poverty, 70 percent are women.
- Biomass fuels account for 80 percent of all household fuel consumption in developing countries mostly for cooking, which is done primarily by women.
- Of the 3 million annual air pollution deaths, 2.8 million are from indoor air pollution, a major byproduct of the traditional use of biomass.
- Nearly one half of the total energy consumed in the country comes from non-commercial sources such as cowdung (gobar) and vegetable waste.
- While oil has an almost equal share in the primary energy consumption compared to the world average, natural gas constitutes less than 8 percent against the world average of 25 percent.

**Source:** Down to Earth, Volume 13, No. 4, July 15, 2004 and Indian Infrastructure Vol. 6, No. 12 July 2004.

Since 1947 India has made significant progress in several areas of development and economy has diversified substantially. Size of its population has grown from 340 million to one billion and although the rural population came down from 82.8 percent to 72.2 percent, in absolute numbers, it increased from 178 m (1951) to 720 m (2001). In a stagnant rural economy there is a continuous migration to the cities (Fig. 2.2).

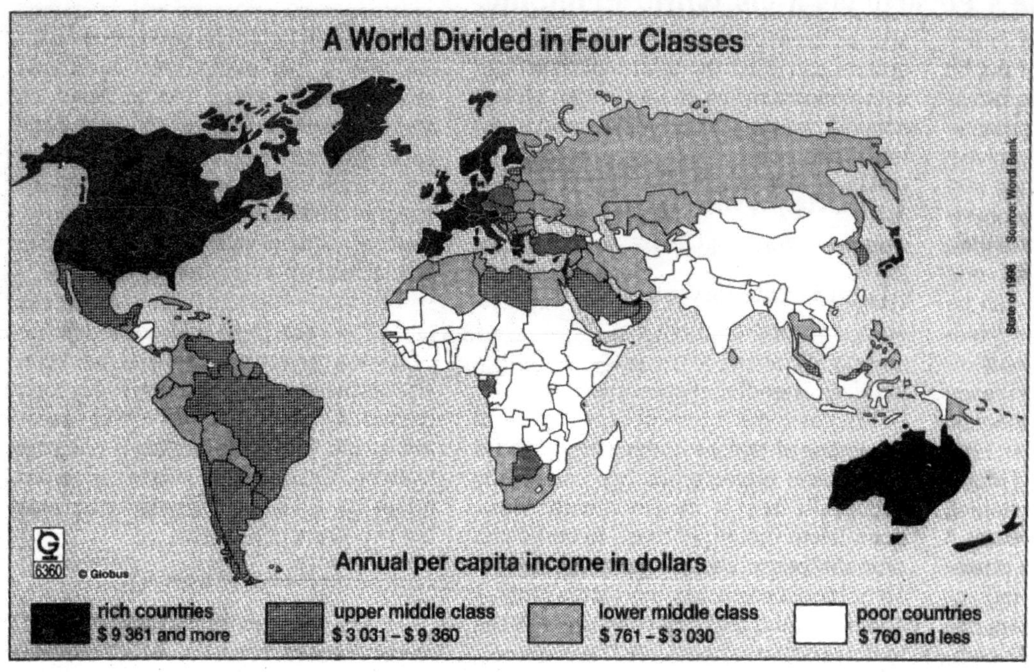


**Fig. 2.1 : A World Divided in Four Classes**

**Source:** World Bank

Despite huge investments in various government programmes, a large population in the country (about one-third) in the rural areas is below poverty line and continue to remain deprived of essential services :

- 63.5% of rural households do not have access to toilet facilities;
- Two-fifth or close to 55 million rural households do not have access to safe drinking water within their premises;
- 2 million cases of malaria, 1.5 million cases of tuberculosis and 4 million cases of HIV have been detected;
- More than 0.5 million women die each year due to pregnancy-related complications;
- Infant mortality rate is at 72 per 1000;
- 65% of the population lacks access to essential drugs;
- Infant immunization rate hovers at about 60%-78%;
- Over 50% of children between 1 and 5 years remain undernourished;
- Rural literacy level was 59.4% in 2001 and female literacy level was 46%;
- More than 45% of villages are yet to be connected by all weather roads.
- 46.5% of rural households are still un-electrified, A large number of villages are not connected to the central grid;

The assessment criteria of poverty often leaves out non-economic parameters, equality and access to services which include shelter, drinking water, sanitation, employment, education and healthcare.

The lack of access to essential services not only has adverse impacts on the quality of life, but also restricts access to opportunities for enhancing livelihood measures, and the social costs incurred due to lack of proper health facilities and education is large.

**Fig. 2.2 : The rural push towards the city**

It is a common experience that the access to rural development and public services is inequitable. Largely the poor, uneducated, women and low caste people remain away from the benefits of development and public investments (Fig. 2.3). There are several reasons for this situation—like the political interventions, official prejudices, social oppressions, corruption, complex procedures, lack of education, etc. To make rural programmes reach the poor and deprived, new ways and means will have to be worked out. Some out-of-box ideas, like bank at village door step, mobile based banking, adult education camps, social reforms, etc. have worked successfully which need to be taken further.

Fig. 2.3 : Inequities in Access to Public Services and Rural Development Programmes

## Understanding Rural Poverty

With the deterioration in the land-man-ratio in the agricultural sector, the rural population in search of livelihoods migrate to the urban areas. With limited possibility of finding a job in the organized sector, the rural migrant is gradually absorbed in the informal activities. Below subsistence levels of incomes inflate the percentage of rural population below the poverty line. The probabilistic models hold that the rural-urban expected income differentials are much larger for the rural poor than the rural non-poor, and hence these poor have a higher propensity to migrate to the urban areas. The migrants enter the urban labour market due to their limited skills and ability to access the formal sector.

Poverty is multi dimensional, the poor are malnourished, lack minimum shelter, sanitation and drinking water, they are illiterate and cannot afford to send their children to the school. Poor are also at various risks, like unemployment, child labour, insecurity in old age, limited access to healthcare or more health expenditure, non-healthy living conditions, no proper housing, etc. The poor occupy a marginal role in the socio-economic life of the community. The poverty manifests the following general features:

- Lack of effective participation and integration of the poor in the larger society.
- The poor do not usually belong to trade unions or other associations.
- They are not regular members of political parties and do not participate in welfare programme, and make very little use of banks, hospitals, etc.
- They face low wages, chronic unemployment and under-employment lead to low income, lack of property ownership, absence of savings, etc.
- Poor housing conditions, over-crowding, material deprivation.
- On the family level, there is absence of childhood, high rate of divorce, desertion by male family head, leaving only female headed households, thereby making children and women the most vulnerable group.
- On the level of individual, the major characteristics are strong feelings of marginality, of helplessness, of dependency and inferiority.
- Many poor people in live in cramped, over-crowded and insanitary conditions on precarious sites who are vulnerable to fires and flooding.
- The poor suffer from unprotected irregular employment or bonded labour conditions poor are highly dependent on public bodies for basic services (water, healthcare, sanitation, etc.). There is abject shortage of safe drinking water, solid waste collection and hygienic sanitation systems and other amenities.
- The poor are often subject to opperssive domination, socio-religious discrimination and feudal exploitation through the traditional customs, like Jamindari self-styled panchayat, religious, political and village leaders. The new form of authorities are emerging causing oppressions to the rural poor which include corrupt and dominating officials, bankers, police, etc.

Participatory learning with the target groups provides useful clues towards understanding, the needs of the rural poor, which can be categorized in the following segments :

1. Survival: Freedom from hunger and malnutrition, food security and employment, right to work and earn.
2. Supportive: Shelter, drinking water supply, power, transport, sanitation, etc.
3. Transformational: Education, literacy, skill development, environmental upgradation and access to information.
4. Empowerment: Equal access to resources, including land, finance and services, justice, participation in decision making, protection of human rights, gender equality, etc.

With a little external support, the poor are often capable of meeting their survival needs where the organized sector has a vital role. The experience indicates that the supportive needs really help the poor in climbing up the economic ladder. The provision of basic services and facilities in the rural context is a major concern, can be grouped accordingly for the purpose of planning, development

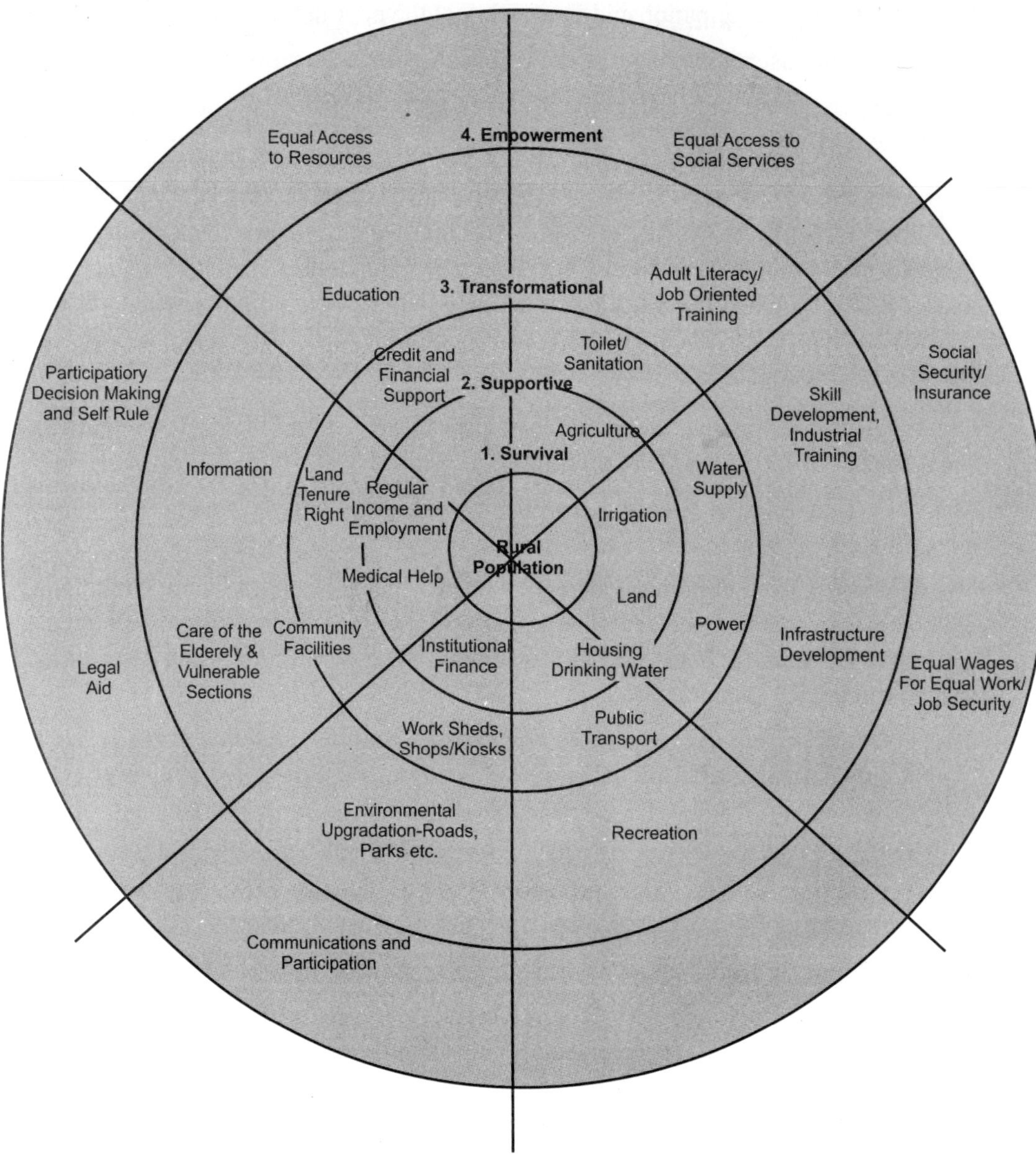


**Fig. 2.4 : Diagramatic Classification Needs of the Rural Population**

and investments. However, no programme would be successful unless it is tied up with community empowerment and addresses to the oppressive traditions, customs and practices. This means evolving a tactical strategy based on community empowerment together with an effective decentralization, devolution and deregulation for a pro-poor, people-centered approach. The plans and programmes should be devised so as to enable the community towards self-rule, self-reliance and self-development.

Rural development by and large is a state subject. The Central government's ideology, policies, plan and programmes are contingent upon the State government agenda, policies, politics, and priorities. The State government's strategies are further dependent upon the district administration, procedurs, rules and regulations. However, the fulcrum in the actual implementation is the local Panchayat/ Block Development Office/village administration. Its functioning is effected by local power structure and equations of party politics, alongwith the ability, capacity and integrity of the officials. The officials on the spot are the field engineer, patwari, self-help volunteers and the local banker. It is often observed that they hardly trained and oriented about the policies, programmes and plans, and contrinue to discharge their duty by carrying out the orders of the higher officers. Very often no attention is given to draw out and prescribe the standard operating procedures and protocols, which result in substandard, ad hoc implementation.

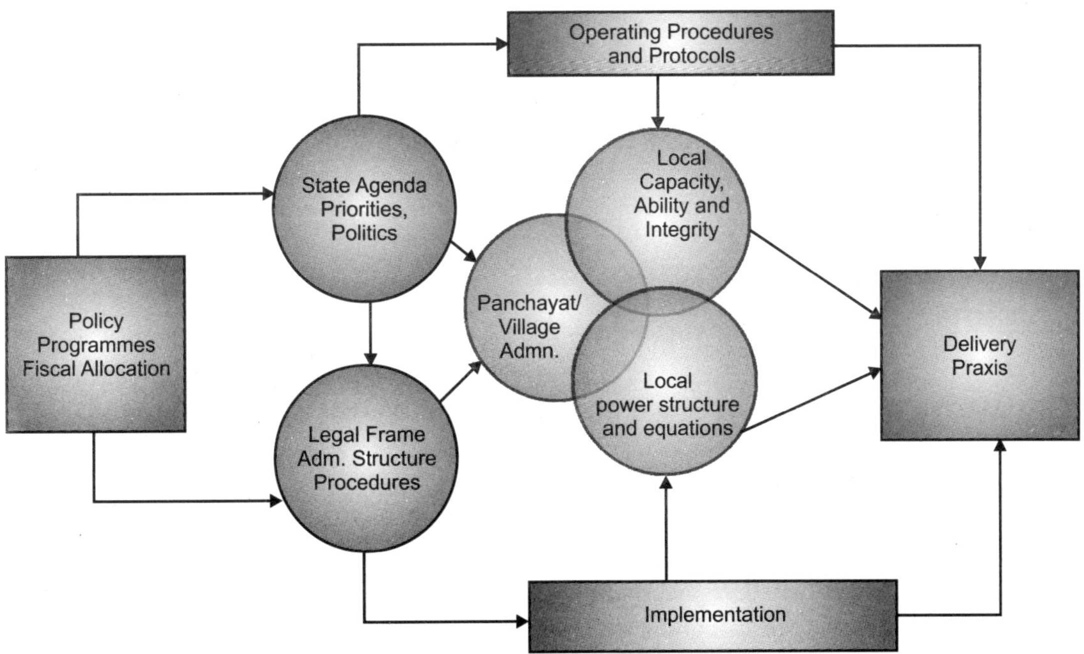


**Fig. 2.5 : Policy, Programmes, Politics and Praxis of Rural Development.**

The process of rural development in the country often starts with a well worked out policy framework, which is detailed out in the form of plans, programs and projects. At the stage of implementation, the projects encounter several hurdles-like local politics, activism, vested interests, corruption, lack of local capacity, outdated procedures, societal oppressions, etc. These result into a truncated delivery and a wide gap between the plans and implementation (Fig. 2.6).

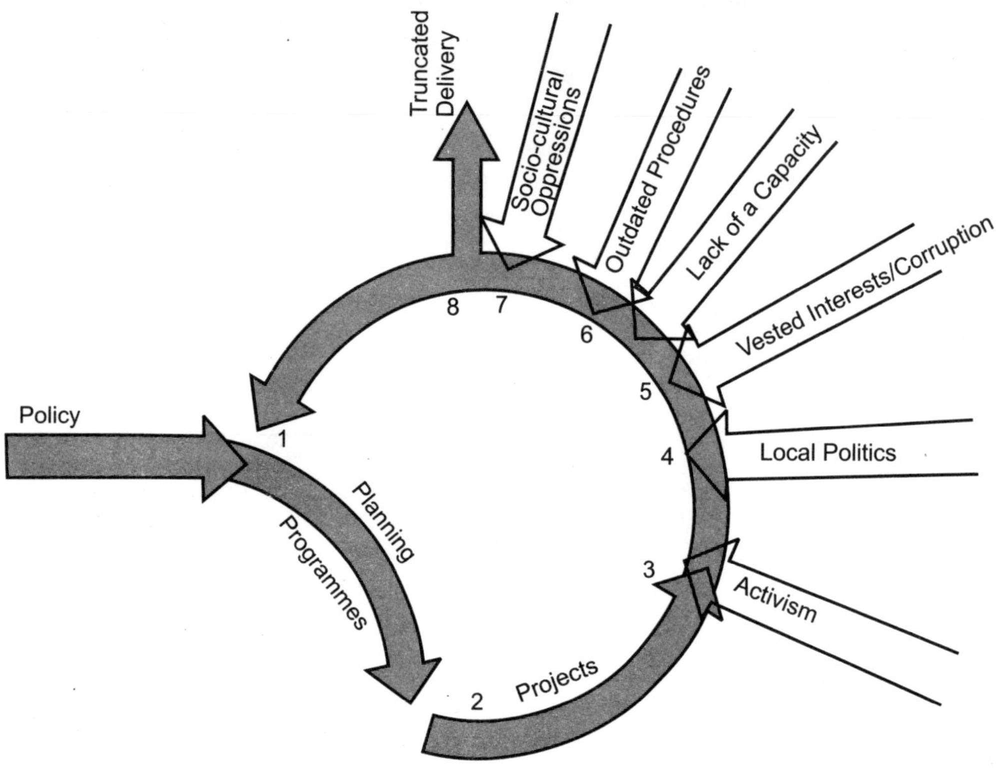


**Fig. 2.6 : The Cycle of Policy—Plans—Projects and Programmes and their truncated delivery**

## Socio-cultural Oppressions

Feudal and oppressive societal practices in India's rural areas and perpetual poverty go hand in hand. Economic development and poverty allevation programmes of the government often fail to succeed as they do not factor the ongoing social oppressions. These practices tend to close the door of opportunities for the deprived, oppressed rural poor. Whether the oppressions can be eliminated is a major issue. For this we have to understand the various forms of oppressions :

- Human Rights Violations

- Feudal, Para-legal practices.
- Communalism and casteism
- Religious fundamentalism and superstitions
- Gender/sex discrimination
- Physical disability
- Lack of education and literacy
- Poverty
- Government servants and other officials, authorities acting as the rulers

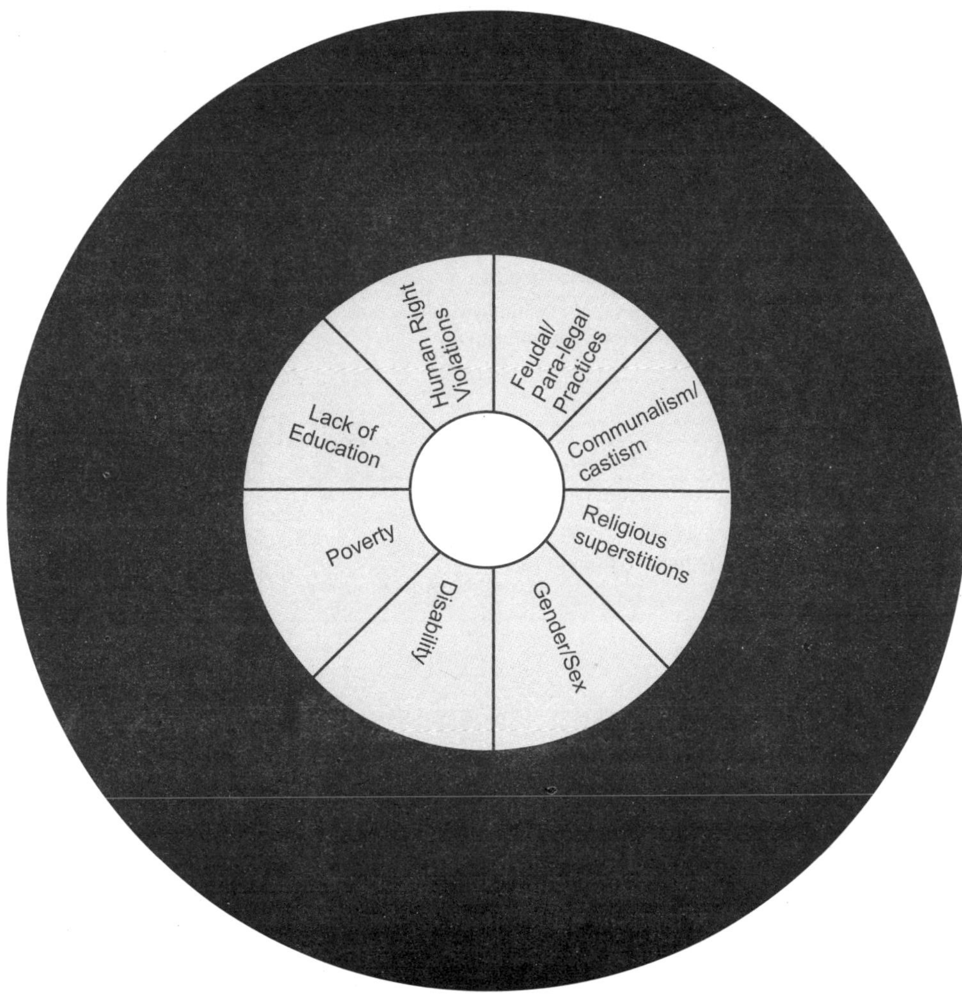


**Fig. 2.7 : Oppressions create a closed world for the deprived rural poor**

**Table 2.1 : Village Oppressions Matrix**

| Levels<br>Oppression Elements | Local/Community | Regional/Public |
|---|---|---|
| **Communalism/caste** | — communal violence and tensions, insecurity<br>— non access to business, vocations, etc.<br>— Superior and inferior caste labels<br>— Segregated housing, work place, cremation, ghats, well/water points, schools, toilets, etc.<br>— Exclusion for non-conformist behaviour<br>— Social discrimination | Caste based Elections/ appointments |
| **Religious Superstitions** | — Forced religious conversion<br>— Non access to temples<br>— Ex-communication<br>— Self-proclaimed mystiques, pandit, guru, healers, tantriks, etc. | Nexus between religious groups and political leaders |
| **Gender/Sex** | — Girl child and child marriage<br>— non-acceptance of inter religious/inter-caste marriage<br>— discrimination of widows | lack of gender equity and community empowerment |
| **Disability** | — Social exclusion, stigma, fake doctors, Superstitions, discrimination | Non-accessible buildings, transport, jobs, etc. non-integration of disabled with society |
| **Feudal/Para-legal Practices and Human Rights Violations** | — Political promises<br>— Voting coercion<br>— Para-legal punishments<br>— Human Rights violations<br>— Feudal traditions | lack of human rights enforcement<br>Non-implementation of Government manifestos/ programmes<br>Police terror/excesses<br>Officials as ruling elite<br>Urban-centric administration, courts and governance<br>Complexity of rules, regulations and procedures |
| **Poverty** | — Economic exclusion<br>— Bonded labour<br>— Child labour<br>— Unequal wages | Market driven approach to basic services, healthcare, education, housing, etc.<br>Diversion and misuse of subsidies, development funds |
| **Lack of Education** | — Inequalities in education<br>— School psychosis | Anti illiterate/complex procedures<br>privatization, diversion of subsidies and grants |

The oppressions often exist at the local level community village and at regional, public level (Fig. 2.7, Table 2.1). The regional, public oppessions refer to those at the level of political, administrative and judicial interventions and are directly related to the governance. The remedy to various types of the oppressions can not be through legal process and by policing, but by a people centric multi-pronged approach. This has to start with education, empowerment and equity. The younger generation have a major role in changing the oppressive traditions. A major area of concern is the political system and election reforms whereby the public representatives only with an umblemished, clean record could fight the elections.

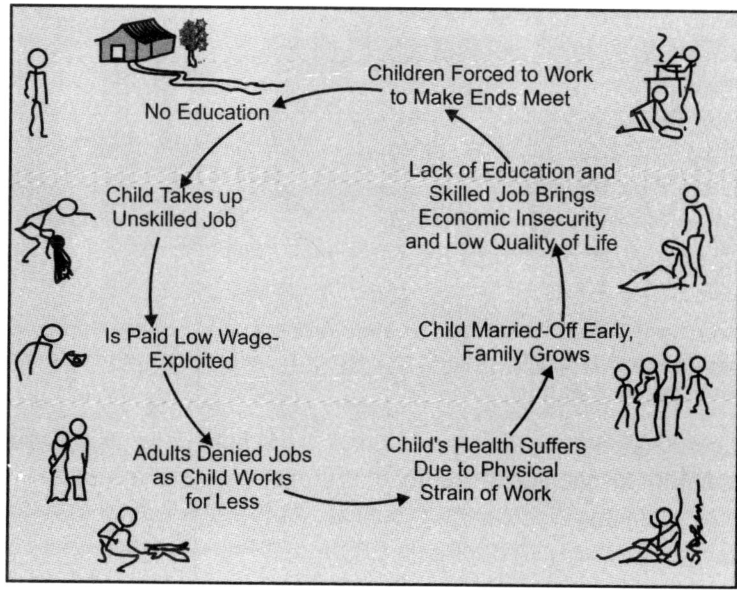


**Fig. 2.8 : The vicious cycle of poverty and child labour**

The village can no more remain the feudal island of social discrimination, backwardness and dark age. In an era of communications and speed, the villages are becoming global for which matching social reforms are needed.

The children of the poor in Indian villages are often deprived of education, health and normal life. A vicious circle of poverty and child labour still exists and children an a tender age have to work on low paid, unskilled jobs. Lack of education/early marriage, responsibility of family and poverty add up to make the entire life of children miserable and of hardship (Fig. 2.8) Although the government has made child education compulsory and a right, child labour illegal and child marriage a cognizable offence, the practice persists. What is necessary is to go beyond the legal and police remedies, and to focus more on social and financial inclusion and 'rights' based approach. The transformation of the thinking of village elders, heads and leadership is necessary, who need to be more sensitive to the evil and conscious of the rights of children.

**Fig. 2.9. Right to education can be a catalyst in eliminating social oppressions which the rural poor face. Adult literacy and schools can be made more friendly by mixing entertainment, sports, financial concessions and food with education**

In Indian villages religions play an important role. It has both—the positive and negative roles at indiviual and community levels. It is difficulty to segregate religion from daily lives, politices and village development. Mahatma Gandhi observed that : "A religion that takes no account of practical affairs, and does not help in them, is no religion." Religious beliefs and practices are central to many people's daily lives, and religious organizations have a major influence on politics, law and government. The studies show that episodes of violence between religious groups, while apparently about religion, are often expressions of other social tensions and demonstrate the manipulation of religion by other social actors. It was also believed that religion is used to mobilize rival groups to compete for political control of local government and for other resources such as land.

While religious organizations play a positive role in providing immediate relief to victims, usually members of their own community, there is little evidence that they play a larger role in long-term reconstruction or in preventing further outbreaks of violence. In villages residential segregation seems to be an inevitable outcome of the conflict, as people seek safer places to live. Those affected by the violence relocate in the short or long term to safer areas. Over time, this is leading to residential segregation. New or relocated places of worship and schools are being built-in segregated neighbourhoods and religious minority communities can not access lands owned by indigenous groups. In addition, vigilante groups are emerging where there is lack of confidence in the police to provide protection.

In the aftermath of the violence, religious organizations play an important short-term role in assisting victims and provide temporary relief and counseling, usually to members of their own faith. However, they have not, for the most part, developed longer-term transformative programmes (such as rebuilding houses or livelihoods) and their attempts to prevent further conflicts have been limited.

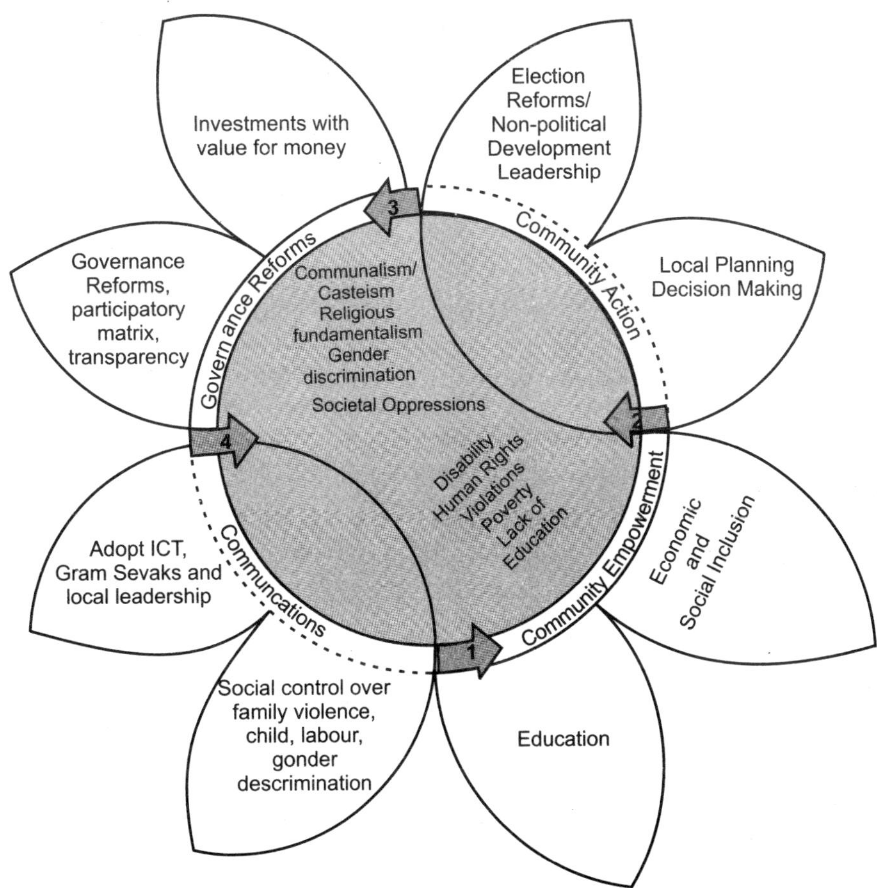


**Fig. 2.10 : Transforming Rural Oppressed Society into an Opportune Community**

Four critical areas, viz. community empowerment, community action, governance reforms and communications are vital for transforming oppressions into a lotus of opportunities. The specific areas to curb the societal oppression are :

(*a*) Within the government domain such as election reforms, non-political representation in local development bodies, local planning and decision making, economic and social inclusion, education, governance reform and value for money investments, (*b*) Within the community domain, such as local leadership, self-help groups, social control over family violence, child marriage, child labour, illiteracy and gender discrimination, and improving the level of education.

(*c*) Information and communication technology (ICT) is emerging as a tool of empowerment of rural poor, savings of time, energy and resources, lesser vists to government offices and enhanced efficiency. In the rural context, the local offices, police, service agencies, bank and panchayat have to gradually adopt communications by e-mail, mobile, e-banking and e-governance, replacing time-consuming and corruption generating paper work. This has to be a fundamental building block of rural development.

**Fig. 2.11 : World is a small Village-Vanishing social oppressions and discrimination by information technology**

Refocusing upon the Key Result Areas and Key Action Areas is necessary to achieve inclusive rural growth (Fig. 2.12). The key result areas are (*a*) financial inclusion, enhanced productivity, employment generation, (*b*) Social inclusion, connectivity, communications, education, healthcare, gender equity, empowerment, human rights, etc., (*c*) Democratic governance, participation, decentralization and localisation, (*d*) Ecological sustainability, including re-engineering, new technology opportunities, and (*e*) Transparency and efficiency. These need focused attention and action, which are often treated as marginal issues. As such rural development plans and programmes should include (*i*) Political, legal, election and governance reforms (*iii*) Social change-from oppressions to opportunities, (*iii*) District and local planning, spatial enblement, and (*iv*) Praxis for co-ordinated and inclusive implementation.

A major focus area of rural development had been the infrastructure. However, to balance between the spread and investments, the government has been emphasising upon low cost, low standard, poorly maintained infrastructure services. This perspective has to change and rural infrastructure need not be inferior to 'state of the art' urban standards (Fig. 2.12)

State of the art rural development can be possible only by a nexus of local leadership, socio-cultural a legal reforms, strategy structure, Institution and ICT system dervised on the basis of local implementation potential A weak area of implementation praxis is lack of institutional and official capacity and orientation, which needs immediate review and strengthening. Spatial planning is another area, often marginalized at the local level.

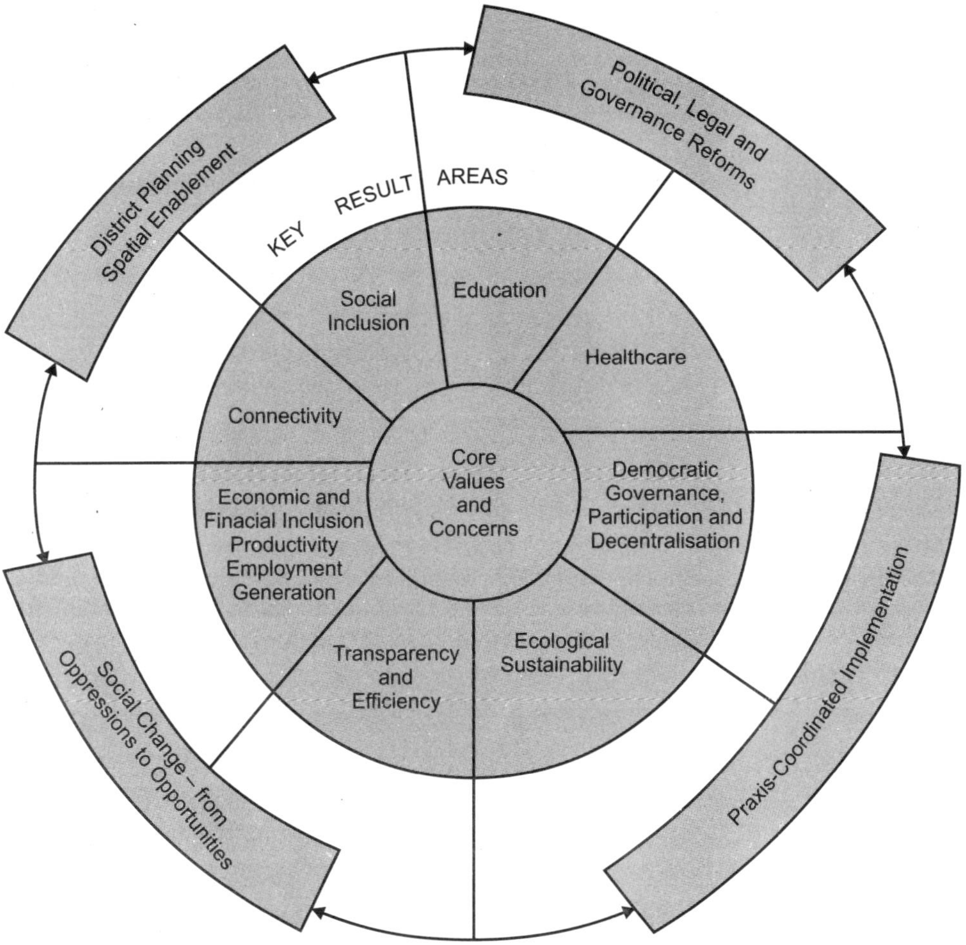

**Fig. 2.12 : Key Result Areas for Inclusive Rural Growth**

**Fig. 2.13 : With the globalization and fast track economic development, the village infrastructure needs are multiplying. These have to keep pace with the demands of economic development and should be state of the art, sustainable and forward looking. 'Low cost' in the modern world may not be critical, as finance is not the issue, but its mobilization by leveraging, partnerships and new paradigms.**

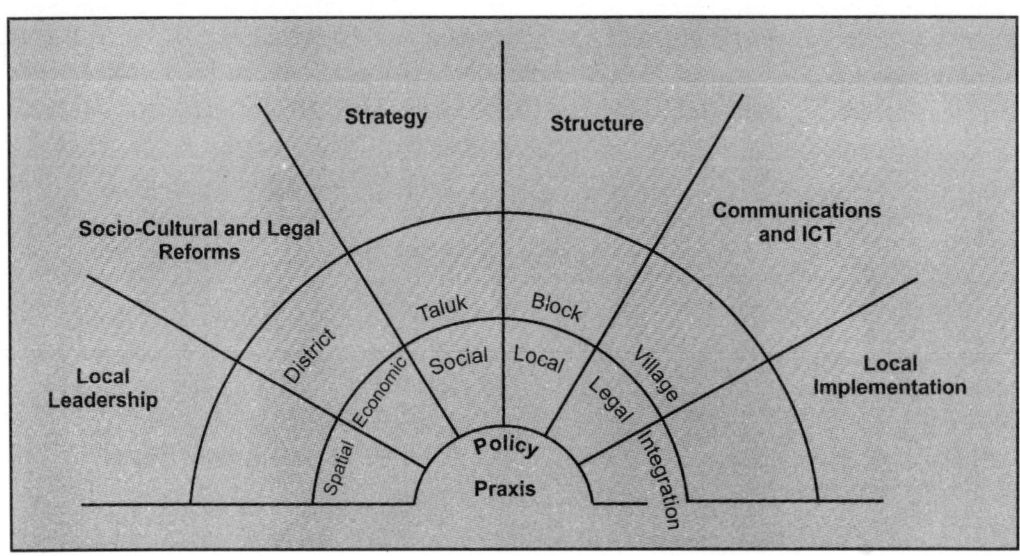


Fig. 2.14 :The Rising Sun-Successful policy implementation is largely contingent upon economic, social and legal integration. This can be achieved by District and Local development planning and socio-cultural reforms.

Chapter **3**

# Politics, Governance and Transparency

*"The power brokers have established their vice-like grip only because democracy has not functioned representatives from electorates as small as a hundred to five hundred persons, the source of power will lie only as far away as the Panchayat Ghar, not some distant state capital or even more distant capital of the country.*

*Their [PRIs] existence has depended less on the mandate of the people than the whims of state governments.*

*The essence of democracy is election. Elections to panchayati raj institutions have been woefully irregular and uncertain. To avoid it enshrine in the Constitution regular, periodic elections to panchayati raj institutions."*

***—Rajiv Gandhi. Selected Speeches and Writings. vol. V, 169. Publications Division, Government of India.***

The paradigm of development adopted by the Indian Government in the initial years was based upon the thought of absorbing the surplus labour of agricultural rural economy into industries through massive industrialisation. It found its mirror image in the political and administrative arrangements set out in the Indian Constitution. E.M.S. Namboodiripad put it very candidly in his dissent to the Asoka Mehta Committee Report. He wrote : 'Democracy at the Central and State levels, but bureaucracy at all lower levels—this is the essence of Indian polity as spelt out in the

Constitution.' The main draftsman of the Constitution, Dr. B.R. Ambedkar was strongly against the system of village panchayats. Characterising the village as 'a sink of localism' and 'den of narrow mindedness' he had observed: 'I am glad that the draft Constitution has discarded the village and adopted the individual as unit.' (Shive Rao B, 1968, The Framing of Indian Constitution, A study by the IIPA, New Delhi). Rajiv Gandhi as the Prime Minister during early eighties visited rural areas in the country and had wide ranging discussions. He was disillusioned by the urban control of rural governance. This was the beginning of the Constitutional Amendments (73rd and 74th) and transfer of power at the local, grass-root levels.

## Panchayati Raj and 73rd Constitutional Amendment

Village communities are characterized by agrarian economies, organized around village headmen. Such bodies, known as panchayats, were the centre of social life, a forum for justice and a basic structure for administration of village affairs. Local self government in India was initiated by a government resolution of 18th May 1882 during Lord Ripon's viceregal tenure, providing for local boards consisting of a large majority of elected non-official members. This is considered as the magna carta of local democracy in India. By 1925 eight provinces in India passed Acts for establishment of village panchayats. By 1948 twenty nine native (princely) states enacted village panchayat acts. However, these statutory panchayats covered only limited number of villages and generally performed only a limited functions.

The 73rd Constitutional Amendment Act passed by the Parliament on 22 December 1992 came as a historical initiative to provide constitutional protection to panchayats and to address their problems. With the passage of this Act panchayats have become a substantial and justiciable part of the Constitution of India.

The Seventy-third Constitutional Amendment Act recognized panchayats as institutions of self government and expanded the jurisdiction of panchayats. Eleventh Schedule of the Constitution of India contains a long list of subjects on which panchayats have jurisdiction now. The list has 29 subjects. However, powers of panchayats are basically executive in nature, and include planning function as well. District Planning Committees in each district and Metropolitan Planning Committees in each metropolitan area will prepare draft development plans for the area under their jurisdiction by putting together the plans prepared by municipalities and panchayats in the district/metropolitan area, and will forward such plans to the state government. Panchayats do not enjoy legislative powers, which rest with the central and state governments. They have no control over police and no judicial role under the new law. Thus, in spite of widening of their jurisdiction in terms of subjects and the recognition as institutions of self government, panchayats under the 73rd CAA continue to have only limited developmental functions.

The 73rd CAA required the States' legislates to pass legislation for their states in conformity to the mandatory provisions and providing details in areas where States were to take their own decisions. States were also expected to make the relevant rules and take other steps to implement various provisions of the new law. This sub-section briefly summarises the progress of implementation and thus describes the present status of PRIs in certain respects. All the 21 States passed the conformity acts (CAs) within the stipulated one year period. The legislation provides for uniform three-tier panchayati raj system. All the three tiers (at village, block and district level) being directly elected. States with population not exceeding 2 million need not have panchayats at the intermediate level. The nomenclature for panchayats at the three levels varies across States. In this document panchayats are referred to as gram panchayat or GP (at this village level), Intermediate Panchayat or IP (at the intermediate level) and Zila Parishad or ZP (at the district level). At the village level there exists Gram Sabha consisting of all the adult citizens in a village. While chairpersons of IPs and ZPs will be elected by and from amongst the elected members of these bodies, the mode of election of the chairperson of GPs is left to state legislatures to decide. In most states chairpersons of GPs are directly elected. An independent Election Commission will be established in each state for holding elections to panchayats.

Although some states had reserved some seats for SCs, STs and women even before the 73rd CAA was passed, this Act provided for mandatory reservation of seats in panchayats at all levels for SCs in proportion to total population of the relevant area, and 30% reservation for women. Both these reservations have to be effected through rotation among constituencies.

Before the enactment of the 73rd CAA many state governments resorted to supersession of elected panchayats at will. This resulted in many panchayat remaining suspended and their work being managed by bureaucrats for long intervals. The new Act provides for a uniform five-year tenure for PRIs, and in the event of supersession of a panchayat election to reconstitute the body to be completed within six months of the supersession.

The Act provides for empowerment of panchayats to levy taxes, duties, fees, etc. It also provides for setting up of State Finance Commissions every five years to review the financial position of panchayats and to make recommendations, among other things, on the principles of sharing of taxes, duties, fee, etc. between the state government and the panchayats. The recommendations also cover principles which should govern grants-in-aid to panchayats from the Consolidated Fund of the State. However, district planning does not find a place in the 73rd Constitution Amendment Act, though it is tucked somewhere in the 74th Amendment Act. One is amazed to find barring a couple of isolated instances, States have been playing ducks and drakes with this provision. The powers, authority and responsibilities of panchayats are stated in Article 243G, which is quoted below :

'Subject to the provisions of this Constitution, the Legislature of a state may by law endow the panchayats with such powers and authority as may be necessary to enable them to function as institutions of self-government and such law may contain provisions for the devolution of powers and responsibilities upon panchayats at the appropriate level, subject to such conditions as may be specified therein, with respect to—

(*a*) the preparation of plans for economic development and social justice;

(*b*) the implementation of schemes for economic development and social justice as may be entrusted to them including those in relation to the matters listed in the Eleventh Schedule.'

Article 243H deals with the funds of the panchayats and their powers to impose taxes. The Legislature of a State may be law, authorize and set out procedures for panchayats to levy, collect and appropriate such taxes, duties, tolls and fees. The State legislature may assign to a panchayat such taxes, duties, tolls and fees levied and collected by the State government for such purposes. Subject to certain conditions and limits, it may provide for making such grants-in-aid to the panchayats from the Consolidated Fund of the State. The State can also provide for constitution of such Funds for crediting all such moneys received, and its withdrawal.

Article 243I states that every five years a state Financial Commission shall be constituted to review the financial position of the panchayats and to make recommendations to the Governor as to the principles which should govern :

(*i*) the distribution between the state and the panchayats of the net proceeds of the taxes, duties, tolls, and fees leviable by the state, which may be divided between them under this Part and the allocation between the panchayats at all levels of their respective shares of such proceeds;

(*ii*) the determination of the taxes, duties, tolls, and fees which may be assigned to, or appropriated by the panchayats;

(*iii*) the grants-in-aid to the panchayats from the Consolidated Fund of the state;

(*a*) the measures needed to improve the financial position of the panchayats;

(*b*) any other matter referred to the Finance Commission by the Governor in the interests of sound finance of the panchayats.

The reservations for Scheduled Castes, Tribes, and women in Panchayat institutions are provided in Article 243D. Article 243E provides for a normal duration of five years for panchayats and a gap of not more than six months between the expiry of the period and the conduct of the elections for the next term of the panchayats. Article 243K invests the authority of preparing the electoral rolls and conduction elections in the state Election Commission. Article 243F empowers the state government to make laws providing criteria for disqualification of candidature from panchayat elections. Under Article 243J, the state can legislate with respect to maintenance of accounts by the panchayats and their audit.

For the rural local bodies, the 73rd CAA provided a three-tier structure called the Panchayati Raj Institutions or PRIs. The gram village panchayat (GP) at the village level; *panchayat samiti* at the intermediate (*block, tehsil, mandal, taluka*) level; and *zila parishad* at the district level form the three tiers of PRIs. Broadly, the functions identified for transfer to PRIs are (*i*) literacy (Adult literacy) and elementary education; (*ii*) primary health and sanitation; (*iii*) rural water supply; (*iv*) rural roads; (*v*) housing for the poor; (*vi*) nutrition, children, women and crèches; (*vii*) livelihood and employment guarantee, and (*viii*) rural electrification.

In conformity with the 73rd CAA, all Indian states have passed relevant legislation establishing a three-tier system of *panchayat*. Political decentralization to local bodies has been more or less successful in India, as a study by World Bank (2000) Points out. With the first round of elections to PRIs and ULBs having been held in most states, a sizeable number of elected representatives (approximately 260,000 to PRIs and over 60,000 to ULBs), who bear responsibility for taking decisions, have been elected in the country's local government system.

Out of more than 22 lakh representatives elected to three levels of panchayats, more than 40 per cent belong to the STs (Table3.1). At the gram panchayat (GP) level, each Panch's constituency comprises about 340 people (70 families), making India the largest and most intensely democratic country worldwide.

**Table 3.1 : Composition of Panchayats**

| Panchayat Level | Number | Elected represent-atives | Women % | SC % | ST % |
|---|---|---|---|---|---|
| District Panchayat | 602 | 11,825 | 11 | 18 | 11 |
| Intermediate Panchayat | 6097 | 1,10,070 | 43 | 22 | 13 |
| Village or Gram Panchayat | 2,34,676 | 20,73,715 | 40 | 16 | 11 |

**Source:** MOPR (2006)

India, with more than 2,40,000 local bodies and almost 2.2 million elected representatives, has the distinction of having the largest number of democratically elected local governments. Together with many strengths and opportunities, the system of elected local governments and Panchayati Raj Institutions (PRIs) presents certain weaknesses and threats. These are:

(*a*) Pre-eminence of the state government/administration leading to the issues of domain, devolution, autonomy and localization of PRIs,

(*b*) Weak finances of PRIs,

(*c*) Issues of corruption, audit and accountability, and

(*d*) Lack of capacity and capabilities at local level.

## Devolution of Powers and Functions (Activity mapping)

In the First Round Table of State Ministers of Panchayati Raj in Kolkata it was agreed that all states and UTs would undertake activity mapping by the end of 2004-05, using the activity mapping model that was evolved by the Ministry of Rural Development in the Report of the Task Force on Devolution of Powers and Functions upon Panchayati Raj Institutions (August 2001). Though this target has not been achieved in all states, there has been considerable progress on activity mapping with respect to each state. Activity mapping involves allocation of the responsibilities across levels of government, including panchayats at the district, intermediate, and village levels through specific and logical steps. Each function ought to be unbundled into activities that are consistent with devolution and each activity is tested against certain 'public finance' characteristics so as to determine where it might be assigned.

The Round Tables of State Ministers of Panchayati Raj arrived at several action points, that are being progressively implemented. These include strengthening the gram sabha, a good system of audit, no mismatch between functional and financial assignments, and having a strong revenue base. The gram sabha can be a powerful instrument of downward accountability, if property empowered and convened regularly. Ideally speaking a good framework for empowerment of gram sabhas would be that at the minimum, it will have powers to approve plans, programmes, and projects before they are taken up for implementation by the panchayat at the village level. It would identify beneficiaries of poverty alleviation and other programmes and issue certificates of utilization of funds by the panchayat at the village level for the above programes. In the context of infrastructure development, this would also mean that gram sabhas have the power to undertake community contracting, both for construction of rural infrastructure projects and their maintenance.

For taking up development activities, many state governments have constituted Rural Development Departments. These aim to facilitate accountable funds management, including parking of funds in commercial banks and proper account keeping through double entry systems. The experience of functioning of these organizations shows that in respect of securing non-diversion of funds they have been effective, however, in planning and in ensuring transparency and participation the achievements are limited. There is an increasing disquiet about such practices and in some states, the discontent is spilling over into court litigations, where panchayats have questioned the locus standi of such bodies to undertake work within the assigned functional domain of panchayats.

With the 73$^{rd}$ Constitutional Amendment Act (1992) the non-governmental organizations are no longer serving only as intermediaries between the rural community and the government, but are more directly linked to the process of decentralization and democratic governance. This has widened the role of civil society and community organizations in rural management. They are becoming an organized voice in the civil society, which make it possible to channel demands, and undertake the development. This requires a fundamental change in the attitudes and approach towards understanding and addressing the urban problems and issues. The old assumptions have to be re-assessed to develop a new vision.

**Table 3.2 : Revisiting Old Assumptions**

| Old Assumption | New Vision |
|---|---|
| 1. Economic development as a vehicle for social progress. | 1. Economic development is not a substitute of socio-cultural integration. Focus on poverty alleviation, sustainable infrastructure development and social mobilization. |
| 2. Social equity by downward fitration. | 2. Focus at the grassroots level and evolve a pro-poor perspective. |
| 3. State intervention for creating a civil society. | 3. State itself is not a creation of civil society. |
| 4. Poverty as indicator of socio-cultural unrest and law and order problems. | 4. Majority of the poor have the 'values of patriots and perseverance of pioneers. |
| 5. Globalization of development and management systems. | 5. Decentralization and localization of planning, development and governance. |
| 6. Political intervention as a hindrance. | 6. Political apparutus essential for people-centred planning. |
| 7. Population distribution and decentralization by regional policies and planning. | 7. Guide population distribution by incentives and integrated economic development. |
| 8. Planning and governance as expert domains. | 8. Bottom-up, participatory approach, rather than top down. |
| 9. Centralized and strong apex organizations for coordinated management. | 9. Decentralised management, devolution and effective horizontalization among actors, resources and people. |
| 10. Government as provider of services and jobs to the poor. | 10. Government as facilitator and catalyst of self-generating economy, self-build and self-reliance. Promote partnerships. |
| 11. Planning for an egalitarian society with modern education. | 11. Promote and preserve local semantic values and heterogeneity. |
| 12. Legal systems for social justice and gender equity and to control social unrest, crimes and corruption. | 12. Many of the problems arise due to complex and too many legislations. Simplify procedures, minimize legal complexity, maximize enforcement and empower the community. Develop regulatory powers. |
| 13. Statutory Comprehensive Planning. | 13. Flexible strategic and action planning, focus on performance. |
| 14. Environmental issues subsidiary to economic development | 14. Ecology and environment (including land, water, air, energy, sanitation, waste management, drainage, transport, building materials, industry and technology) as the basic criteria of economic planning and development. |
| 15. Monopoly over information. | 15. Resort to Right to Information GIS, GPS, tele-communications, internet, web, virtual conferencing, networking, intelligent systems, etc. |

There is an urgent need of transition towards a post-modern, post-European civilization for a people-centred approach. This requires giving up old assumptions and embrace a new vision and evolving a governance index encompassing the principles of effectiveness, equity, participation and accountability of services. This will help in 'actualising' the process of new governance model on the ground. For this a set of 'tools' are to be identified for planning, management and implementation. These should be based on local priorities, profiles and situation (e.g., poverty, environment, safety and community participation), which are derived on the basis of consultation process. The keywords of sustainable development are decentralization, democratization, empowerment, participation, local ownership, benefit sharing, equity, justice and public accountability.

With people and resources in place, the District Plan needs to set a strategic direction for growth in a manner acceptable and supported by the people. There must be good match between the planner's perspective and the people's aspirations. This can be expressed from different perspectives which nevertheless converge to become an all-round set of shared values. Simulation models should be developed to explore the blue-sky of future livelihoods, life-styles and time-use. The breakthrough concept of lifetimes—a human time-use base resource accounting system enables life cycle time-use accounting and imputed economic value simulation. This would cross-link environmental accounting systems with human capital and should determine the broad direction and investments for the sustainability transmission scenario.

In order to address to the needs of the majority of the people, that is poor, a major focus area has to be local economic promotion and poverty reducation. Among young people there is a widespread perception that the future holds nothing for them, as a result, a large number of the unemployed are forced to take on informal, illegal or uncertain jobs. While entrepreneurial potential and development opportunities lie untapped, the state villages lose out on tax revenue. This sort of situation is not attractive for investors, the economic development stagnates, and the vicious circle of poverty perpetuates. As such, there is an urgent need to focus on the promotion of small and medium sized enterprises (SME) and the local and regional economy of the region. The growth opportunities of existing enterprises, value added chains that are labour intensive, facilitating business start-ups and attracting new business will enhance the competitiveness of the State/District, while also meeting the basic human needs, as given in the Millennium Development Goals.

## Millennium Development Goals

Goals 1 : Eradicate extreme poverty and hunger

Goals 2 : Achieve universal primary education

Goals 3 : Promote gender equality and empower women

Goals 4 : Reduce child mortality

Goals 5 : Improve maternal health

Goals 6 : Combat HIV/AIDS, malaria and other diseases.

Goals 7 : Ensure environmental sustainability

Goals 8 : Develop a global partnership for development.

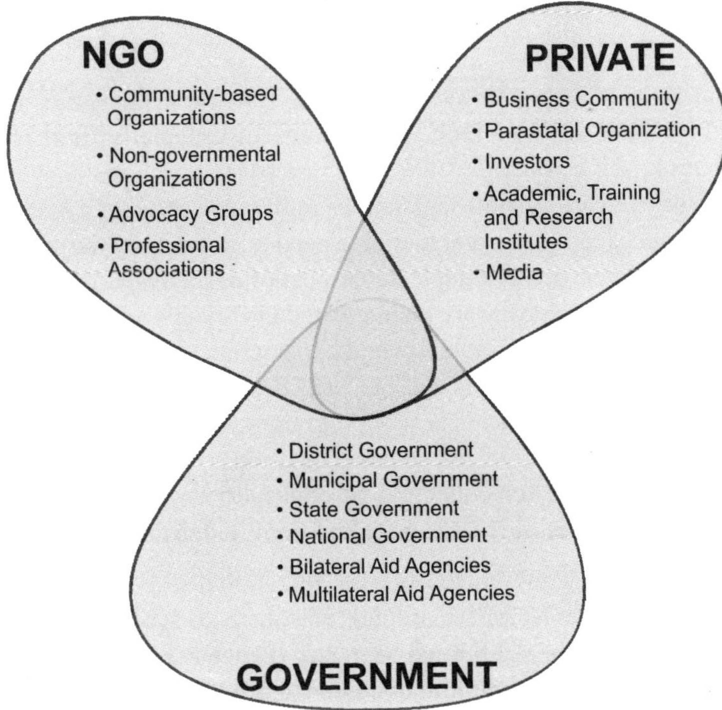


**Fig. 3.1 : The form of governance prevalent in the country is generally bureaucratic and involves conservative controls. Inspite of conflicts and retardants, private sector and non-government organizations have assumed a growing degree of protagonism within the more open context of democratic dialogue. Without doubt private sector and non-governmental organizations are going to play an important role in the future of democratic governance.**

## Financial Base of Local Body/Panchayat

The finances of *panchayats* consist of :

(*a*) Own sources, i.e., taxes assigned by the state *panchayat* Acts to the local bodies, which are levied and collected by them. Own sources also include non-tax revenues such as fees and fines, user charges for services, and rent from property.

(*b*) Shared taxes that are collected by the states with a share of the proceeds being disbursed among the local bodies of the state;

(*c*) Grants from the state/central government (which may be tied or untied).

The PRIs are heavily depends on external financial resources, most of which tend to come from the central/state governments. The degree of self-reliance also varies across the tiers of the PRIs, which are dependent on transfers from state and central governments. The position of *gram panchayats* is much better than the other two tiers, namely, Panchayat Samitis and District Panchayats.

The First Round Table of State Ministers of Panchayti Raj at Kolkata recommended that steps be taken to encourage PRIs to raise their own resources, especially through the provision to 'appropriate' revenues raised by them for their own purposes, in accordance with Article 243H of the Constitution. A study of various state legislations indicates a menu of 24 taxes, duties, tolls and fees levied by village panchayats. However,there is a need to utilize fully the potential of panchayats to raise taxes. In several states, this is a neglected aspect of panchayat empowerment. While there is a popular impression that panchayats are disinterested in collection of taxes, that the poor would suffer and that this is politically inadvisable, several good practices are emerging where panchayats, on their own, have taken steps to collect taxes. The confidence in panchayats raising local revenues is also reflected in a number of economic action programmes (EAPs) and CSSs are now insisting upon a local community contribution for scheme sanction—obviously, this would require the participation of local panchayats for collection of contributions. Prominent among these is the Swajaldhara scheme (Department of Drinking Water Supply), housing, and sanitation sectors.

In order to come up with specific modalities for operationalising the objective of the National Common Minimum Programme (NCMP) that funds that are to go to panchayats are neither delayed nor diverted, a Committee with the Additional Secretary (Panchayati Raj) and representatives from Ministry of Finance among others, went into this issue and submitted its report in May, 2005. The Committee's terms of reference included an examination of the feasibility of maintaining a data base of the bank accounts of all the 240,000 Panchayati Raj institutions, feasibility of electronic transfer of funds under the current banking system and feedback mechanism on actual crediting of funds into the accounts of PRIs. The Committee concluded unanimously the maintenance of data base of panchayat accounts state-wise and setting up of feedback mechanism. Implementation of the recommendations of the Committee is being attempted in sending funds to be devolved by the 12$^{th}$ Finance Commission to panchayats through bank accounts from the consolidated funds of states.

## Issues of Corruption, Audit and Accountability

Corruption in public works is almost universal and has become incurable. It exists irrespective of caste, creed, colour or religion. In spite of plethora of religious and moral protocols and sermons, huge vigilance organizations, punitive laws, frequent enquiries and punishments, the cancer of corruption is ever-spreading. Corruption works both ways—as an organized activity and as an individual, unorganized activity. It is not confined to the government sector, but cuts across all the borders. It would be innocuous to consider financial misappropriate as the ultimate form of corruption. Other forms of corruption which are widely prevalent and conspicuous are administrative discretion, discrimination, inefficiency, favours and inaction; manipulations and non-payment of taxes and public service bills, public land appropriation; sexual exploitation, child labour, social oppressions, misbehaviour and violations of human rights. Table 3.3 shows a broad matrix, ranges and zones of corruption at individual and

**Table 3.3 : Corruption—A Broad Matrix**

| Levels/Corruption zone | Individual/Unorganised | Political/Systemic |
|---|---|---|
| **Financial Misappropriate** | – Award of works and PPP<br>– Cuts in giving loans, advances, wages/payments to contractors/ suppliers<br>– Misuse of public facilities, transport, time and resources | – Misuse/diversion of subsidies budget, grants, etc.<br>– Huge administrative expenditure from development funds<br>– Dummy contracts/supplies on behalf of officials/political leaders |
| **Administrative** | – Discretionary and discriminatory appointments and excessive use of authority<br>– Favours in posting, work allocation<br>– Deficient/inferior services, payment against poor delivery<br>– Absence, late coming of officials, delays in work output/ delivery/disposal<br>– Lack of transparency, non-implementation of RTI Act. | – Non enforcement/violation of Rules and Regulations pertaining to conduct, environment, labour, agriculture, land, etc.<br>– Complicated/opaque/confi-dential procedures<br>– Fictitious NGOs, companies, village associations, political parties, etc<br>– Lack of accountability, trans-parency and monitoring |
| **Land and Public Services** | – Encroachment on public land, roads, etc<br>– Property ownership transfer manipulation<br>– non-payment of taxes, bills for public services, theft of water and power | – Underhand land transactions<br>– Agriculture land use conversion (SEZ, Industrial Park, Farm house, etc.)<br>– Regularisation of unauthorized and *post-de-facto* use conver-sion<br>– Illegal transfer of ownership, land registration |
| **Gender/Human Exploitation** | – Sexual graftification/abuse/ exploitation<br>– Bonded/underpaid labour, child labour<br>– Misbehaviour | – Slow/non-implementation of Human Rights<br>– Misuse of police & state machinery<br>– Slow Judicial process<br>– Para-legal interventions |

political/systemic levels. Looking at the diagnosis, the present medicine dominated by vigilance, police and legal actions is grossly inadequate. In fact, the medicine is worse than the illness. The vigilance and police itself tend to become a wheel of corruption of the magnificient machinery. The solutions at the social, political and systemic levels have always been more difficult and hence are underplayed.

**Fig. 3.2 : Corruption and communalism dismantling the vision of Mahatma Gandhi**

There is a need to establish simple and comprehensible audit and accounting standards for PRIs to cap, reduce, and eventually eliminate scope for corruption. These standards could focus on identifying when transactions should be looked into, what should be monitored, transaction documentation, and transaction disclosure. A system for internal audit needs to be established to complement external audit. There is a need to establish Public Accounts Committee (PACs) or PR Committees specifically for PRIs. This will have to be complemented with an appropriate Fiscal Responsibility Act for elected local authorities. Outsourcing of accounting by panchayats through standard contracts and automation and computerization of accounts would be imperative. Social audit systems will have to be implemented at gram sabha and higher levels. Preparation of Social Audit Policies based on best practices available in different states and their adoption by state governments is required. The Right to Information legislation provides a powerful tool for accountability.

**Fig. 3.3 : The extent of paper work is inversely proportionate to transparency and delivery on ground**

## CHECKING CORRUPTION BY SOCIAL AUDIT

Dungarpur district, bordering Gujarat and nestled in the lap of the Aravalli mountain range, has some of the poorest socio-economic indicators in Rajasthan, so, implementation of welfare schemes is critical.

Purna Chandra Kishan, collector of the tribal Dungarpur district in Rajasthan, had quite the task on hand: battling the corruption undermining the Union government's flagship welfare programmeμthe Mahatma Gandhi National Rural Employment Guarantee Scheme, or MGNREGS.

The country's first social audit was held in Valota in 2006 by the Soochna Evam Rozgar Adhikar Abhiyan—a right to information and employment campaign by a group of not-for-profit bodies and the government. Since then, *gram shahas* in the district have become animated affairs, with people asking questions of the elected heads and demanding quality work.

"When we check the work in the presence of villagers and officials, it becomes a kind of social audit," says Kishan. "Poor people come forward to lodge complaints and corrupt *sarapanches,* secretaries and junior engineers are publicly embarrassed. The work automatically improves."

Some 70,000 to 100,000 people migrate from Dungarpur every year in search of jobs. No official data is available on this, but Kishan expects the migration to decrease by about 40 per cent as a result of the employment scheme.

Even the usually skeptical non-profit bodies approve of Kishan's work. "He has pulled up officials and controlled corruption in material. *Sarpnches* and 'mates' (site supervisors) have been blacklisted, work site boards have been put up," says Hari Om Soni, an activist who works to improve livelihoods and the local governance system.

Kishan also organized a workshop on constructing gravel roads, "We constructed a stretch of 100m of quality gravel road as per specifications in one day in Jaisela *panchayat,* "he says, adding that the people who claimed quality gravel roads could not be constructed by *gram panchayats* and NREGS labourers were proved wrong.

He says that the problems in the scheme arose mainly because the projects are not decided by the labourers, as required under the Act. He has now passed an order that for illiterate labourers, the application entry should read 100 days or maximum.

"In seven *panchayats,* where *sachivs* were regular offenders, I personally filled up job application forms for average 500 labourers for 100 days in each panchayat, "says Kishan, "I told the secretaries that if they failed to provide employment, I would process unemployment allowance. They forgot all *netargiri* (politicking) and fell in line."

**Source :** The Hindustan Times, New Delhi, 9 August 2010

## Capacity and Capabilities at Local Level

The existence of countrywide 2,40,000 elected local bodies is both a triumph and a tragedy of democracy. It is a tragedy because of the mismatch between the functions of local bodies which demand planning, poverty alleviation, infrastructure development, financial management, etc. and the qualifications of the elected officials. There is a widespread vote bank politics and manipulation of the election process through propaganda, bribes, threats and by creating cleavages among in people in the basis of caste, creed or religion. There is a need to review the election process for the local bodies. The national and state level political parties may have to give way to the locals, with or without political party affiliation, but dedicated to local development. It may not be an impractical idea to ban the political parties from contesting the elections of rural and urban local bodies, i.e., panchayat, gram sabha, municipal body, etc. The qualifications of individual candidates can be prescribed on the basis of tasks, e.g., infrastructure delivery, provision of the village services, employment generation, community participation, planning and management, etc.

Several key issues of good governance stand out in the Indian context. These are decentralization, integration of the poor and marginalized, environmental sustainability, mobilization of local finance, transparency and civic engagement, better local governance and capacity building. In the context of local bodies, these issues do not stand alone, but are inextricably linked to each other and mutually reinforce the strengths that each brings to the process of good governance. These linkages, however, are not automatic, and the improper structuring or management of one issue contains the potential to impact negatively on some others. As such, the rural local bodies/PRIs need to develop the following capabilities:*

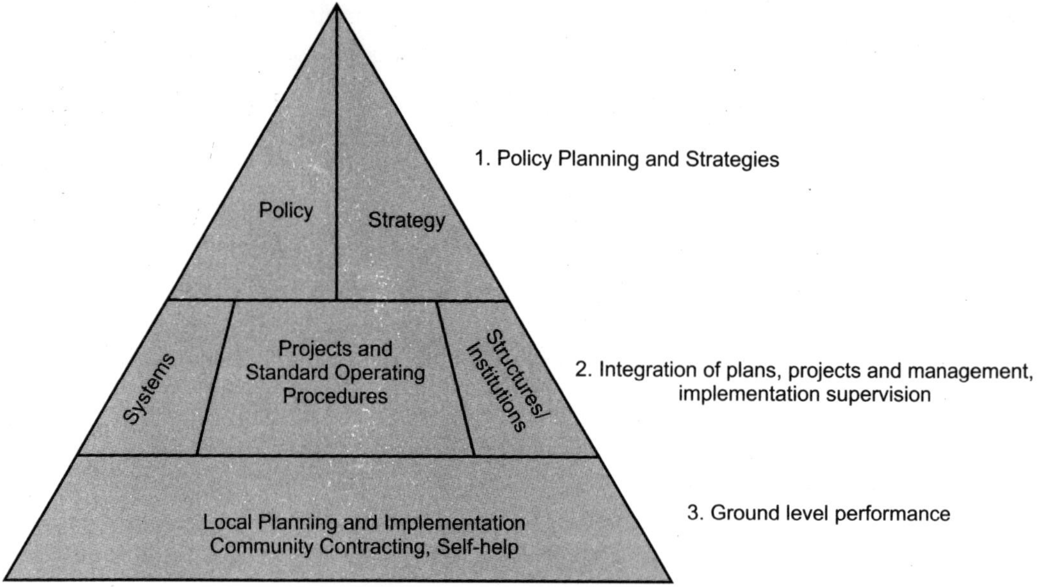


**Fig. 3.4 : The hierarchy of policy, plans, strategies and performance**

* The Department for International Development (DID) study 'Strategies for Achieving the International Development Targets : Making Government work for Poor People', (2000).

- To operate political systems which provide opportunities for all people, including the poor and disadvantaged, to organize and influence state policy and practice.
- To provide macro-economic stability and to facilitate private sector investment and trade.
- To develop a policy framework which can meet the poverty eradication targets and to raise, allocate and account for resources in accordance with pro-poor policies.
- To guarantee the equitable and universal provision of effective basic services.
- To manage accountability and to resolve differences between communities before they develop into violent conflicts.
- To develop honest and accountable local government that can combat corruption.

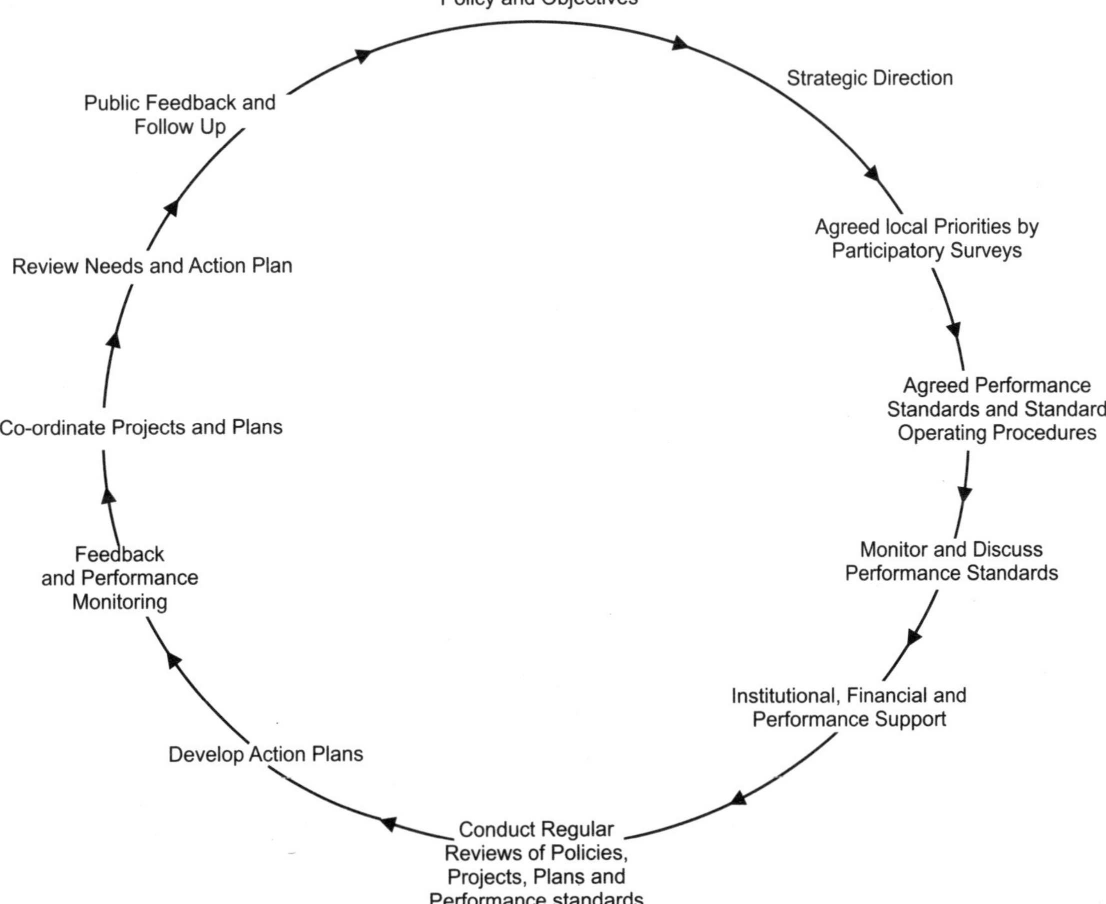


**Fig 3.5 : Performance Cycle is based on the principles of subsidiarity and engaging the right actors and stakeholders at the right level. In many situations, establishing the practice of good performance entails setting up new procedures and institutions and devolving responsibility chains and reporting structures.**

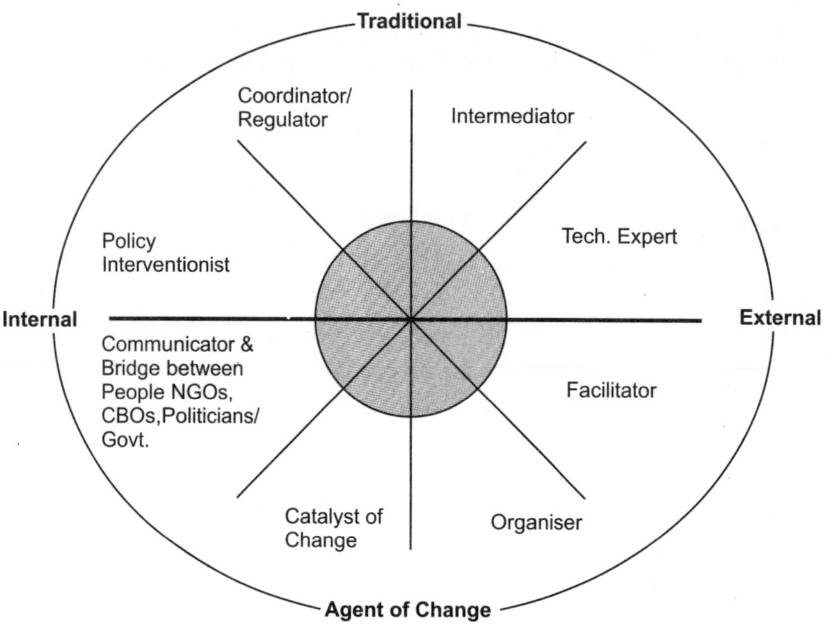


**Fig 3.6 : Changing Role of Rural Manager**

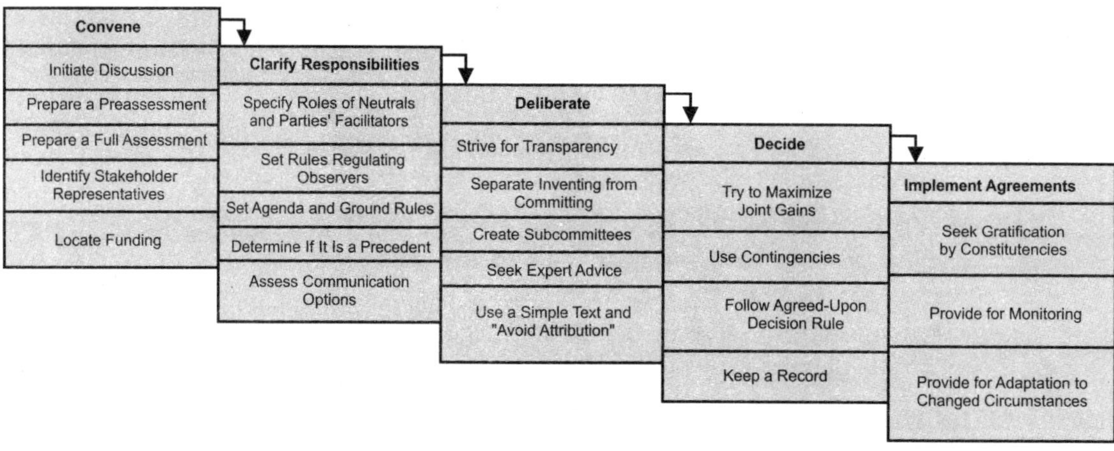


**Fig. 3.7 : Consensus Building—Essential Steps : India has the distinction of having the largest number of democratically elected local governments in the world with more than 240,000 local bodies and 2.2 million elected representatives. One of the basic task of elected local bodies is consensus building through participatory decision making. This involves a series of steps– to convene, to clarity agenda, functions and roles, to deliberate, to decide, to agree and to implement (which includes monitoring). Clearly the local officials at in PRIs have to develop the capacities to involve the community in decision making by way of a systematic and meaningful participatory process.**

**Source:** The Consensus Building Handbook

The process of rural development is intimately linked with the system of governance, elections, articulation the participation of civil society, issues of transparency and ethics and democratic decentralization of decision making process. It has direct bearing on the aspects of the livelihoods, poverty, infrastructure/basic services, equity and capacity building, which are linked to the role of officials. The role of the rural manager has to change from that of a technical expert, co-ordinator or office manager to an organizer, facilitator and a bridge between the people, NGOs, CBOs, politicians and the government (Fig. 3.6).

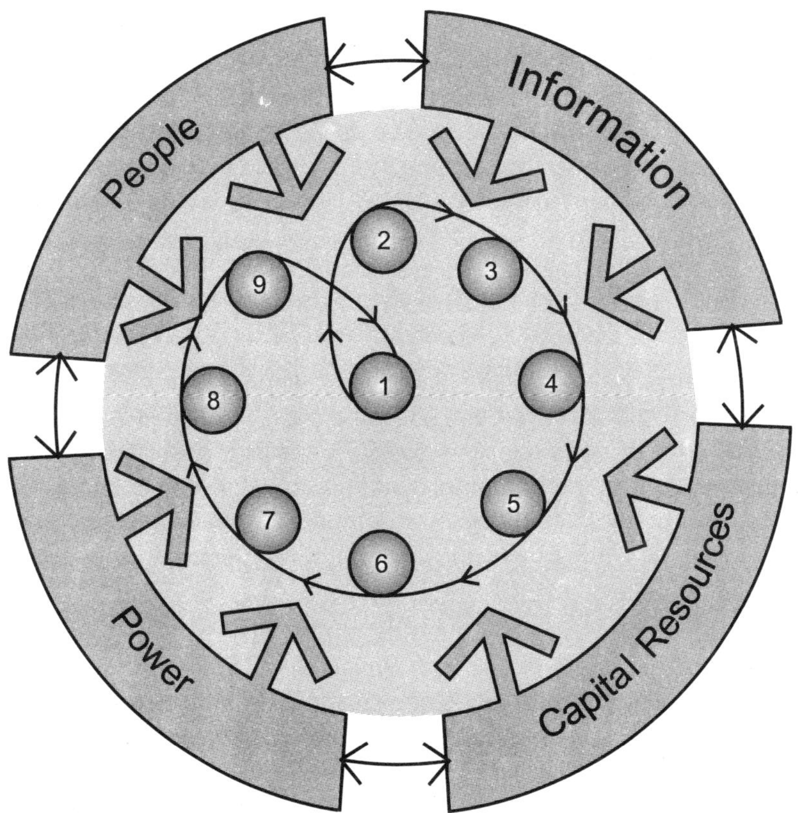


**Fig. 3.8 : Rural Governance Cycle is the integration of people, power, capital resources and information in the context of place and time. Governance is the process of decision making that recognizes, respects and engages all the potential actors and *stakeholders* (1 to 9) who will be affected by the decisions that are made. Therefore it is inclusive and participatory, involving and bringing together actors from central government (service delivery agencies, health, education, etc.), local government (both political decision makers and technical/administrative officers), civil society (NGOs, community groups) and the private sector enterprises and associations.**

## SUCCESS STORIES : SELF-HELP INITIATIVES BY WOMEN

The Community Development Societies (CDS) are grass root level organizations constituting solely of women drawn from families identified by the poverty index that uses nine non-economic criteria formulated by the Government of Kerala. The CDS mechanism has three-tier organizational structure and at the grass-root level, 25.30 women from a Neighbourhood Group and 2 or 3 such Groups in each Ward constitute an Area Development Society that finally converge at the city level as CDS. This novel experiment incorporates and mechanism of encouraging the beneficiaries to deposit an initial amount with the CDS account, which is functioning as an informal bank of the poor. The accumulated amount is used by the CDS to offer credit to the beneficiaries for multi-purpose activities with priority for self-employment. This successful experiment in micro-credit is now extended to housing sector too. The shelter scheme under CDS envisages part contribution from beneficiaries, which would be dovetailed with a subsidy from the state government and local bodies and supplemented by soft loan assistance from HUDCO. A saving of 15% of house cost in Public Deposit Scheme, in addition to acting as a cash security from HUDCO. A saving of 15% of house cost in Public Deposit Scheme, in addition to acting as a cash security also ensures substantial growth during the repayment period. The recovery is done from the beneficiary family through the CDS network at the grass roots.

The *Shri Mahila Sewa Sahakari Bank,* a bank of the poor self employed women workers, started initially providing finance to the self employed women it has been enlarged to cover security insurance of water supply delivery. In addition to extending loans for housing, it has also implemented schemes for improvement of water supply system and sanitation facilities. Extensively supporting promotion of self-help initiatives in employment generation through micro-enterprises, the SEWA experiment has a substantial replication potential.

The *Society for Promotion of Area Resource Centres (SPARC)* has been facilitating access to credit through a community based collaborative mechanism. In addition to its activities in promotion of self help initiatives which would make the women economically self-reliant, a substantial capacity building efforts are also attempted to ensure participation of women and low income groups in the problem conception and solution evolving processes. With its effort in mobilizing the savings from the people, this institution has been able to address the multiple credit requirements of the low income population.

Kerala, Kudumbashree, is a State Mission working through village panchayats and urban local governments to foster a self-help movement among BPL families through their women folk to combat poverty. Even in a sharply adversarial political set up, village panchayats have uniformly supported the women's network, which in turn has matured into a powerful demand factor. Similarly, the World Bank supported Rural Water Supply Project is implemented through village panchayats, which in turn use beneficiary groups for project planning, execution, and asset management.

## CASE STUDY

## The Grameen Bank Housing Programme, Bangladesh

Bangladesh is one of the world's poorest, most densely populated and least developed nations. With a population in excess of 125 million it is the eighth most populous country in the world; with an average per capita income of $250, it is also one of the poorest. Situated in a low-lying delta where four major river systems come together, the country is blessed with highly fertile soil, but also suffers regular and severe problems of flooding. Despite their many problems the Bangladeshi people retain considerable optimism and pride in their nation.

Grameen Bank grew out of an action research project initiated by Professor Muhammed Yunus in 1986, who recognized that it is poor people's lack of access to capital rather than their capacity to repay that perpetuates their poverty. The action research project started in Chittagong University, provided credit facilities for a small number of poor rural families and enabled them to set up small income-generating businesses. These tiny loans of a few dollars, issued without formal collateral, enabled the poorest of the poor to get out of their downward spiral of poverty and exploitation by money lenders. Building from this, the Grameen Bank was formally incorporated in 1983 and is today the largest rural credit institution in Bangladesh with 2,400,000 borrowers, 95 per cent of whom are women. It provides services in 38,659 villages (more than half of all villages in Bangladesh). The average loan size is $167.

The Grameen Bank operates as a specialized bank for the poor, charging interest on its loans and is not reliant on donor funding. It specialized in the provision of financial services, including credit, savings and insurance to the poorest of the rural poor. It obtains funds from the Central Bank of Bangladesh and lends them on to its borrowers at a higher rate of interest. It is able to operate profitably due to its high loans recovery rate of 98 per cent and makes a small annual profit.

In 1984 the Bank started to lend money for housing loans and to date 450,000 houses have been built using these loans. An average of 7,000-8,000 new loans are made every month. The housing loans are available only to existing Grameen Bank borrowers who have a 100 per cent repayment record and have completely repay their first two loans for income generation activities, but after a natural disaster Grameen Bank developed a special housing programme in which the above criteria were relaxed. The housing loans are usually repaid over a 10 year period with a simple interest rate of 8 per cent.

Poor families typically live in small shelters of jute stick, strew, grass thatch, bamboo and dried mud. Each year a family has to spend about $30 to repair the house after the monsoons. For an equal amount of money a family can repay a housing loan for a strong, well-constructed house with a floor area of 20m$^2$. The Bank views housing loans as investment rather than consumption, since a secure and well-constructed house aids the health and well-being of the family and helps them break the vicious circle of poverty. The house can be used for their small businesses and time and money are saved in not having to continually repair the jute-shelters. The Grameen Bank has developed two standard house designs. The smaller one costs $300 and a larger version costs $625. In many cases the family add their own savings to the loan and are spending up the $800-$1,000 on their home and its furnishings.

The houses vary in appearance throughout the country but have the same basic structural components. There are four reinforced concrete pillars on brick foundation at the corners of the house and six intermediary bamboo or concrete posts, with bamboo tie beams, wooden rafters and purlins supporting corrugated iron roofing sheets. This provides stability in the flood and strong monsoon wind and protection from the heavy rain during the monsoon season. In cases of severe flooding the house can be dismantled and the components stored and reassembled later. A sanitary latrine must be provided with each house. Families can build the houses themselves, with the help of friends and neighbours. Local skilled carpenters carry out the roof construction for many families. Many houses now have an electrical connection which powers an electric light, a fan and a TV or radio. All houses have raised sleeping areas so that the family do not have to sleep on the floor and in each house there is a table with school books for the children to work on when they come in from school. Cooking is done outside and cooking pots and utensils are stored in the houses. Loans are also available to purchase homestead lands if a family has no land on which to build its house.

The title to the house is vested with the borrower and in 95 per cent of cases this is the women. By having title to the house the woman obtains financial security and an improved status within the family and society. The borrowers repay their loans on a weekly basis at the Centre meeting when the manager of the local branch office of the Grameen Bank comes to their village. The collateral system of peer support means that families help each other out with payments if necessary to ensure that all repayments are made on time. There is a 98 per cent loans recovery rate, compared to 25-30 per cent for other banks.

The Grameen Bank is dedicated to meet the needs of the poorest of the poor. It employs 12,600 people, most of whom are based in the branch officers in the rural areas. All the staff have a sense of pride and mission in their work and an identify with the borrowers. Branch staff treat the borrowers with obvious respect and liking and are held in high regard. The organization prides itself on being free of corruption and is innovative and progressive. It is constantly seeking to develop new opportunities for income generation and services for its borrowers and h as established sixteen new enterprises to provide these services on a commercial basis (including electricity supply using solar energy, a mobile phone network for the villages and a marketing organization for the high quality hand-woven fabrics, which are manufactured by the villagers).

The Grameen Bank micro-credit model is already being replicated throughout the world. Another organization known as the Grameen Trust, is in charge of the international programme, which seeks to promote micro-credit for the poorest of the poor throughout the world, in both developed and developing countries. To date, micro-credit programmes based on the Grameen Bank experience have been established in 56 other countries.

According to Professor Muhammed Yunus the beggars turn to dignified business by micro-credit and their own home:

"In Bangladesh 80 per cent of the poor families have already been reached with micro-credit. We are hoping that by 2010, 100 per cent of the poor families will be reached. Three years ago we started an exclusive programme focusing on the beggars None of Grameen Bank rules apply in them. Loans are interest free, they can pay whatever amount they wish, whenever they wish. We gave them the idea to carry small merchandise such as snacks, toys or household items, when they went from house to house for begging. The idea worked. There are now 85,000 beggars in the progam. About 5,000 of them have already stopped begging completely. Typical loans to a beggar is $12. We encourage and support every conceivable intervention to help the poor fight out of poverty. We already advocate micro-credit in addition to all other interventions, arguing that micro-credit makes those interventions work better.

## CASE STUDY

### Nepal-People Pursing Development

According to an ADB technical assistance project to reform the water supply sector in the Kathmandu Valley, the peri-urban village of Dhulikhel has proven the people-led development can reap a number of successful outcomes. By pursuing a more reliable and safe water source, the people of Dhulikhel also solved their sanitation problems. An ADB report tells an interesting story of pursuit and success:

The people of Dhulikhel faced a water problems that was compounded by the time and effort the women spent to walk to the sprout, gather water, and carry it home. At first, the people approached His Majesty's Government of Nepal, which said, "Tomorrow." But tomorrow never came, so the people took the matter into their hands. They were aware of the work Deutsche Gesellschaft fur Technische Zusammenarbeit (GTZ) was doing in Bakhtapur, so they went to Bhaktapur and managed to elicit GTZ interest. With GTZ assistance, they found a good source of water; designed and built a pipeline to carry it 14 km to the town; and worked with people in the villagers along the pipe's length to arrange for right-of-way—some of which were secured by building a school in the nearby village. The mayor noted that these side projects (along the pipeline) have helped build a good, familiar feeling between the town and the villages nearby. When the water first came through the pipe, the towns people celebrated.

The 14-year effort bore considerable fruits. Dhulikhel has ample water. Water use has increased as women use it more for washing dishes and clothes. Every house is connected to the system and most homes have toilets. As a result, gastrointestinal disease has markedly decreased. But, the most significant result was the community spirit that developed and the sure knowledge that they can solve their own problems. When asked what advice he would give to the Mayor of Kathmandu, the Mayor of Dhulikhel answered that the people must be "thirsty" to energise them to fix a water problem. Also, if people pay for a system and work hard to build it, they will more likely to take care of it. And finally, it was public participation and a "never give up" attitude that saw them through from start to finish."

The Nepal case study proves that people can solve their problems and enlisting communities is one way of scaling up to meet the Millennium Development Goals.

## CASE STUDY

### Pakistan – A Little Mobilisation Goes a Long Way

Many people in Pakistan recognize the need for wastewater management and sanitation, yet these remain neglected issues in the majority of villages in part because people assume that the Government is responsible for funding and implementing the necessary infrastructure. Dr. Rashid Bajwa in his paper on "Successful Approaches to Improving Wastewater Management and Sanitation in Pakistan" points out that mobilizing villagers can overcome their inertia and address critical problems. By doing just that, the National Rural Support Programme (NRSP) in Pakistan, working with donors and the Pakistan Poverty Alleviation Fund (PPAF), has implemented more than 400 projects, benefiting more than 85,000 households. Over the course of the NRSP projects, an approach to community mobilization evolved, which includes the following seven steps:

***Step 1 :*** Social mobilization begins when NRSP "Social Organisers" engage in dialogues with members of rural communities. These dialogues are founded on two things: first, it they form one or more Community Organisations (COs), each with members of 15 to 20 households, and second, if they poor their human and financial resources, members of rural communities can meet their development needs.

***Step 2 :*** Once a CO is formed, community members priorities their needs, with many identifying sanitation schemes as their first priority because they understand the connection between insanitary conditions and disease very well.

***Step 3 :*** Members of NRSP's Physical Infrastructure and Technology Development Department – all of them qualified engineers – assess the needs identified by community members and then create a Project Digest, which identifies the technical, economic, and environmental requirements for the specific project. In an Integrated Project, this usually includes:

- Water harvesting and storage systems;
- Distribution systems, street paving, and installing connections to the drainage system in each household;
- Installing sewers, building filtration, and water treatment tanks; and
- Installing pipes to safely carry treated waste away from the village—either into the fields where it can be used as fertilizer or into a water channel.

***Step 4 :*** The next step for NRSP and COs is to sign a formal Terms of Partnership (ToP) agreement. At least 75% of the community representatives must be present in a meeting to sign this agreement. In the meeting, NRSP staff explains every detail of the project. Before they sign, everyone involved knows the specifications, contributions required from all parties, disbursement schedule for funds, implementation process and procedures, time required to complete the project and estimated annual operation and maintenance costs. They are also aware of the roles and responsibilities of NRSP and other partners.

***Step 5 :*** CO then constitutes a Project Committee, which assumes responsibility for the overall implementation of the project, and the management, and operation of the project after its completion.

***Step 6 :*** After signing the ToP, CO opens a project bank account. NRSP disburses the grant in installments, as each stage of the work is completed. The Project Committee forwards a request to NRSP for the release of the funds in the form of a resolution signed by at least 75% of the members. NRSP's accounting staff checks the expenditure vouchers, and the engineers check the progress and quality of the work. Before releasing the final payment, the NRSP engineer ensures that the work has been completed satisfactorily and that the best materials have been used.

***Step 7 :*** NRSP arrangers training programs for the members of the committee established by COs. The members learns how to manage the construction process, how to keep records, how to procure high quality materials, and—after project completion—how to properly operate and maintain their projects. The are also encouraged to adopt participatory ways of working: holding regular meetings, ensuring attendance of at least 75% of members in meetings, and ensuring that CO members are saving regularly. Members learn how to maintain accurate records and to link the village organization with relevant organizations.

Following lessons are learned using this approach:

- Once people have seen how well these projects can work, they are ready to tackle other development projects that are vital to their communities; and
- Although many rural residents are quite poor, they are willing and able to contribute funds and labor for community development.

NRSP's approach to the social aspects of organizing communities to meet their sanitation and waste water needs reflects that of its exemplar, the Orangi Pilot Project in Karachi, Pakistan's largest slum and informal settlement.

## CASE STUDY

### Bangladesh – Partnership for Empowerment

A study by Ms. Rokeya Ahmed on "Shifting Millions from Open Defecation to Hygienic Practices" discusses a case study of Water Aid Banladesh and the NGO Village Education Resource Center

(VERC) partnering to help Bangladesh achieve 100% sanitation. The study summarises the background of the problem and the approach the partnership took. The Government of Bangladesh plan to achieve total sanitation by 2010. According to a survey, average sanitation coverage is only 32%. Traditional approaches to improving sanitation have focused on latrine construction rather than on health and hygiene education.

Wateraid Bangladesh and its rural partner VERC jointly developed an integrated, empowering approach in collaboration with community people living in rural areas. VERC's approach is based on the assumption that once the issues have been understood, communities have the commitment and ability to overcome their water and sanitation problems themselves. The approach has proven effective in establishing safe water supplies, environmental sanitation, and promoting good hygiene practices.

The approach is based on the following key principles:

- **Integration :** Safe water supply, environmental sanitation, and hygiene promotion are addressed simultaneously. Projects are appropriate, sustainable, and affordable for the community;
- **Participation :** The whole community, including the hard-core poor, are actively involved in project planning, implementation, monitoring and evaluation. Individuals in the community are trained to become trained to become trainers; the community determines the best water supply and sanitation infrastructure option and hygiene promotion education inputs are facilitated; and
- **Empowerment :** People's capacities, skills, and indigenous knowledge are recognized and valued support is provided in the form of capacity building to strengthen the ability of individuals who emerge as leaders to work as agents of change within the community; communities act as facilitating agents in their neighboring areas; empowered communities increase their confidence to analyse and voice their needs constructively to local government agencies in other development programs.

## Key Aspects of the Approach

- People's skills, abilities, and knowledge are valued;
- 0% subsidy for latrine construction;
- "Whole community" approach;
- Use of participatory research tools to analyse the problems;
- Formation of village development committees (local engineering groups);
- Identification of potential community leaders and involve them as community "catalysts";
- Mobilisation of local resources; and
- Involvement of local government.

The Department for International Development's (DFID) assessment of VERC results in areas with improved water facilities and 100% sanitation indicates the following :

- Cases of diarrhea have fallen by 99% dysentery by 90%, and stomach-related problems, such as intestinal worms in rural areas, by 51%,
- Monthly medical costs for common illnesses are 55% lower;
- Working days lost due to illness have fallen from 77 to 35 per year in rural areas;
- School days lost due to illness have fallen from 16 to 7 per year in rural areas; and
- Expenditure on food and clothing has risen by 6%.

These outcomes are phenomenal—demonstrating the power of an approach that depends on the community as project drivers and combines safe water supply, sanitation, and hygiene promotion.

Chapter 4

# District and Rural Planning

*"The earth provides enough to satisfy everyman's needs, but not everyman's greed."*

*"A time is coming when those who are in the mad rush today of multiplying their wants, vainly thinking that they add to the real substance, real knowledge of the world, will retrace their steps and say: 'What have we done?*

***—Mahatma Gandhi***

The 73rd Constitutional Amendment Act, 1992 has provision for the establishment of panchayat at village level. Article 243ZD creates Committees for District Planning at the district level, which shall consolidate the plans prepared by the panchayats and the municipalities in the district and prepare a draft development plan for the district as a whole. The committee has a composition that gives representation to both members of panchayats and municipalities in the district. In preparing the draft development plan, the District Planning Committee (DPC) shall clearly spell out the way forward for the integrated development of infrastructure and environmental conservation and the extent and type of available resources, whether financial or otherwise, in matters of common interest between the panchayays and the municipalities including spatial planning, sharing of water, and other physical and natural resources. The duty of the DPC is to forward the development plan, as recommended by such Committee to the government of the state.

The Eleventh Schedule (Article 243G) of the same has listed 29 items for consideration in development plans. Panchayats have power to prepare plans for economic and social development and implement schemes for such development in their respective areas. Various items as per Eleventh Schedule include the following :

Item No. 1 : Agricultural Productivity

Item No. 2 : Land Improvement

Item No. 3 : Minor Irrigation

Item No. 4 : Animal Husbandry

Item No. 5 : Fisheries

Item No. 6 : Minor Forest Products, etc. are related to economic development of rural area and hence they should be incorporated in development plan.

Certain items aim at welfare of the people,, Provision of better education facilities, health services, recreational facilities, etc. and change in social condition of the people :

Item No. 10 : Rural Housing

Item No. 11 : Drinking Water

Item No. 14 : Rural Electrification

Item No. 17 : Education

Item No. 18 : Technical and Vocational Education

Item No. 19 : Adult and Non-formal Education

Item No. 24 : Family Welfare

Item No. 25 : Women and Child Development, related to social development which should be a part of development plan.

The development of rural area basically depends on location of various economic and social activities, their integration and proper linkages within and outside the areas. Similarly, anticipated development activities, set up of organizational framework at different level, etc. also affect the size of existing settlements, emergence of new settlements and overall development of the area. Item No. 13 (Transport and Communication), Item No. 8 (Small Scale Industries), Item No. 9 (Village and Cottage Industry), etc. decide the location of various functional units. Hence, development plan of rural area needs to take care of all these aspects for proper and balanced development.

It is mandatory for State Government to constitute District Planning Committees (DPCs) to consolidate plans prepared by panchayats and municipalities. The preparation of development plans requires exploring the potential of the districts, priority of various schemes, financial details, environmental sustainability, viability of the projects, etc. for achieving integrated development of the district.

In connection with preparation of Draft District Development Plan, DPC shall have regard to matters of common interest between panchayats and municipalities including spatial planning, sharing of physical and natural resources, development of infrastructure and conservation of environment, etc. Similarly, DPC may also co-ordinate various schemes and programme at district level such as Minimum Needs Programme (MNP), Integrated Rural Development Programme (IRDP), National Rural Employment Guarantee Act Scheme (NREGA), Bharat Nirman, Drought Prone Area Development Programme, etc. Both the MG-NREGA Scheme and PURA envisage the preparation of District Development Plans. However, this is the last priority and the District Administration/PRI hardly have any expertise of spatial-economic development planning.

In India the settlements can be grouped as below (2001) :

| | | |
|---:|:---:|:---|
| 35 metropolitan areas | : | 120m people (12%) |
| 619 Districts | : | 80m people (8%) |
| 4,000 Towns/Cities | : | 100m people (10%) |
| 5,75,936 Villages | : | 700m people (70%) |
| Total | : | 1000 million people |

India has a three tier system governments :

| | | |
|---|:---:|---|
| First Tier | : | Central |
| Second Tier | : | States (28 + 7 UTs) |
| Third Tier | : | Local (Urban and Rural) |

Spatial planning, land, housing, slum improvement, local self government, physical and social infrastructure, urban transport are in State List.

Environment and heritage protection, education, health, regional transport, bulk services, industrial growth and tourism are in Concurrent List. The 73rd CAA requires that District Planning Committee (DPCs) be created for all districts. So far about 10 states have legislated in favour of DPCs. At present, the planning functions are carried onto as given below :

| | | |
|---:|:---:|:---|
| First Tier | — | Policy level/5 Year Plans/Regional Plan |
| Second Tier (State) | — | Strategy Level /District Plan |
| Third Tier (Local) | — | Action level/Local plans |

There are overlaps in planning function, which is mostly performed by the state/central governments and third tier elected representatives have very little say in the process. Public participation is almost well nigh nil. As a continuity of first tier policy plans, the district and local planning is almost missing. Nor the policy plans emerge from local, grass root level.

According to EFN Ribeiro, former Chief Planner, Government of India (2003): The process of governance and investments through a spatial plan does not necessarily downplay the continual top down equation in developmental import through the tested equation. However, it enjoins a stronger central-state down-top process through an improved LSG—state partnership. It implies a people' involvement in the development process at panchayats and ward levels and understanding of investment frameworks, disaggregated from state/district/taluk levels. Thus, planning is envisaged through:

(*a*) A 20 year broad Spatial Strategy Plan as rolling plan with 5 yearly programmes — revised every 5 years based on annual investments;

(*b*) A disaggregated 20-year District/Spatial Structure Plan as a rolling plan with 5 yearly programmes—revised every 5 years based on annual investments.

(*c*) Disaggregated Sub District/Taluka/Tehsil Spatial Structure Plan as a rolling with 5-yearly programmes.

Ribeiro further suggests that the wards as LSG units could offer answers to several of the obligatory functions of LSG as indicated in the CAA schedules. Plans at a spatial scale (1:5000 or larger), can be the canvas for the councilor and the entire community to understand and work for development with peoples' participation. Currently these are the prerogative of a centralized bureaucracy with little or no participation of the stakeholders. Wards of 30,000 persons (6,000 families) constitute an ideal community for planning.

**Fig. 4.1 : Due to lack of planning, the development of villages in India is often ad hoc and fragmented. The individuals build their houses, while the government/local bodies do not keep pace of development of roads, water supply, sanitation and public amenities.**

With the policies of democratic decentralization and empowerment of local bodies in India in the early nineties, the Districts have a greater autonomy and role in planning. Planning skills involve new ways of seeing, thinking, learning and acting. They are often referred to as 'generic' skills, because they can be shared, transferred between, and learned from all those with a stake in the sustainable development of settlements – planners, politicians, academics, community leaders and citizens. Planning is a part of management and management is part of planning. Therefore those involved in planning – both professionals and non-professionals–need management skills.

Over the last decades there have been concerted attempts to reform public administration. This movement, often referred to as New Public Management, typically advocates market testing, contracting out and privatization of public services, full cost recovery (which may exclude the poor), internal competition mechanisms and more. However, enhancement of management skills for planning does not require endorsement of this agenda. For example, 'marketization' and internal competition often fragment service delivery and set up structures that hinder integration and an understanding of the whole, and are likely to work against sustainable development. Other aspects that have figured strongly in public service reforms are consistent with the revamped understanding of planning, such as decentralization, citizen involvement, partnerships with NGOs, strategic planning and visioning. New management skills are part and parcel of planning for sustainable development where the challenges of poverty have to be addressed. Management is about being accountable for the use of resources–time, property, people and budgets. A radical shift is required to put sustainable development and poverty alleviation at the heart of planning. The participation and partnerships are the two essential hallmarks of planning and management in a democratic extent.

Participation is the involvement of people in the planning and management of development programmes and projects. There is a wide range of levels of participation, extending from perfunctory consultation or 'using' people as unpaid labour to deliver projects cheaply (participation as a means) to engaging people, community leaders and their organizations in the design and management of development initiatives to the extent that they take a measure of control over the process (participation as an end). The 'participants' are participating in someone else's (governments') initiative.

Partnership, on the other hand, implies shared responsibility, shared risks and shared benefits – partners have equal status, though they may, and usually do, have different roles and interests. In these circumstances government and communities are in it together. However, 'partnership' has taken pride of place in the current development jargon and is widely and indiscriminately used to cover everything from subcontracting to the excesses of political arm-twisting.

The plans of rural development have to begin from the grassroots levels, keeping in view the need to provide a network of day to day facilities and amenities to the people. As such the plans are to be based upon the critical aspects of community development, funding, administrative reality, equity principle, employment creation, integrated development, poverty alleviation and basic needs provision. Based on accessibility, a shell like graph can be developed for an evolving provision of rural facilities (Fig. 4.3). The plans have to be pro-poor, participatory and meaningful for the local rural population. A matrix developed by Alison Bailey for rural planning and management (2001) provides useful clues in this task (Table 4.1):

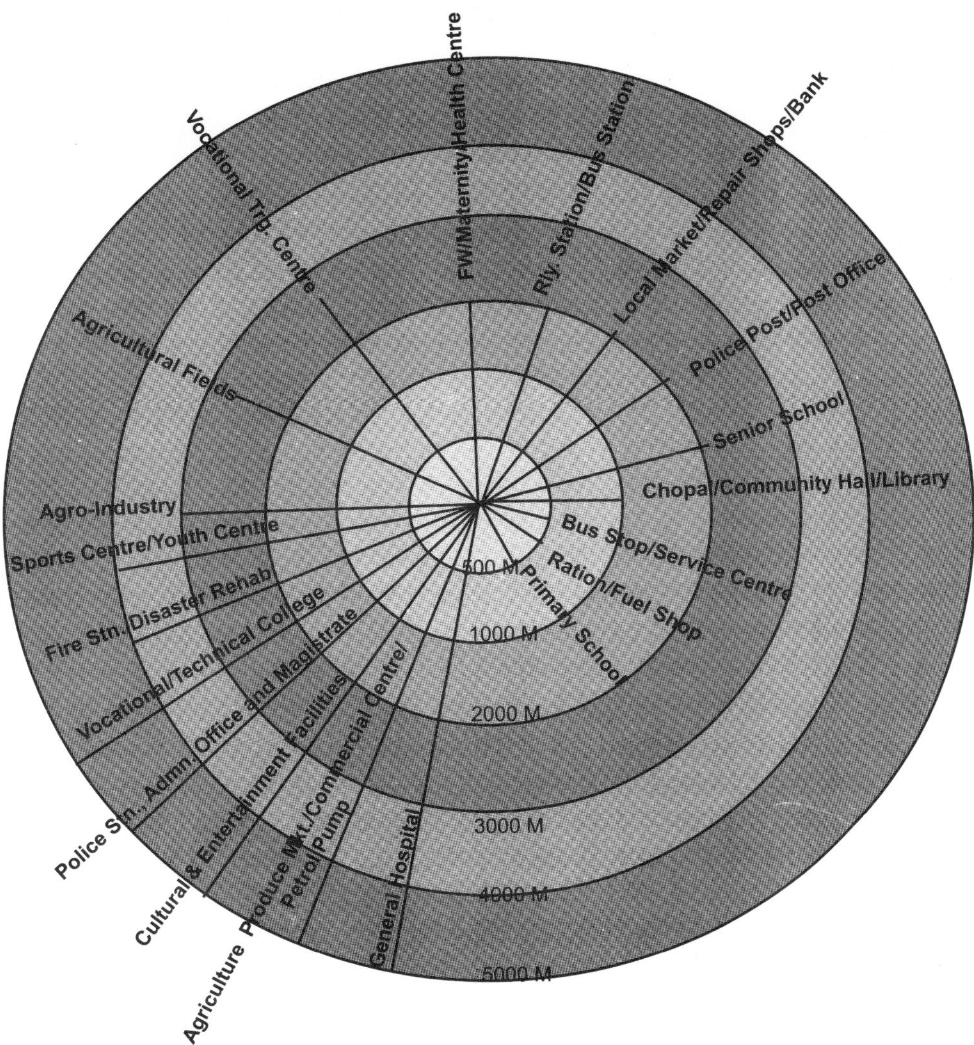


**Fig. 4.2 : Conceptutal Accessibility Standards for Local Facilities, as the basis of Rural Planning**

## Translating the Macro-vision at Local Level

The eleventh Five Year Plan recognises that the major weakness in the development process is that the growth is not perceived as being sufficiently inclusive for many groups, especially for the rural population, Scheduled Castes, Scheduled Tribes, minorities and the poor. Although India has reached the high economic growth of 7 to 9 percent, it also suggests that the economic achievement is still far from redeeming the pledge for ending of poverty, ignorance, disease and inequality of opportunity.

The central vision

**Table 4.1 : Major alternative Instruments for Implementing Rural Development Strategies**

| Strategy emphasis or key instrumentality | Agencies particularly associated with strategy | Key planning concept(s) | Typical plan components |
|---|---|---|---|
| 1. Self-help community development | Ministries and departments of Community Develop-ment, NGOs | Local participation and small group self-help with technical and In-kind assistance | Small scale production and social service activities outside sectoral programmes. |
| 2. Rural development funds | Rural Development Ministries Local Governments | Self-help and assistance in kind | Community infrastruc-ture or production activities identified by rural communities or their leaders. |
| 3. Administrative area based public invest-ment plants | Government Departments in districts, horizontally coordi-nated by administrative officers. | Project 'shopping lists', Physical plans | Government buildings, roads, water supply, power, land settle-ments, etc. |
| 4. Local-scale rural 'equity institutions'. | Governments with strong rural equity ideology (Maoist China, Israel, etc.) | Economies of scale; cooperation, mecha-nization; moderni-zation, mobilization and control. | Collective farms, communes, state farms, village councils, etc., sometimes Incorporating diversi-fication (non-agricultural) activities. |
| 5. Rural employment creation | ILO, WFP, UNIDO assisted | Local-level develop-ment projects to diversity rural economy and create out-of-season wage employment or permanent self-employment. | Diversification projects including crafts and small-scale Industry; physical infrastructure through labour-Intensive methods; grants/ credit for self-employment of poorest. |
| 6. Integrated Rural Development | 6.e.g. GTZ, SNV donor agency implemented or NGO assisted | Multi-sectoral area-based plans; horizontal integration; participa-tion; self-determina-tion. | Multi-social develop-ment plans with strong agricultural compo-nents based on family farms. |
| 7. Poverty alleviation via small farm productivity gains | IFAD assisted | 'Agriculture plus' projects; target groups below poverty line; small farmer, rationality poverty line and efficiency | Agricultural projects for small farmers, usually cash crop based, with supporting infrastruc-ture. |
| 8. Basic needs provision | ILO Initiated; NGOs | Target groups below thresholds for nutrition, income, housing, etc; participation; self-help. | Comprehensive pla-nning with multiple special targets, inclu-ding social services (health, education, water, housing). |

| Abbreviations | | |
|---|---|---|
| | ILO | International Labour Office |
| | WFP | World Food Programme |
| | UNIDO | United Nations Industrial Development Organisation |
| | GTZ | Gemeinschaft for Technische Zusammenarbeit |
| | SNV | Netherlands Development Cooperation |
| | NGO | Non-governmental organization |
| | IFAD | International Fund for Agriculture Development |

**Source :** Alison Bailey (2001) in Rural Planning and Management, Elgar Reference, Chetenham, UK

The central vision of the Eleventh Plan is to build on the strengths to trigger a development process which ensures broad-based improvement in the quality of life of the people, especially the poor, minorities and women. The broad vision of the Eleventh Plan includes several inter-related components:

- **Rapid growth and poverty reduction,** with a decisive reduction in poverty and an expansion in economic opportunities for all section of the population.
- **The employment challenge** is answered by generating an adequate number of productive employment opportunities as a major factor on which the inclusiveness of growth will be judged.
- **Access to essential services** will be improved because a person is categorized as a poor because his/her endowments of capital, labor and skills are meager, and also because of his/her access to public goods and services and natural resources is limited. Without access to these services one cannot be considered to have equality of opportunity.
- **Social justice and empowerment,** the vision of inclusiveness must go beyond the traditional objective of poverty alleviation to encompass equality of opportunity, as well as economic and social mobility for all sections of society. The plan says that there will be an improvement in the opportunities for economic and social advancement.
- **Environmental sustainability,** including a clear commitment to pursue a development process which is environmentally sustainable.
- **Gender equity,** by acknowledging the women's special needs to ensure that their needs, rights and contribution are reflected in every section of the Plan document.
- **The improvement in governance,** which would make government-funded program in critical areas more effective and efficient.

The major strategy for inclusive growth in the Eleventh Plan includes macro-economic framework. Agriculture, irrigation and watershed development, industry and minerals, infrastructure requirements, education and skill development, health and nutrition, science and technology, poverty alleviation and slum development are the important components of the Eleventh Plan.

Planning activity is the integration of time and resources in a spatial dimension. It is usually divided into 3 interconnected phases-Long Term, Short term and Annual Plan. Long term plans are usually policy, programme, short term are strategic plans (usually for 5 years) and annual, local, project plans are operational, action plans. The continuity and linkage of these phases is obtained by planning cycle comprising survey and Analysis, Plan Preparation, Plan approval, Plan Implementation, Plan Monitoring and Plan Review.

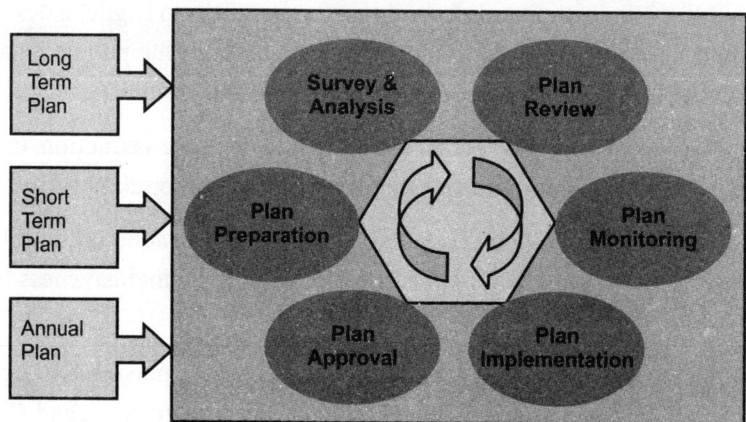


**Fig 4.3 : Integration of Time and Planning**

The interlinkages among Development Planning and Projects in Indian context aim to achieve social welfare through inclusive economic growth employment, equity and social justice. National Development Plans are the blue prints to organize population, economy, resources and mobility over space. Regional Development Plan aims at orderly development, efficient functioning and enhancement of the quality of life. Sub-regional/District Development Plan attempts to translate activities, life supports system, transport, social and physical infrastructure in terms of space and time. This is further detailed out in specific projects by operational action plans at village project levels.

Planning is a roadmap towards reaching a destination and shows the best way to get there in time. It is targeted towards achieving certain objectives, goals or results. Objectives or goals are the ends towards which activity is aimed. Planning attempts to device integrated systems, which are essentially a set or assemblage of things to form a complex unity. As such it sets certain parameters, norms and benchmarks planning has four important goals:

(*i*) to off-set uncertainity and change

(*ii*) to focus attention on objectives, benchmarks, norms and systems

(*iii*) to make operations economical and time bound

(*iv*) to guide managers to control and implement.

Broadly speaking, planning is done at three levels, viz., policy, strategic and operational, which are all interconnected. Policies are plans in the form of general statements or understandings which guide or channel thinking and action in decision making. All policies are not statements, since they are often merely implied from the actions of managers. Policies limit an area within which a decision is to be made and ensure that the decision will be consistent and contribute to achieving an objective. Policies help decide the issues before they become problems. Since policies are guides to decision making, it follows that they must allow for some discretion.

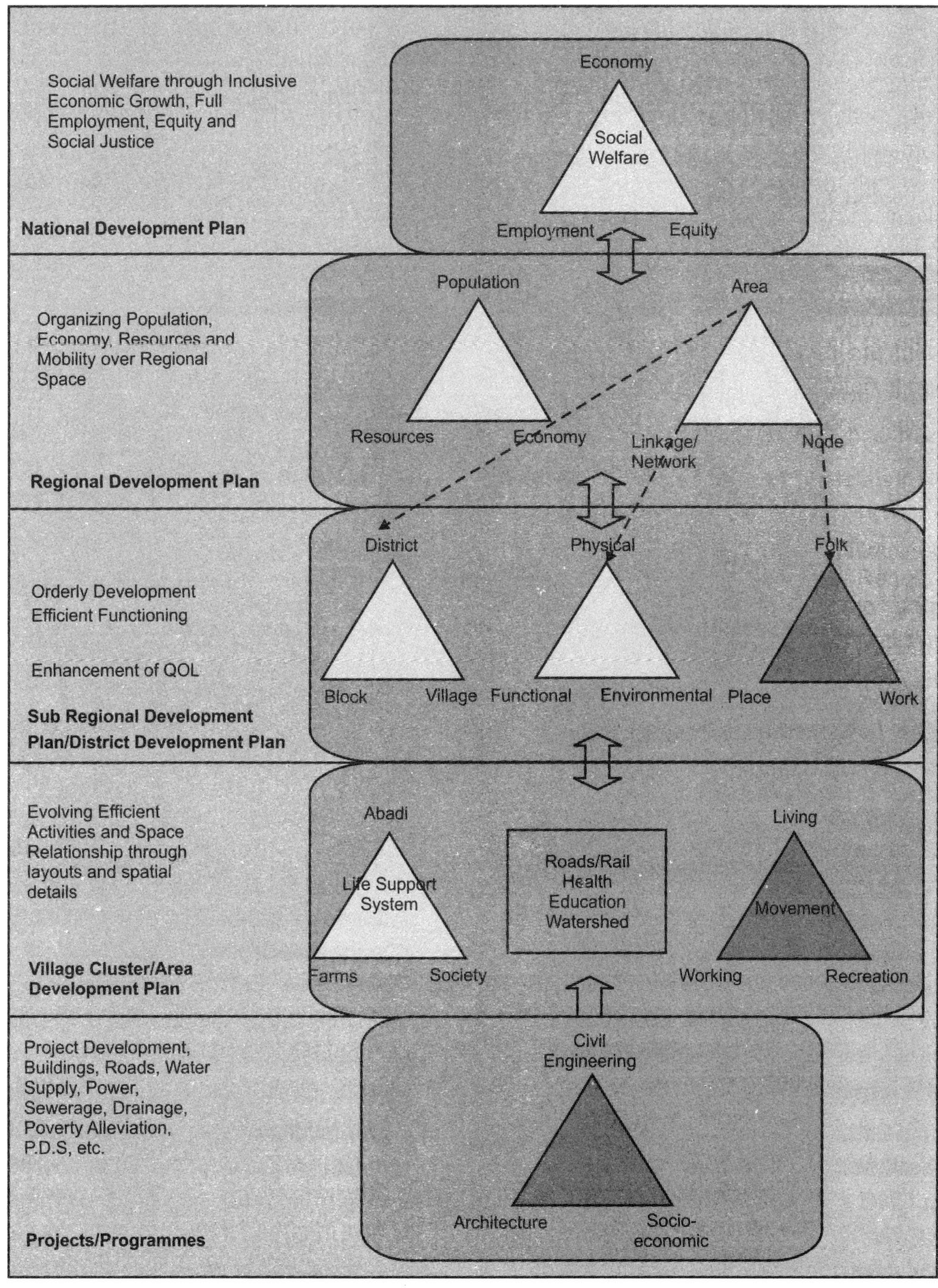


**Fig. 4.4 : inter-linkages between Development Planning and Projects**

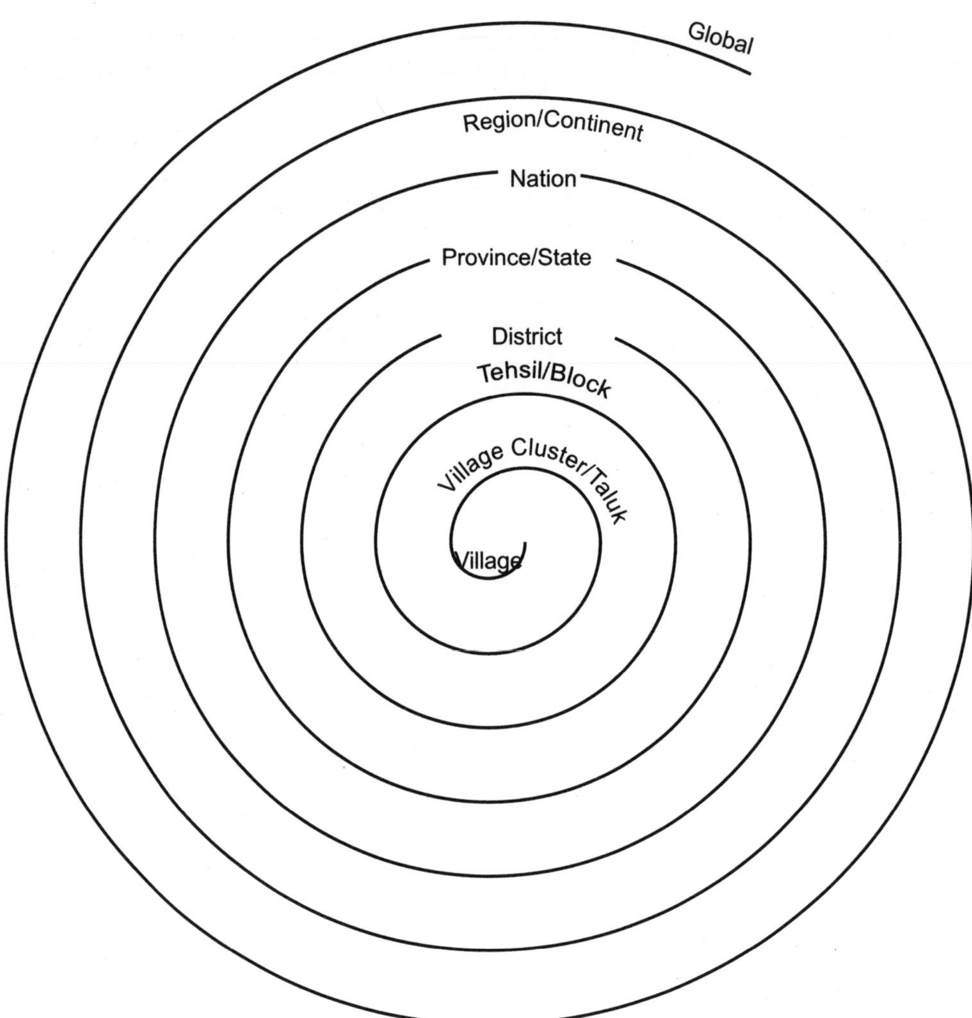


**Fig 4.5 : In view of the globalization trends, the Indian settlements are no more the islands of poverty or prosperity. They have to consciously link with the spiral of the state, nation, continent and global networks. However, in this process, care is to be exercised that they do not loose their positive cultural, artistic and heritage values.**

Strategies indicate a program of action and development of priority areas/sectors and resources to attain comprehensive objectives. The programme of objectives of an organization and their resources are used to attain these objectives and policies governing the acquisition, use and disposition of these resources. The determination of the long term objectives and the adoption of course of action and allocation of resources are necessary to achieve these goals.

Action plans are the operational and technical plans that establish a method of handling future activities. They are guides to action and detail the exact manner in which a certain activity must be accomplished in a chronological sequence. It also spell out specific action required or non-action allowing no discretion. Action plans are usually the simple type of plans which prescribe the procedure as sequence of rules. A rule, however, may or may not reflect a managerial decision that some action must or must not be taken. An action plan will have a programme. Programmes are complex of goals, policies, procedures, rules, assignments, steps to be taken, resources to be employed and other elements necessary to carry out a given course of action. They are ordinarily supported by necessary budget.

All the above components of planning are inter-linked in a sequence (Fig. 4.6), focusing upon the problems, objectives and opportunities.

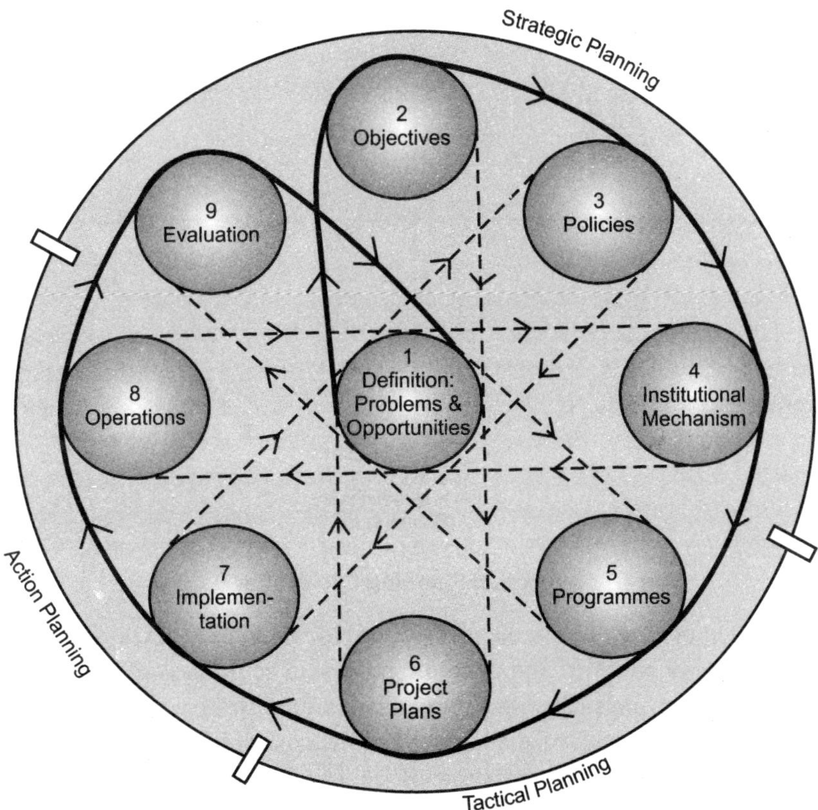


**Fig. 4.6 : Planning comprises a continuous and inter-linked cycle of problem definition, objectives, policies, strategies, Institutional structure, programmes, projects, implementation, operation and evaluation.**

Planning today has become a complex process. The planners often find it difficult to cope up and strike a balance among various levels and competing demands—political, economic, social, environmental, governance, physical/spatial, etc. A perplexed planner finds that the transitional planning paradigms like 'survey, analyse and plan' have become redundant. This needs starting again from the basics.

(*a*) Organizing timely and relevant information,

(*b*) Identifying the pertinent issues and problems,

(*c*) Conceptualizing options, solutions and plans, and

(*d*) Converting the plans into implementation, monitoring and feedback.

Baum's cycle simplifies the planning process into these four major steps.

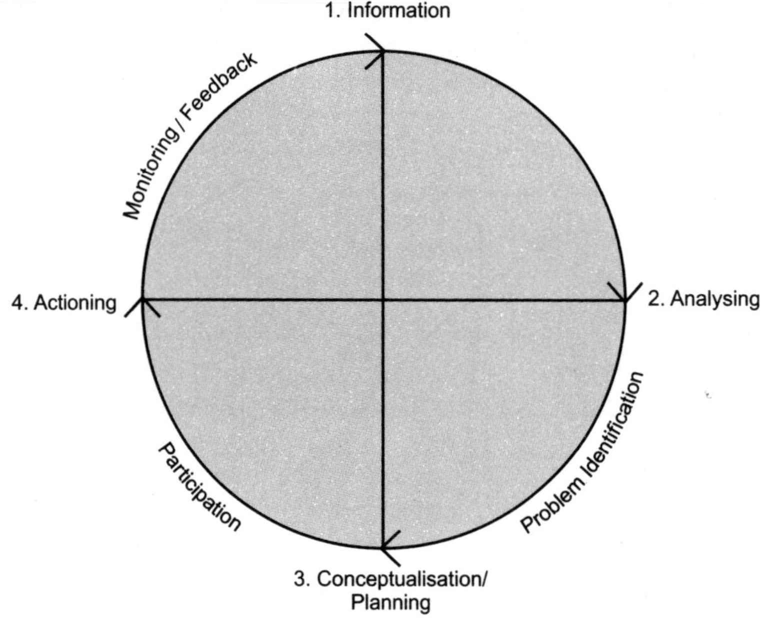


**Fig 4.7 : Simplified Planning Cycle (after Baum)**

Planning, as an attempt to synthesise the diverse activities, perspectives, aspirations and resources into a composite whole is a complex and dynamic process. The process of planning depends upon the political, socio-economic, physical, infrastructural and administrative realities. During last decades the people's aspirations and focus of planning have become enlarged – from the local, spatial, infrastructure, housing, and functional aspects, to global, environmental, organizational, governance, conservation of heritage, urban, aesthetics, employment and poverty alleviation, human dignity, empowerment and participation.

With people and resources in place, the plan aims to set a strategic direction for growth in a manner acceptable and supported by the people. There must be a good match between the planner's perspective and the people's aspirations. This can be expressed by the planning perspective which nevertheless converges to become an all-round set of shared values and sustainable development.

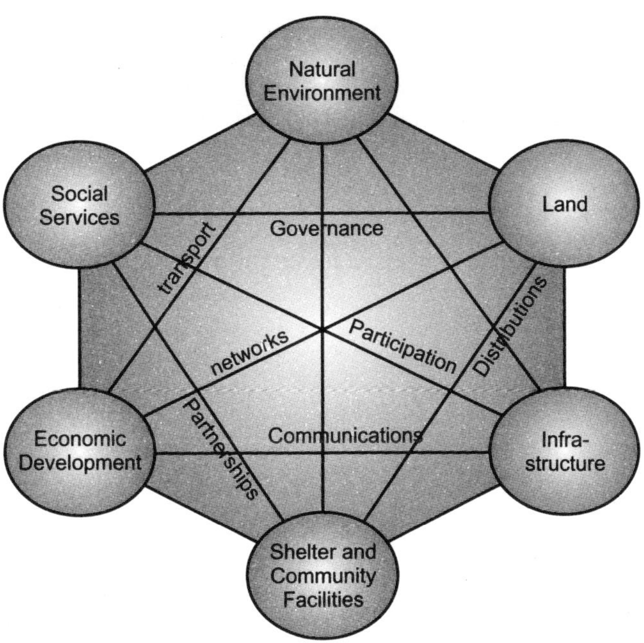


**Fig. 4.8 : The planning attempts to synthesise the resources (natural environment, land, humans) with infrastructure services, shelter, community facilities, social services and economic development. Governance, communications, service networks, transport, etc. constitute the linkages among the resources and development.**

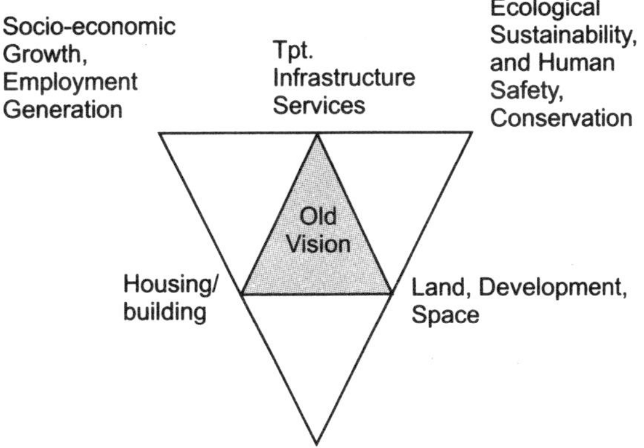


**Fig. 4.9 : Enlarged Paradigm of Planning**

As such, a development plan should essentially synthesise various components of sustainable development, such as :

- The potential carrying capacity, water conservation/supply and ecological footprints of growth.

- Economic development and poverty related challenges.
- Energy, transportation and water resources constraints and opportunities.
- Environment, pollution control and climate change challenge
- Heritage and conservation potential.
- Governance and institutional capacity.

The sequence of planning can be expressed in the following starting with 'P'

1. Position, perceptions, people and projections.
2. Problems
3. Possibilities
4. Proposals, policy, principles, parameters
5. Plan
6. Process/procedures/programmes
7. Practice/performance
8. Projects, product, partnerships, participation.

It is important to remember that it is not the plan that is important, it's the planning." As such, planning is a continuous process. Planning exercise involves working from both ends—from whole to part and from parts to whole. It should be able to grasp an overview as well as the ground reality. The perceptions of providers and consumers both are reflected in a balanced perspective. The sectoral study provides a synoptic picture, which usually focuses on the performance of the providers. 'The whole to part' approach often marginalizes the 'have nots' and wishful plans and proposals camouflage the ground reality. Area based approach is often context oriented, although it tends to overlook the scenario in totality. For a realistic assessment, and to bridge this gap, a study from both the sides, i.e., overall study and specific area studies, which are useful to triangulate the providers' and consumers' perceptions. The objective should include assessment of performance with focus on financing and management issues. This requires the following inputs and relevant details:

(*a*) Context-Physical, Environmental, Social and Economic

(*b*) Operation/Systems of Delivery and Distribution

(*c*) Plans/Proposals

(*d*) Financial management

(*e*) Governance, including administrative, legal, institutional frame, organizations involved and their linkages.

For exploration of relevant indicators and their sources, "who, how, what, and when" can be adopted as the basic questions, which derive the checklists. In this respect, framing of 'correct' questions assumes utmost importance, as no answer can be correct if the question itself is not correct.

## Planning for Change

The new economic policies and democratic decentralization envisage a shift from command economy to market economy, from centralized to decentralized system, from deficit spending to structural adjustment, from government domain to public private partnership, and from high subsidy regime to user pay principle. (Table 4.2) The challenge is to find ecologically sustainable, socially just, economically viable and culturally transferable planning, technological and managerial innovations. The traditional role of government and local bodies is changing from 'provider' to 'facilitator'.

**Table 4.2 : Changes in Policy Context**

| From | | To |
|---|---|---|
| Command economies | ➡ | Market Econimies, privatisation |
| Low environmental awarencess | ➡ | High environmental awareness |
| Centralised System | ➡ | Decentralised System (73 & 74th CAA) |
| High deficit spending | ➡ | Structural adjustment |
| Govt. Domain over Land, Infrastructure & Housing Dev. | ➡ | Incentives for Infrastucture investments & Private Sector Participation |
| High subsidy Regime | ➡ | Users pay principle, low subsidy |
| Programmes and Sectoral Projects | ➡ | Inclusive Growth with focus on marginalised/ valuerable population and areas |

The policy changes reverberate in the paradigm shifts in planning approach. This demands action oriented planning, management of development, enabling a partnership approach. The scope of planning is enlarged to include institutional, financial and legal aspects, together with an enabling and participatory process.

With the changing socio-economic conditions, the emergence of a stronger private sector, political intervention, inadequacies of centralized approach, rising unemployment and redundancy of old technology, new models of infrastructure planning, district planning and local management are emerging, which

**Table 4.3 : Paradigm Shifts in Planning Approach**

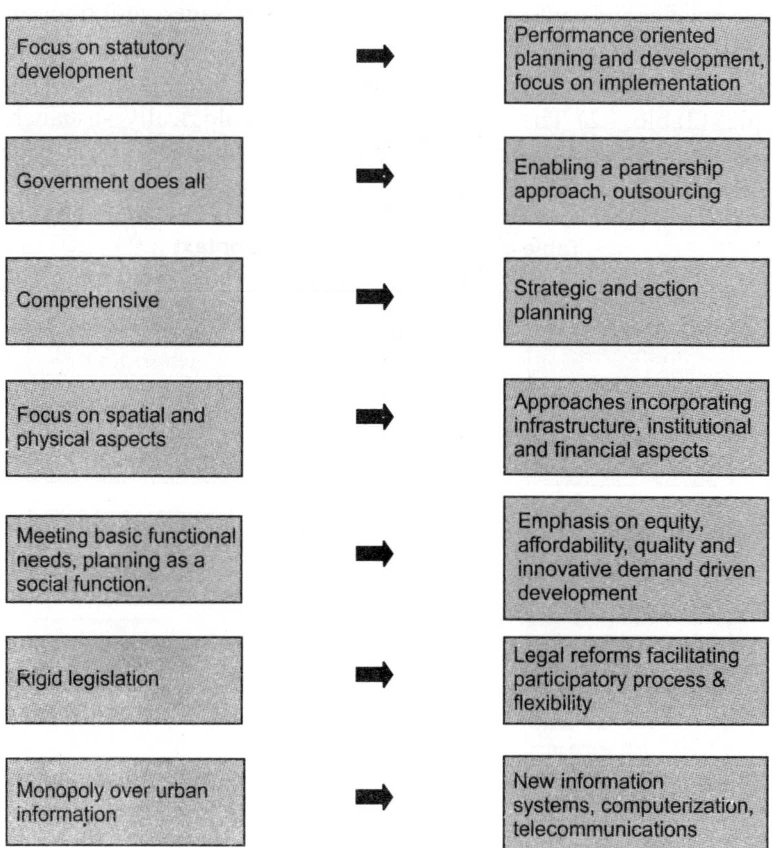

| From | | To |
|---|---|---|
| Focus on statutory development | ➡ | Performance oriented planning and development, focus on implementation |
| Government does all | ➡ | Enabling a partnership approach, outsourcing |
| Comprehensive | ➡ | Strategic and action planning |
| Focus on spatial and physical aspects | ➡ | Approaches incorporating infrastructure, institutional and financial aspects |
| Meeting basic functional needs, planning as a social function. | ➡ | Emphasis on equity, affordability, quality and innovative demand driven development |
| Rigid legislation | ➡ | Legal reforms facilitating participatory process & flexibility |
| Monopoly over urban information | ➡ | New information systems, computerization, telecommunications |

emphasise interventionist approach and revitalization of infrastructure, business and employment generation. This requires the adoption of a new strategy to public sector intervention, whereby a new coalition is forged between the local government/authority, the private sector and the community with a view to mop up various resources for infrastructure development, transportation, power, water, sanitation, etc. A leveraging strategy can trigger a chain reaction of private sector investments. Market led development based on short term partnership may not be viable in the long run and could adversely effect the labour welfare policies, social security, service and equity.

The concept of public-private partnership aims at 'rolling back the frontiers of state' and revitalizing the enterprise. A basic purpose of the partnership is to reduce the burden of state's investment and to attract private sector efficiency and resources. However, it is yet to be seen whether direct private sector investments can be mopped up for infrastructure projects, like solid waste management, trunk sewer, water supply, roads and bridges and social housing, without adversely affecting the nature of 'social service' which such projects provide.

With globalization, economic liberalization and devolution of power to local bodies, participatory decision making is becoming institutionalized. This means redefining the goals and objectives. This process requires (*a*) investigation, information and ground truth base, (*b*) analysis, identification of problems and prospects, and (*c*) synthesis, formulation goals and objectives and strategy formulation (Fig. 4.10)

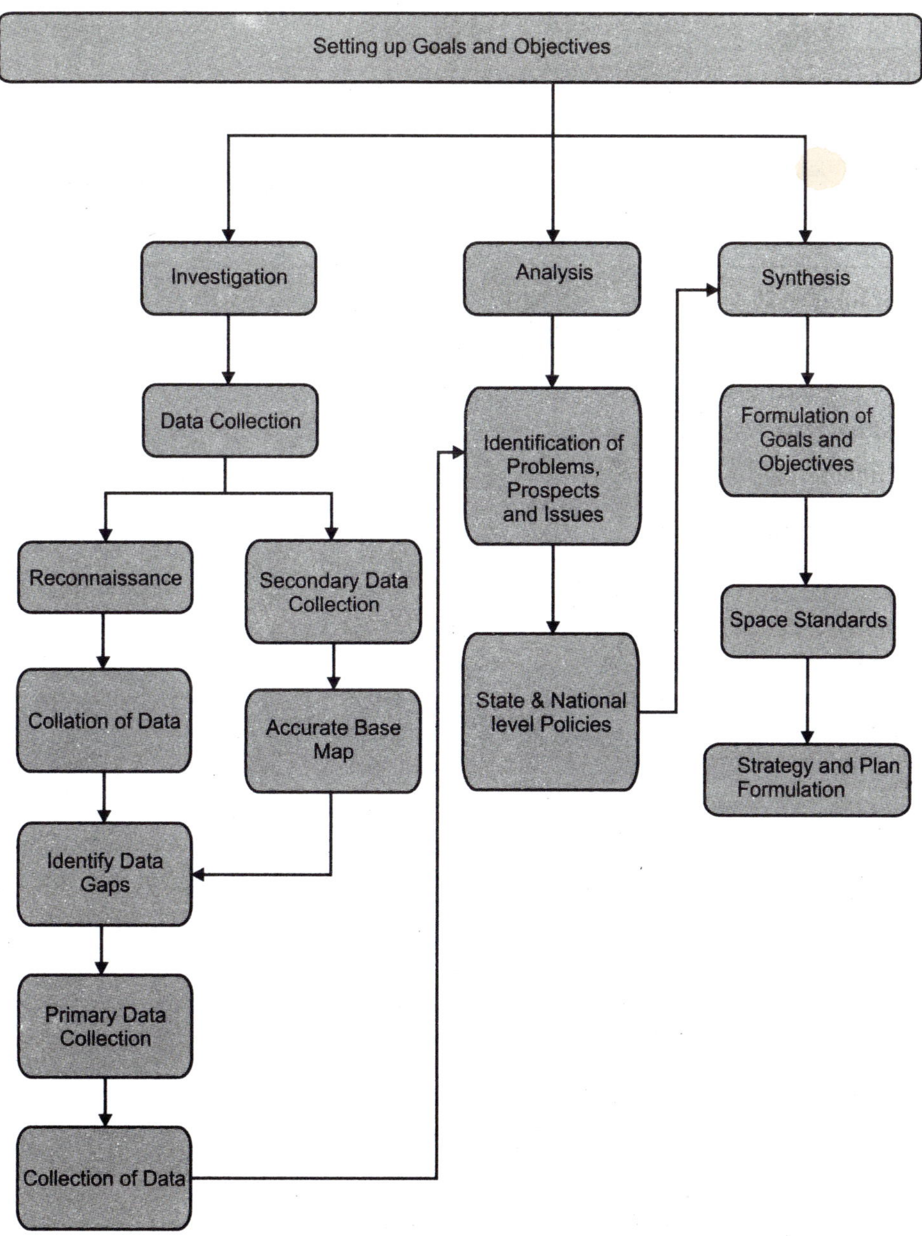


**Fig. 4.10 : Redefining Development Goals and Objectives**

Hyrum Smith explains the concept of goals as follows :

"Values explain why you want to accomplish certain things in life. Long-range goals describe what you want to accomplish. Intermediate goals and daily tasks show how to do it. When you set goals, I suggest you make sure they are SMART goals". SMART goals are :

- Specific
- Measureable
- Action-oriented
- Realistic
- Timely

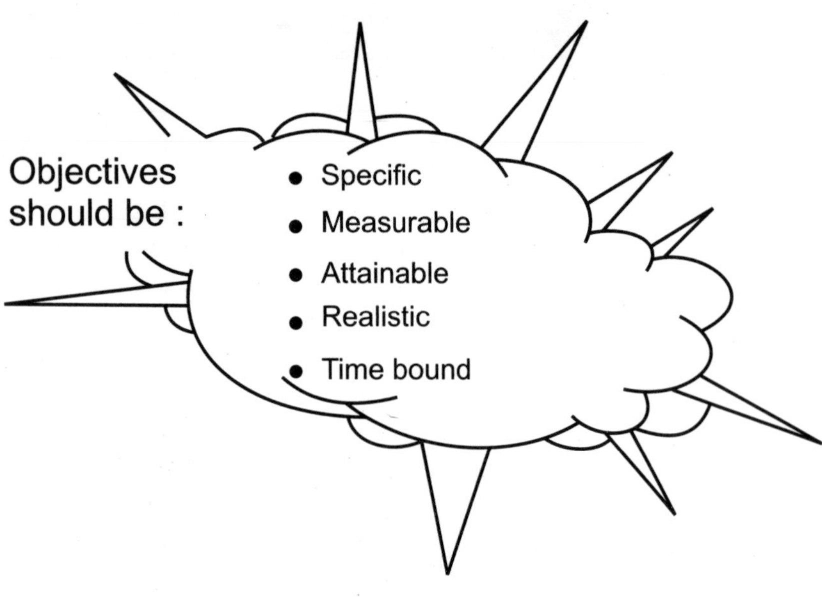


Fig. 4.11 : "Smart" Objectives

Someone once said that an unwritten goal is merely a wish. Writing the goals forces you to be specific, you will have a hard time knowing whether or not you have reached it. You can improve what you measure. Goals should always focus on actions, rather than personal qualities. Goals must be realistic. It's good to aim high, but if we aim too high, we can get discouraged, and the goal-setting process can become just another fruitless activity. Goals that are too easily reached are just as useless and unrealistic as goals that are too far beyond our reach. Goals must also be timely. Don't give yourself so much time that the goal becomes meaningless.

Following the evolution of Smart goals (Specific, Measureable, Action-oriented, Realistic and Timely), the steps below are to be taken up for District Planning :

- Setting up the benchmarks for physical and social infrastructure and facilities
- Preparation of the development plans at policy, strategic and operational levels and exploring a needs based approach for a basket of facilities, services and amenities.
- Strategic planning for priority projects/areas and sectors and a timeframe
- Action Planning and participatory management
- Institutional/organizational framework and governance
- Legal framework and procedural reforms
- Financial Planning and harnessing the potentials of private and community sectors

In view of the above, the following sequence can be adopted in the process of planning (Fig. 4.12)

1. Mission Statement and Objectives.
2. Translating the above into SMART goals.
3. Baseline Information and participation learning.
4. Identifying the issues and Key Action Areas.
5. Conceptual Framework with respect to policy options, strategic planning, benchmarks and standards.
6. Evaluation of planning options by SWOT analysis, matrix analysis, financial implications, cost benefit analysis, feasibility and viability assessment.
7. Develop a Plan disaggregated into sectoral plans for various services and key action areas.
8. Resource Planning and Governance :
    - Shared governance and decentralisation
    - Identifying key issues *via-a-vis* resource assessment
    - Empowerment of the community
    - Participatory Action Planning

The entire superstructure of planning and development rests on the three pillars :

- Organisational/institutional structure;
- Finances; and
- Legal Framework.

No Plan, however good, can be implemented unless it is supported by the people and stakeholders who have to participate at all levels of decision making and implementation. Coordinated spatial, financial and institutional planning necessitates an effective delineation of actions at various levels-national, state, district and local. The respective roles of the different levels of government and other agencies involved in planning, financing, provision of services and other activities should be clearly defined, together with coordination of physical, financial, social and political aspects. The plans of rural development need to be based upon the foundation of community development, equity principle, employment creation, poverty alleviation and basic needs provision. The plans have to be pro-poor, participatory and meaningful for the local population.

## Participatory Learning and Identifying the Key Issues

The basis of planning is the information, for which a systematic, scientific and flexible approach is necessary. This involves working out flexible check lists and semi-structured cross examination of various sources of information. The salient features of such approach are as follows :

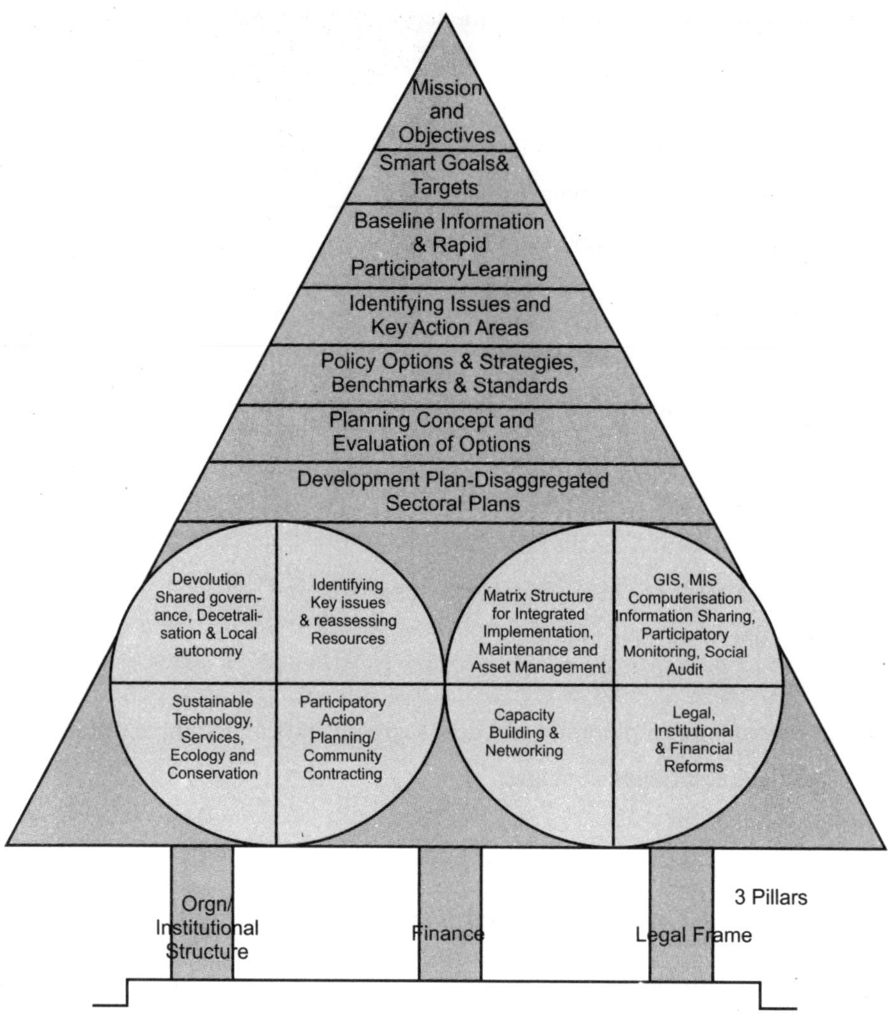


**Fig. 4.12 : Pyramid of Rural Planning**

(*a*) To collect information as an incremental learning process,

(*b*) To relate information and inputs with reflective observations, conceptualization and experimentation,

(*c*) To recognize the limitations of optimal ignorance and precision,

(*d*) Adoption of triangulation process for a three dimensional perception,

(*e*) Proxy indicators as an aid to information and perceptive understanding,

(*f*) Quality control *versus* quantitative/statistical approach, (*g*) Use of triangulation technique for performance assessment,

(*h*) Recognizing the principle of "less is more" (time/information/resources).

## Surveys and Mapping

A map provides the ground base for planning. It is the spatial dimension of development. For various levels of planning, appropriate kinds and scale of maps are required. Apart from field surveying, maps are now available through internet, satellite, geographic information system and aerial photography. New technologies are emerging which bring up maps providing hidden/underground information (like service lines, minerals, geology, sub-soil water, temperature, etc.). However, for general purpose a map will have the following characteristics:

- **Geometry (accuracy of position and dimensions/area) :** The geometry of a map is achieved through a set of ground control points, called stations and leveling Benchmarks (BM). These stations may have the utmost accuracy of a geodetic station. BM's are, presently, being provided by the Survey of India (SOI). The position of these stations is given in the form of coordinates expressed in terms of latitude and longitude. In most of the cases, accurate information about the stations and the BM is restricted.
- **Contents of a map :** The earlier technology of the ground based methods (plane-tabling, etc) has been replaced by the aerial photography (photogrammetry) and satellite imagery. The resolution of the modern day satellites has reached a level of one metre. This enables contents of the map to be based on high-resolution satellite imagery on desired scales.
- **Updateness :** It is a natural desire of a map user that the map is reasonably updated. Here the satellite imagery is of great utility, as it visits the same spot at a regular interval of say, one month, or so. Therefore, technologically the problem of updating the maps, to a large extent, can be resolved.
- **Scale :** The scale of a map can be chosen according to its planning purpose, such as given in Table 4.4 :

**Table 4.4 Scales for Maps**

| Functions | Scale |
|---|---|
| Regional Plan/District plan | 1:40,000 |
| Master Plan/Taluk Plan | 1:20,000 to 1:4000 |
| Ward Plan/Village Plan | 1:4000 to 1:10,000 |
| Housing/Industrial Layout Plan | 1:2000 to 1:400 |
| Engineering Plans/Roads/Services | 1:2000 to 1:400 |
| Revenue/Land related Records | 1:2000 to 1:200 |

The revenue maps traditionaly were drawn at a scale of 1 inch = 330 feet, that corresponds roughly to 1:4000, as such surveys at 1:4000 scale can be layered with land ownership/shajra maps.

**Land Information Technologies :** Various options are now available for obtaining land information, which can be suitably used according to the function :

- Field Surveying, Total Station Survey by electronic equipments
- Global Positioning System, photogrammetry and Aerial Photography
- Satellite Imagery and Remote Sensing
- Geographic information System (GIS)
- Cadastre/spatial Data Infrastructure
- Air Borne Laser Terrain Modelling (ALTM)
- Reader Interferometry
- Transmitting graphic (map) information on-line by application of internet, compression of data

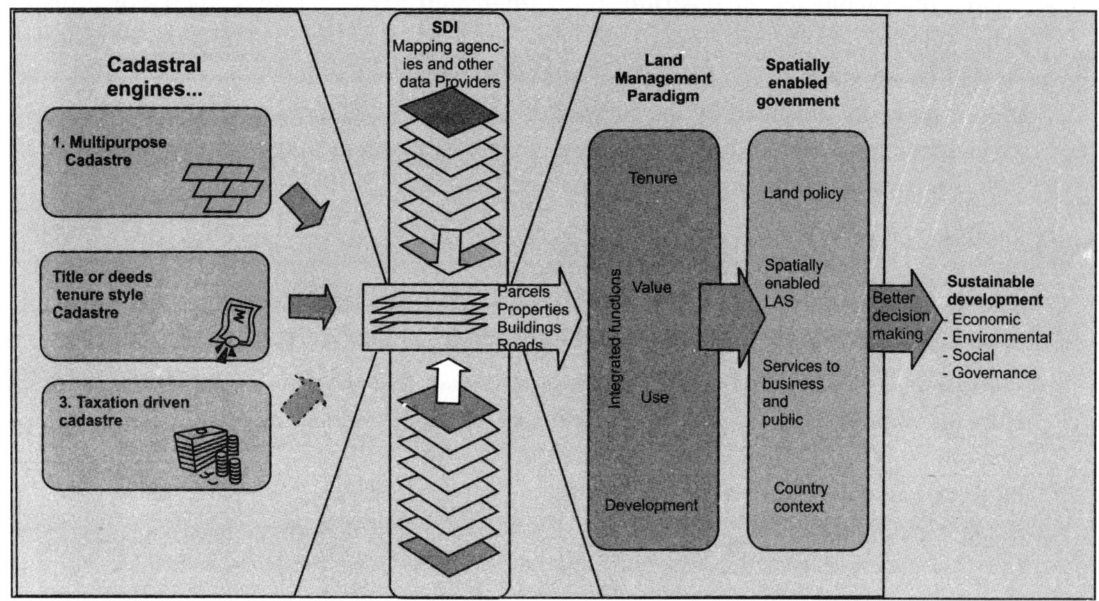


**Fig. 4.13 : Land information is an important tool to develop spatial Data Infrastructure (SDI), land policy and management and spatial enabled governance. It enables better decision making for sustainable planning and land use, besides improving land revenues for local body.**
**Source:** Significance of the Cadastre (Williamson and Wallace, 2007).

## Reconnaissance Surveys

In order to have an overview of the physical context, its topography, urban sprawl, form, and also for selection of study area, following types of reconnaissance surveys are useful:

(*a*) Aerial triangulation/synoptic survey

(*b*) Windscreen survey at ground level

(*c*) Ground Surveys

(*d*) Interpreting remote sensing maps and overlaying them on ground surveys

## Vector Mapping

The Survey maps (Survey of India, etc) are superimposed and corrected by ground survey, administrative revenue maps, aerial maps, satellite images and other available maps, such as environmental, ground water, etc. All these should be mechanically enlarged or reduced to the same scale (popularly 1 : 4000 which corresponds to revenue maps of 1″ = 330 ft). These provide useful vector maps for planning, without need for elaborate, time consuming fresh surveys.

## Collecting the Data

There are two kinds of data sources—primary and secondary data. Primary data is first hand information, gathered from original sources, for instance through interviews or going out and directly observing the phenomena that is being studied. Secondary data is second-hand data that someone else has gathered but that is available and may fit one's needs. Data collection by the Census of India, published and stored in the library, becomes a secondary source for everyone's use.

## Interviews

They can be face-to-face or by internet or telephone. Face-to-Face interviews are more accurate but any sort of interviewing is expensive. Interviewers must be trained and since one shot surveys can not hire full time staff, surveying becomes difficult. In these circumstances, survey and research centers, often affiliated with universities or with large businesses with experienced staff are frequently used for survey and research.

## Direct Inspection

The direct inspection of conditions or activities is employed in making traffic counts, housing conditions, jobs, income, land use surveys, water quality studies, and many other kinds of surveys where human communication is not required to elicit the information directly. However, this is not always as easy as it sounds. A well known direct technique is participant-observation. The technique was developed by anthropologists in the study of community life. The surveyor becomes a resident of the community and lives among the people, learning their way of life by participating in it. It has been very effectively used by some social scientists in contemporary western cities to investigate problems of middle class and ethnic life.

The question of choice of techniques of observation rests primarily on two criteria-bias and cost, both of which are inter-related in such a way that reducing one results in increasing the other.

The choice of technique is a problem of striking a balance of these two criteria. The mode of observation is often largely determined by the form and the substance of the questions being asked.

The questions of a survey are called the variables of the survey. This means that each question constitutes an item for which we seek information about variations in the population being surveyed. Family income, as a variable or question in a survey, tells us how family income varies among those being surveyed. There are three basic variations that are used in structuring the questions of a survey. These are—nominal, ordinal, and interval.

A properly chosen sample of the whole is usually adequate to estimate the information accurately for the whole population. Where estimates from samples cannot be trusted, and adequate resources are available, the whole population can be surveyed. This is called a 100% sample. But a smaller sample is often the only feasible alternative. The problem is to make certain that the sample accurately represents the population. A sample that is not representative is called a biased sample. If the population to be surveyed is very large and the sampling proportion is small then the test can be done with the target population. Otherwise, as not to bias the real sample, an alternate but similar population should be used for the test. The test run will allow more accuracy to estimate costs in terms of time per interview or per question, allowing final adjustments in sample size or number of questions. It will also help one to spot the ambiguous questions, areas of misinterpretation, poor layout on the forms and will help in formulating the special instructions and training that must be given to the survey persons. When surveys are conducted by trained interviewers or observers, some system of monitoring is advisable to discourage improper practices.

## Multiple Index Surveys

To assess a particular aspect/condition, such as poverty, the multiple index survey can be adopted by means of a sieve map (or quantitatively by calculating average multiple index). This helps to determine the areas having worst (shown by incidence of all the bad factors in that areas), moderate (few bad factors) or fair (no bad factors) conditions. Some of the factors chosen for the purpose may be, for example:

- No bath room
- No latrine
- No electricity
- No. of rooms per family/house
- Rooms excessively small
- Structural condition.

Average Multiple Index is calculated for different areas, which can be given different weightages depending upon the gravity of a factor in contributing to condition of buildings, poverty or environment.

## Transect

Transect as a schematic device can be extremely useful to obtain an overview of a particular area and its problems and issues. This is a diagrammatic illustration and record of major characteristics, events, profiles or issues. While conducting windscreen or reconnaissance, freehand transects can be prepared, which can supplement the diary or field record book.

## Proxy Indicators

Proxy Indicators are short-cut to time consuming data collection and an alternative to unstructured observations. Information about these indicators may be readily available, which has to be applied on the basis of past experience, common sense and certain assumptions. For example, the growth in the number of banks in an area may indicate its economic base or a greater number of fast food restaurants may represent a youth dominated society.

After a rapid, synoptic and windscreen survey one can identify areas of representative nature on the basis of the criteria for selection of case studies. Depending upon the objectives, the following could be the basis for selection of study areas:

(*a*) category of settlements/sectors;

(*b*) level of consolidation;

(*c*) representative nature of the area.

## Search for Questions and Indicators

Accuracy, timeliness, reliability and cost effectiveness are important qualities determining the usefulness of data for formulation of policies. These factors should be kept in view while deciding the data that needs to be collected for a study. It is always useful to deliberate over the question as to what data needs to be collected. To collect quality information, the key informants should be selected carefully, so that those who are knowledgeable in the field are approached. In addition to public agencies, other sources of information, viz., cooperatives, residents' groups, women's organizations, traders' associations, etc., can be useful to augment information obtained from primary and official sources. Secondary sources of data, such as, reports and literature can also provide useful information.

## Triangulation

Triangulation is an important method to cross-check information obtained from different sources. Multidisciplinary teams are useful in triangulation, so that the data and information can be cross-checked by observation, discussions and by inter-disciplinary perspectives. This way, the reliability of information obtained through rapid surveys/appraisal can be enhanced.

## Exploration

A preliminary visit can be very helpful to work out a handy semi-structured check list and a framework of indicators for actual survey. Simultaneously, a semi-structured questionnaire for interviews with people and organizations concerned can be prepared.

The information thus obtained should be triangulated from time to time to make sense out of it. Information related with observations can be transformed into abstractions in order to make use of it. The information gathered should be crisp and clear so that it can be digested, codified, analyzed, and then synthesized to arrive at the results and for conceptualization.

## Problem Analysis and Options

Both the sectoral and area studies highlight important issues. The issues and problems have different priorities as per the perceptions of official agency and the consumers. These need to be reconciled before and options can be evolved and debated. The issues and aspects can be grouped and analysed in various categories, e.g.:

- Institutional
- Financial
- Delivery/Equity
- Managerial
- Environmental
- Maintenance
- Technical, legal

Analysis is a process of disaggregation. It has to be studied both from 'Consumers' and 'Providers' points of view. Whereas from one end, the problem and issues need to be studied in a comprehensive and synoptic manner, on the other, these are to be seen from their actual delivery on the ground. The official information has to be triangulated and cross-checked with the residents and functionaries. The findings should be based on the views expressed by consumers and corroborated with their observations. A synthesis of the findings and analysis would indicate the critical issues.

## Triage

Triage is a useful method for assessing social, economic, institutional and technical performance of alternative options, systems or technology. It is particularly concerned with the technical aspects and design process and therefore, is relevant for project planning and design. Under this method, various components of a system are given a score and a screening criteria is evolved. For this, the results of technological systems and performance are reviewed and scored as low, medium or high, as the case may be.

## Impact Analysis

The purpose of impact analysis is to assess the impact of a particular service, project or facility. A preliminary impact analysis may be essential at the planning stage. For this, the intended or planned activity is placed at the centre and its direct and indirect, positive and negative results are listed in the boxes around the activity. The arrows linking various boxes indicate the linkages, directions and causes. The effects may be comprehensive, which can be categorized under physical, environmental, social, economic, political, institutional, legal and other impacts. For example, the impact of intended regularization of unauthorized colonies can be analysed by evolving a set of Impact Diagrams.

## Sustainability Analysis

Amongst various planning alternatives, sustainability is a key consideration in making a viable selection. For this, various stages and steps involved in implementation are listed. Against each, major problems are systematically located with their possible solutions. This allows exploration of possible options at various stages of implementation. This exercise can help to arrive at logical decisions or conclusions among various alternatives and options.

## Force-field Analysis

Force-field Analysis is a well established management tool. It allows the analysis of a problem, or an opportunity in a manner that helps to generate innovative but realistic actions. The actions generated may range from use of certain technology to manpower development and choice of partners in development. As such, it has become increasingly recognized as an appropriate tool to help develop innovative solutions to help solve urban management problems. In the context of better use of private sector participation to improve urban service delivery and accessibility, force field analysis can be used to develop and test appropriate line of action. (Fig. 4.14)

## Matrix Analysis

Matrix Analysis helps in identifying the critical strategic issues, potential barriers and bottlenecks, which the project is likely to encounter. On one side verticals are identified:

1. **Physical:** such as land required, location, access, land ownership, power and water, services, raw material, markets, etc.
2. **Investments/Finances and other resources,** such as budget, bank loans, institutional finance, taxes, human resource, subsidies, cost benefit, market potential, pricing, etc.

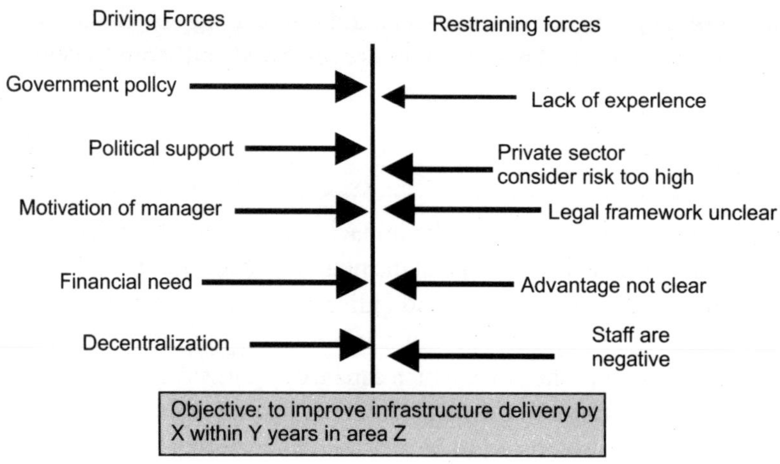


**Fig 4.14 : Force-field analysis**

3. **Environment factors:** such as, pollution, EIA, carbon emissions reduction, waste recycling, water, energy efficiency, etc.
4. **Organisation/Management/Legal issues,** such as law, rules, regulation, labour, organizations involved, contracting procedure, competition, regulatory system, political support, time lines, etc.
5. **Technology:** level, import potential, skills, safety, retrofitting, repair, maintenance, impact, etc.
6. **Service Delivery and Marketing:** consumers, society, local community benefit, jobs, etc.

On the other side Critical Strategic Issues are listed—which can be external or internal. By fuzzy logic these can be given a conceptual weightage and then accordingly action required to tackle the issues is outlined. This way matrix chart provides a clear picture of the problems, difficulties and risks which need to be tackled. In certain cases, the situation could be –

1. Impossible,
2. Can be remedied with additional inputs/efforts, but with risk, and,
3. Can be nipped in the bud by pre-planning, or by internal action.

In most of the rural development projects, a congenial relationship with the political apparatus and local community is necessary which can be achieved by proper PR, communications, offer of jobs to the locals, cultural promotion, religious, healthcare and educational programmes, etc. For certain critical issues, it may be necessary to appoint the consultants, peer advisory group or outsource the difficult components of work.

Triangulation technique can be adopted to co-relate the critical factors (verticals) and project aspects (horizontals). (Figs. 4.15 and 4.16) These can also be represented a 6 by 6 pyramid (Fig. 4.18)

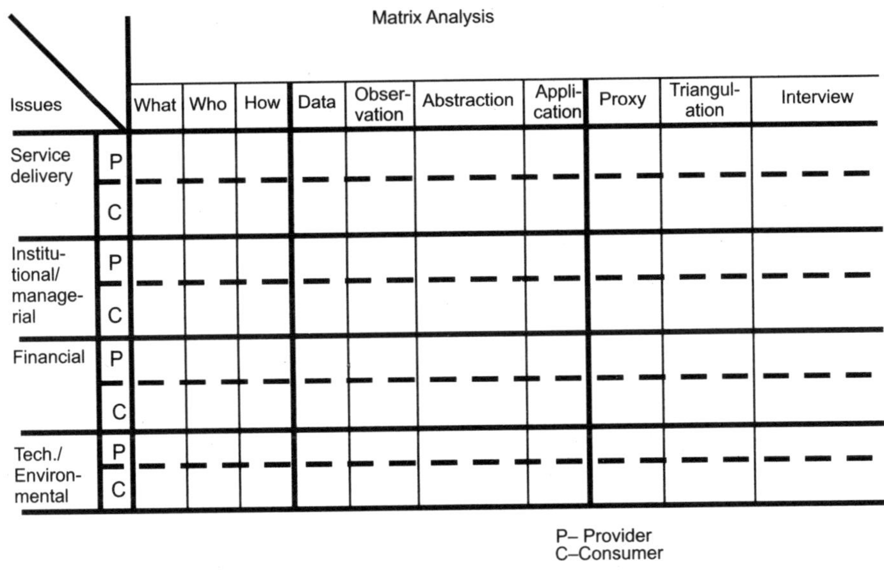


**Fig. 4.15 : Matrix Analysis by Evolving Semi-structured Checklists**

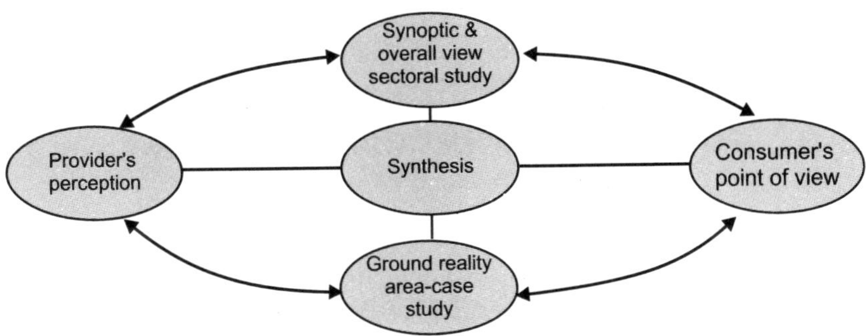


**Fig. 4.16 : Integration of Synoptic/Sectoral Study with Ground Reality/Area Studies; Provider's Perception and Consumer's Point of View**

## District and Rural Planning Process and Practice

In spite of laudable statistics, the rural schemes often suffer from lack of linkages with the livelihoods, health and well being, ecological sustainability and poverty alleviation programmes. The spatial dimension of schemes is either missing or is too narrow. The plans are prepared and implemented by the technical professionals and the departments with urban mindset. They hardly belong to the people. The convergence among central, state and local, and among regional, district and village plans is often missing. Even local programmes of health, education, roads, services, housing, etc. are

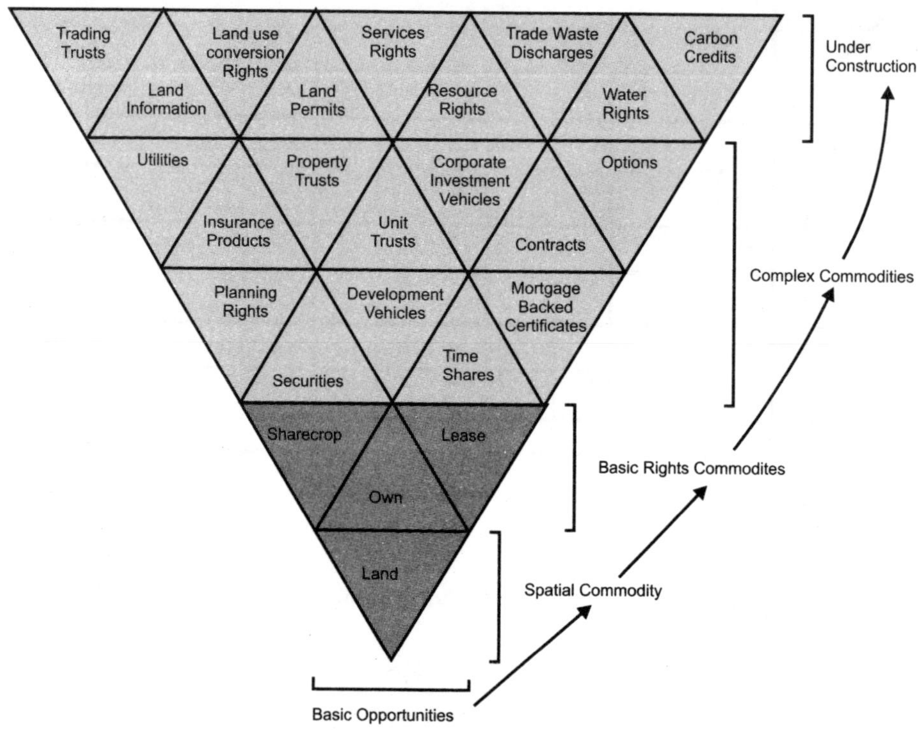


**Fig. 4.17 : 6 × 6 Pyramid Matrix for Land Management**

**Source:** Wallace and Williamson, 2006

taken up in isolation without proper coordination. However, some success stories are available, which can provide useful lessons for rural development. The rural-urban integration in Kerala by District Planning Committee is one of such examples. It reinforces the idea of interdependent rural-urban networks, rather than stand alone District Planning or rural settlement plans.

The state of Kerala launched a highly participatory planning process through formation of 14 DPCs which have undertaken the task of integration of the Panachayat Plan (rural areas) as well as those prepared by 55 municipalities and 3 municipal corporations (urban areas). This is a bold attempt to take the planning process to the grassroots level with maximum involvement of the masses. It is known as People's Planning Campaign. The common people are encouraged to actively participate in identifying local problems and finding solutions. The unique feature of Kerala experiment is the high level of autonomy to the local bodies to determine their own priorities. The planning process of preparation of District Plan involves various stages, which includes formation of strategic perspective for development, formulation and preparation of Annual Plan of gram panchayats/ municipalities. The preparation of district plan is taken up based on feedback from below. The planning of rural-urban integration at the district level is achieved through DPCs by preparing a plan for the whole district.

The state of Kerala while planning has adopted the quality of life approach which synergizes basic, well-being opportunity and amenties needs of the people. All the departments of the District Administration are involved so that their schemes converge into a comprehensive planning framework.

## Kollam Model of Integrated District Planning (Kerala)

In an effort to institutionalize the decentralized planning process in Kerala, which was initiated in campaign mode, the 10th Five Year Plan gave emphasis to spatial planning by the Local Self government Institutions. This helped in linking the spatial planning to the decentralized planning process of Local Self-government Institutions.

The District Planning Committee, Kollam initiated the preparation of Integrated District Development Plan for the District (IDDP) and a Local Development Plan (LDP) for each Local Self Government Institution in the district (Fig. 4.18). The matter was taken up to State Planning Board and a Kerala Government Order (GO (MS) 62/03/Planning dated 1-8-2003) was issued to prepare these plans as a pilot project in Kollam with Town and Country Planning Department as the nodal agency. Subsequently a Handbook for the preparation of IDDP and LDP for Kollam was prepared which was issued by the State Planning Board.

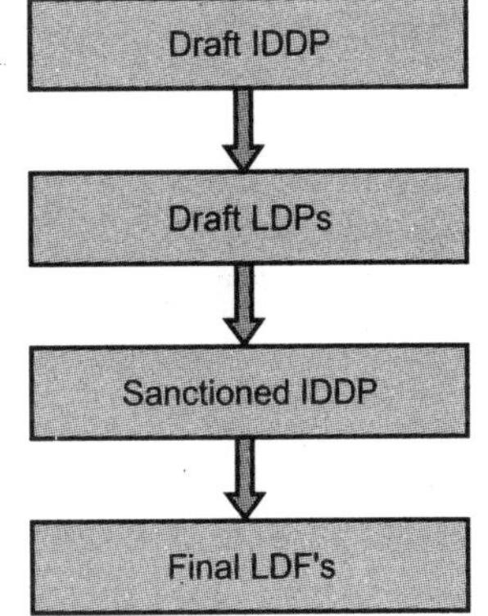


**Fig. 4.18 : Local/Village Plans form part of Integrated District Development Plan Framework**

The process of preparation of IDDP and LDP started with the training programmes for various stakeholders of the project and primary data collection at the Gram Panchayat and municipality levels was carried out for one and a half year. About 12000 stakeholders, ranging from DPC members to NGOs at the Gram Panchayat level were given training which created awareness about the project among stakeholders.

The process of preparation of the Plans then proceeded with the analysis stage. The sequential steps of plan preparation are almost prarallel for both the plans i.e. IDDP and LDP (Fig. 4.19). Based on the analyses, the district level development issues are identified and the development goals and objectives are set. Based on that, Draft IDDP is prepared for the district incorporating suggestions of LSGIs (Fig. 4.20 to 4.23). The Draft IDDP thus prepared is an input for the identification of development issues and setting up of development goals. Each LSGI gives a framework within which the Draft LDPs are prepared. Based on suggestions and proposals of the Draft LDPs the Draft IDDP is modified and finalized. Once the draft IDDP, approved by the DPC, is sanctioned by the State government, the Draft LDPs are finalized.

Block and Jilla Panchayat Development Plans are prepared based on policies and strategies of sanctioned Integrated District Development Plan and sanctioned Local Plans within their administrative boundaries. The projects and programmes, based on the policies and strategies of District and Local Level Plans, are implemented by the Jilla and Block Panchayats. (Fig. 4.24). An important highlight of the planning is a focus on provision of facilities and infrastructure in the rural areas which provide a comparable quality of life with the urban area (Table 4.5)

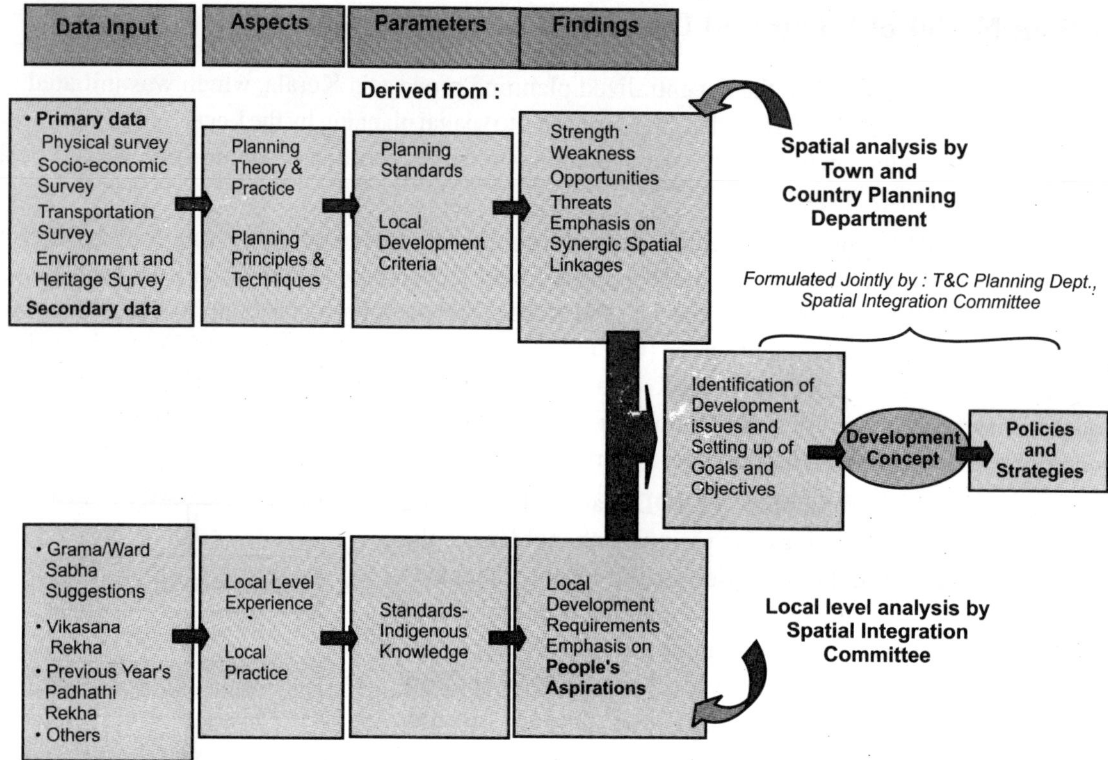


**Fig. 4.19 : IDDP and LDPs are prepared based on top down and grassroot up approach. The data collection, analysis and carving out of local level proposals are done at the grass root level which is later modified, based on the policies derived at the District level while preparing the IDDP. At the same time the policies are formulated taking in to account the proposals at the local level (LSGI level). State of the art technology – GIS, GPS, satellite imagery are utilized in the preparation of LDP and IDDP.**

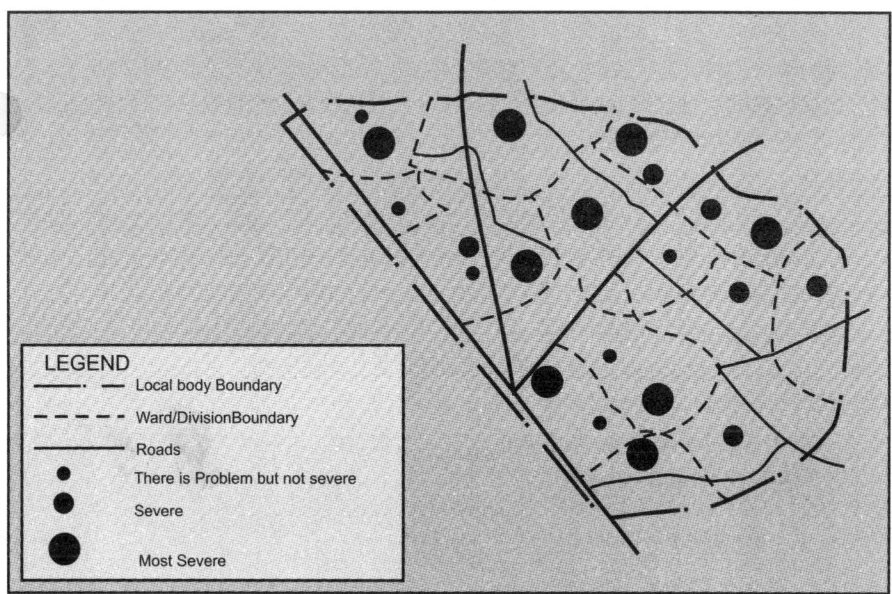


Fig. 4.20 : Integrated Distt. Development Plan : Problem Severity Map

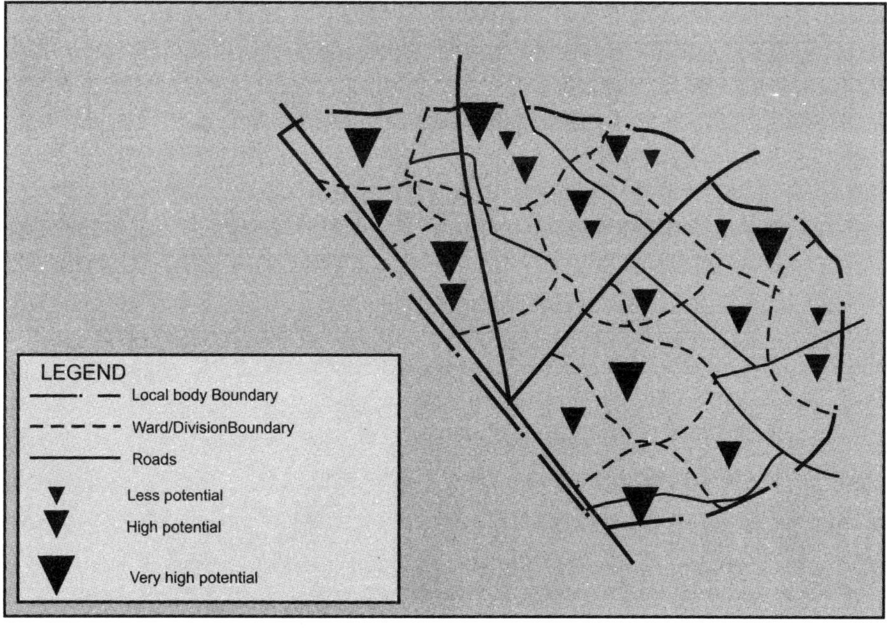


Fig. 4.21 : Integrated District Development Plan : Potential Map

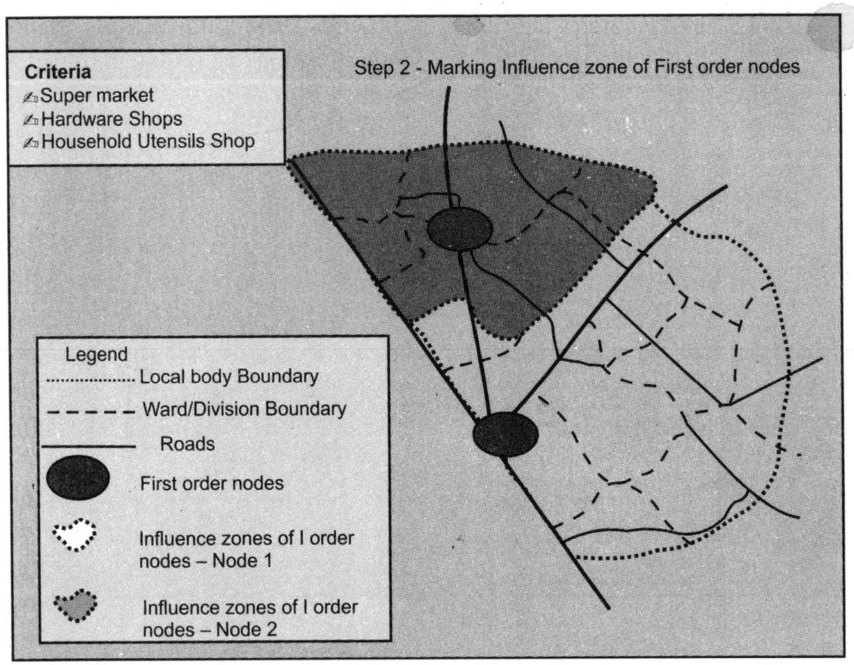


**Fig. 4.22 : Map showing Influence Zones of First order nodes**

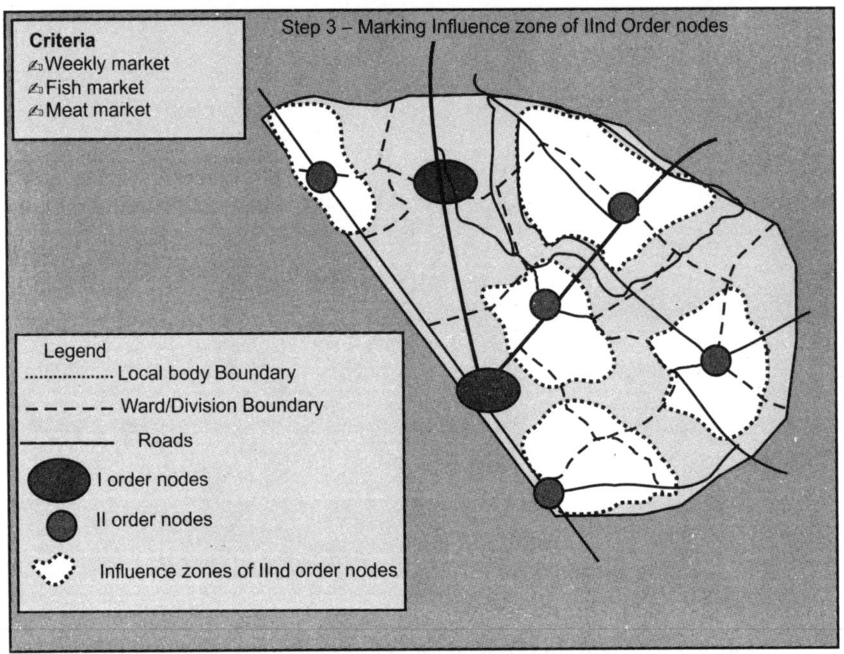


**Fig. 4.23 : Map showing Influence Zones of Second order nodes**

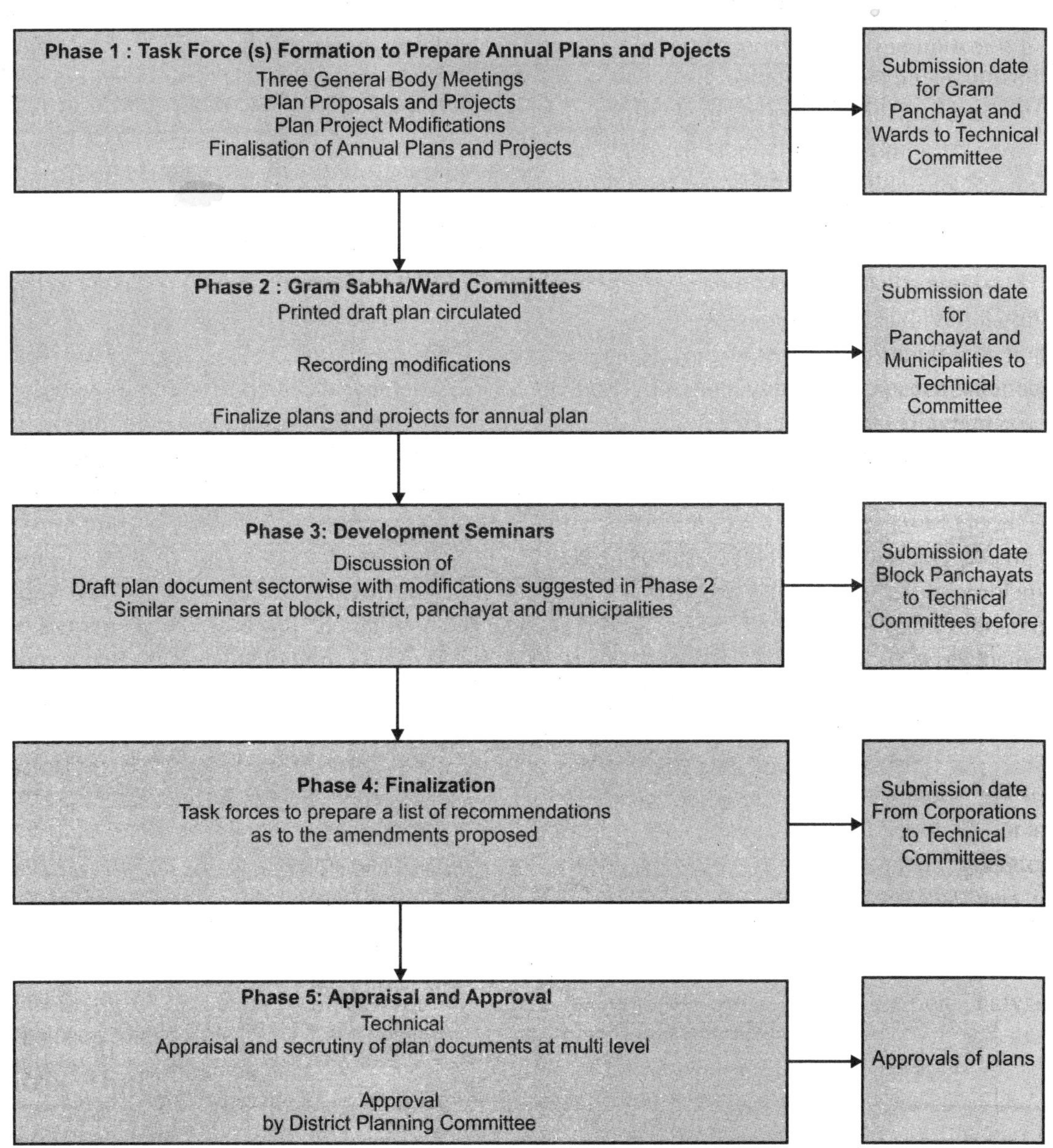


**Fig. 4.24 : District and Local Plan Formulation Procedure**

**Table 4.5 : Comparison of urban and rural areas based on quality of life**

| | | Index of Comparision | Rural | Urban |
|---|---|---|---|---|
| Basic Life Needs | Food | % Below Poverty line | 26.32 | 24.16 |
| | Housing | Housing Condition | | |
| | | % Pacca House | 80 | 85.38 |
| | | % Houses Electrified | 69.41 | 63.23 |
| Well Being Needs | Health | No of physicians per 20,000 Population | 3.52 | 13.54 |
| | | No of Hospital/1 Lakh Population, | 15.14 | 17.38 |
| | | Hospital beds/Population | 12.11 | 92.33 |
| | Safety | Number of police station/One Lakh Population | 1.01 | 1.52 |
| | Employment | Male wage rate | 118 | 130 |
| | | Female wage rate | 105.5 | 116.62 |
| | | Work Participation rate | 22.49 | 22.94 |
| | | Main workers | 88.98 | 92.71 |
| Opportunity Needs | Transportation | Black top road length per thousand persons (km) | 4.29 | 1.9 |
| | | Road Density Per thousand Population | 4.17 | 4.23 |
| | Infrastructure Facilities | Parks and Recreational Area (Ha) per one lakh Population | 0.3 | 0.3 |
| | | Stadiums | 1 | 1.83 |
| | | Gymnasium and Health Clubs | 0.73 | 2.13 |
| | | Cremation Centers | 2.18 | 1.52 |
| | Communication | Telephone Connections | 26.26 | 54.01 |
| | Information Facilities | No of Post Officers and Private Couriers/10,000 population | 1.6 | 1.62 |
| | | Public Telephone Booths/10 Thousand Population | 4.14 | 10.45 |
| | | Cyber Cafes/1 lakh Population | 0.49 | 1.93 |
| | Savings Facilities | Bank per 10 thousand Population | 4.16 | 3.93 |
| | | Agricultural Bank | 1.156 | 3.394 |
| | | Commercial Bank | 0.3 | 0.54 |
| | Equality | Public Distribution System | 0.3 | 0.54 |
| | | No of Shops per ten thousand Population | 3.52 | 3.38 |
| | | Percentage Card Holders | 91.27 | 84.09 |
| Amenity Needs | Recreation | No of cinema Halls/1 lakh Population | 2.82 | 4.57 |
| | | Seating Capacity of cinema halls/1000 Population | 17.54 | 24.95 |
| | Social | Public Library and Reading Rooms/15,000 Population | 4.17 | 7.935 |
| | | Kindergarten | 4.26 | 2.78 |
| | | Community Hall and Auditorium/1 lakh Population | 1.09 | 3.05 |

**Note:** Table generated from Panchayat Level Statistics, Department of Economics and Statistics, Government of Kerala.

**Source :** Firoz, M. (2006) An Enquiry into the Quality of Life and Infrastructure delivery in the Rural Urban Continuum- A case study from Kerala, Journal of Institute of Town Planners India, Vol. 3, No. 1, pp.48-52

## Village Planning

The Gram Sabha/Panchayat are required to prepare village plans for its development and as an input for the District plan. However, hardly any village plan has been prepared in India. This exercise involves proper understanding of the spatial structure, community, their needs and priorities for development of a village plan.

The spatial structure of the villages in India corresponds to occupational division. The unclean occupations cluster on the periphery—low lying areas or in the west. The cleaner or dominant groups occupy the prime locations, usually high lands, central areas or north side. The patches of occupational clusters are separated by open ground and community facilities, e.g. chowk, chopal, temple and bazaar, allowing all levels to interact. Sometimes the boundaries are simply common walls of houses or courtyards, or streets between groups of houses. The village structure represents a closely knit orthogonal fabric with an introvert character of built environment. The patches and clusters within a village are clearly defined in terms of social structure. An inhabitant traditionally relates to his mohalla, i.e. a geographical area that defines the neighbourhood patterns of rural communities. Increasing social mobility now makes it difficult to relate the occupation of a man to his Mohalla, but groups related by practice or customs and geographic origin continue to cluster in mohallas.

The power structure within the community reflects a hierarchial order, which is often made up of sub-caste, numerical strength, wealth, education, age and political power. Often few households are grouped together around a common courtyard with separate areas for men and women. The custom of purdah required that women be shielded from the gaze of passers by, so that a street view presents high blank walls. Women's courtyards are located in the rear, behind the men's quarters.

## Community Space

The focal point of mohalla in a traditional village is the chopal. This is often a semi-public open space at the junction of streets, or at the termination of gali, which acts as a connector between different mohallas and communities. Though chopal apparently appears as left over spaces in a confined environment, the fact that there is no encroachment a is an indication of the great value that the community attaches to them. It is worth nothing that squatters do never encroach over a chopal. The chopal has a sacrosanct and symbiotic imagery in a village, where panchayat often meets to take the decisions and to pronounce judgments. Its sanctity is accentuated by a temple, invariably located adjacent to the chopal. Around a chopal there is generally a commercial, communal or service activity (like a well) serving the daily needs. The chopal serves the immediate community and becomes a focal point where the inhabitants of mohallas meet. There is general community agreement and unwritten principles of its use and sequence of events: washing of clothes, playing, smoking hookah, meetings or occasional festival, marriage or other rituals. The temple is an important land-mark in a village. It does not only enshrine a deity, but serves as an institution of learning and centre of community activities for the villagers.

The privacy is protected by a series of envelops according to the spatial continuum. First degree of privacy is provided by the interior courtyard which is the exclusive domain of women. Second degree of privacy is defined by the land outside the door, which is accessible to the members of family and their relations. Third degree of privacy is the boundary of the mohalla, which is the domain of the local residents. These zones of privacy are reflected in a sequence of public, semi-public and private domain of spaces, including streets, chowks and chopals.

The compact maze of buildings produces a pattern of houses having a close relationship. The contacts established by women are on a more personal level. Through the use of parapet walls, or even scaling low walls. Women have a second layer of circulation open to them which is forbidden to the men-fork. The proximity of structures acts as a deterrent to unauthorized entry of the outsides. The pattern of meandering and narrow streets helps in maintaining the privacy. Different staircases are built for privacy within a house.

## Spatial Pattern and Structure

An outside observer sees the streets as a pattern of dark voids between buildings and is apt to arrive at an erroneous conclusion of chaos. Behind then narrow dark lanes, bounded by blank walls, are sunny courtyards where most of the activities take place. The courts act as the node of horizontal and vertical circulation. The transitional elements, e.g. verandah, entrance and gate are highly pronounced in the built environment. The services are invariably located on the periphery of the houses.

The traditional spatial structure has a sieve like porous form. Closely knit fabric of structures help to keep out the harsh sun and provides shaded courtyards and streets. During the night, the open courtyards radiate out the heat and creating a cooling effect. Thus the form, based upon the principle of thermal comfort through passive means, presents a framework of energy conscious design. The indigenous settlement is a working model of closely knit and self-contained community. Its spatial structure is a logical outgrowth of viable sets of social and economic norms governing community and individual behaviour. Their complex organism presents pluralistic and multiple patterns of morphology reflecting socio-cultural and historical layers. Traditional settlements are not just agglomeration of buildings, streets, land use and deities. They are the spatial embodiment of certain social systems with their ceremonies, rurals, festivals, social network, institutions and family life. It is the inter-relationship of cultural adaptation to physical form which manifests in the continuity of communities providing security, stability and diversity of human experience. Uncontrolled invasion of non-compatible activities has led is disintegration of the homogenous community structure of village.

The spatial structure of a village provides valuable clues to the resolution of planning, housing, and related community development problems arising from continuing rapid growth. Low-income groups and migrants, who constitute the bulk of the population, find in the indigenous urbanized villages and environment where opportunities exist for economic betterment. The life in traditional villages, which is regulated by institutions and social interaction, is often more compatible than the barren imagery of new areas resulting from outdated planning concepts and manipulation of the spatial environment.

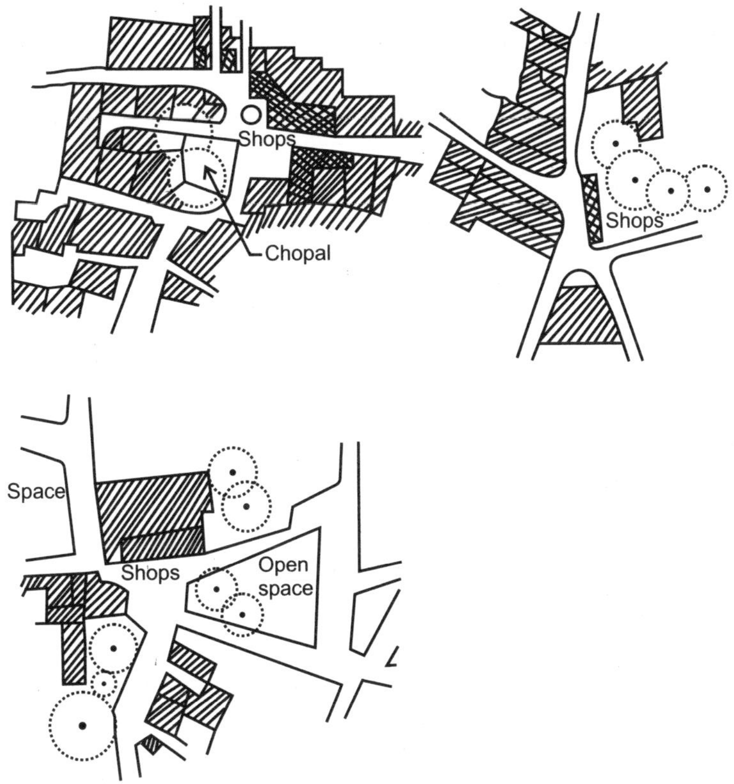


**Fig. 4.25 : Chopal as the focus of community is embellished by trees, well and places of worship. People get together, gossip and exchange news of the day. Enclosures are irregular, linear or square.**

Analysis of the morphology demonstrates that the indigenous settlements have a variety of typologies and characteristics. No single approach can offer optional basis for understanding their morphology. Within a village settlement, it is difficult to have a uniform typology and approach. Variations in physical, cultural and socio-economic conditions are discernible among the villages and also within every settlement. The core area inhabits mostly local population in a high density closely knit pattern of clusters with permanent structures. It has a low-rise, compact and organic pattern, that evolved through the history. This area has predominantly high income, high caste, land owning population and the physical form reflects their status in the village. The houses are in the form of katras, with courtyards as their hub. This area constitutes the core of the settlement. The marginal areas of the settlement, which evolved mainly as a result of migrants, are distinguished by their poor inhabitants and kutcha dwellings.

The essential services like water supply (individual taps) and privies are generally non-available. This area, from official point of view, is usually illegal and non-conforming. The land tenure is usually disputed or it is under unauthorized possession of a non-resident landlord, who extracts rent from the residents. Low-incomes of the residents and status of tenure do not permit immediate improvement of the buildings or reconstruction.

Since such fringe developments are illegal from official point of view, there is a whole range of formal and informal agents patronizing them. Due to their illegality, political pressures coupled with underhand dealings have been instrumental in achieving the levels of services which corresponds to the strength of the patrons and their proximity to the power structure. By and large such developments, although of recent origin, enjoy a better level of services, as compared to the marginal areas of villages.

## Issues of Concern

The main issues of common concerns for the villages are as given below:

(*a*) Protection of traditional habitations, which are often viewed as slums, and squatting,

(*b*) Tenancy/land titles, and;

(*c*) Extension of rudimentary infrastructure (water supply, sewage, electricity, public roads/ transport and social amenities.

The fundamental premise of sustainable village development is based on a process of self-help, public participation and arousing consciousness among the masses, spiritual, ritual and religious connotations. This facilitated a harmonious relationship of man and environment. Today, unless environment is a concern of everyone, mere government and centralized efforts, finance and legislation cannot be successful. To make a breakthrough it is essential to rediscover simple and pragmatic measures, which establish a holistic integration of the five elements of nature, with space, mankind and time. Man is, indeed, an embodiment of the elements and forces of nature—the environment. He is the one with the capacity for consciousness, self-reflection and transcendence. With this premise, there is a need to rediscover the organic culture which provides an innate and all embracing survival. Existing settlements clearly illustrate the potential for improvement that could be released by an overall change in the present attitude of planners. To evolve alternative concepts and strategies for growth and planning of traditional villages, it is necessary to understand the processes which have generated these settlements as the spatial embodiment of the communities.

The selection of village extension site should be part of a District Plan framework which addresses the pertinent issues of land availability, jobs, transport (highways, railways, major roads, etc.), the level of land which is safe from floods, availability of employment opportunities and its potential to be serviced by water supply, power, drainage, sanitation/ sewerage, health, education and such other infrastructure. A linear pattern of agro-

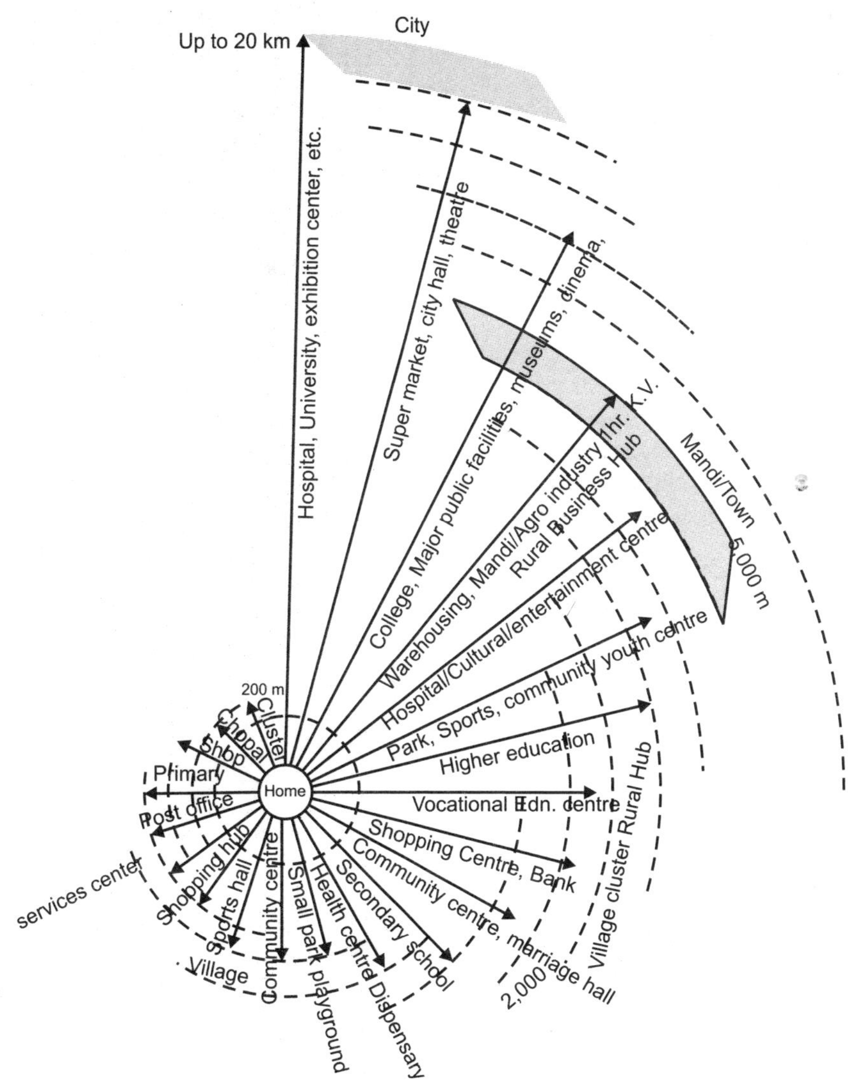


**Fig. 4.26 : "Local Rural Hub" within a District Development Plan**

**Hierarchy of Facilities based on easy accessibility and catchment population**

| | | |
|---|---|---|
| 6-12 km radial | Urban facilities | University, Higher Edn., Shopping Centre, Hospital Agro-industry Centre Warehouses, Bus Terminal, Rural Business Hub |
| 4-6 km | Mandi Town | Theatre/Multiplex Sports centre, Library, Weekly Market/ Panchayat/ Services, Marriage Hall, etc. |
| 1-4 km | Rural Hub | Health centre, Community centre, Bank, Post Office, Schools, etc. |
| Within 1 km. | Local hub/village | Primary School, Ration/Fuel shops, Chopal, Gram Sabha, Village Services Centre, Park/Playground |

**Fig. 4.27 : The rural morphology, though irregular and organic, manifests the social organization of the community in the form of courtyards, chopal, temple, village pond, narrow shaded streets, joint family, occupations and frequent religious and cultural festivals where the whole village participates**

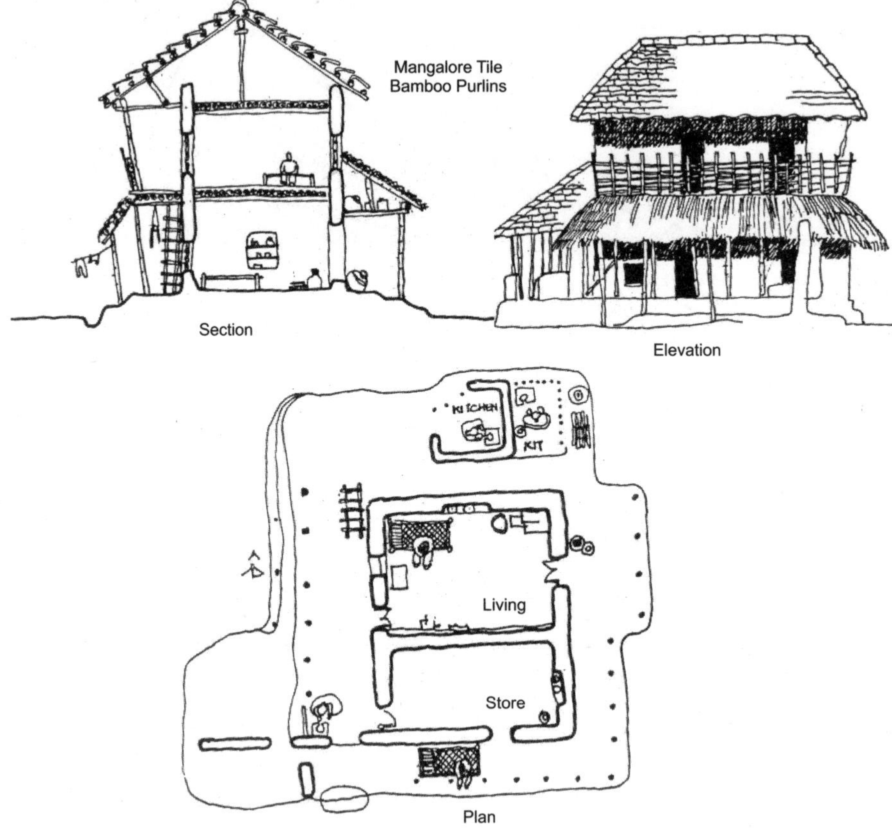


**Fig. 4.28 : A Typical House, Radhaballabhpur. Midnapore. In villages, many of the functions take place in open and semi-open space and therefore every house is enveloped by wide veranda has a and courtyard.**

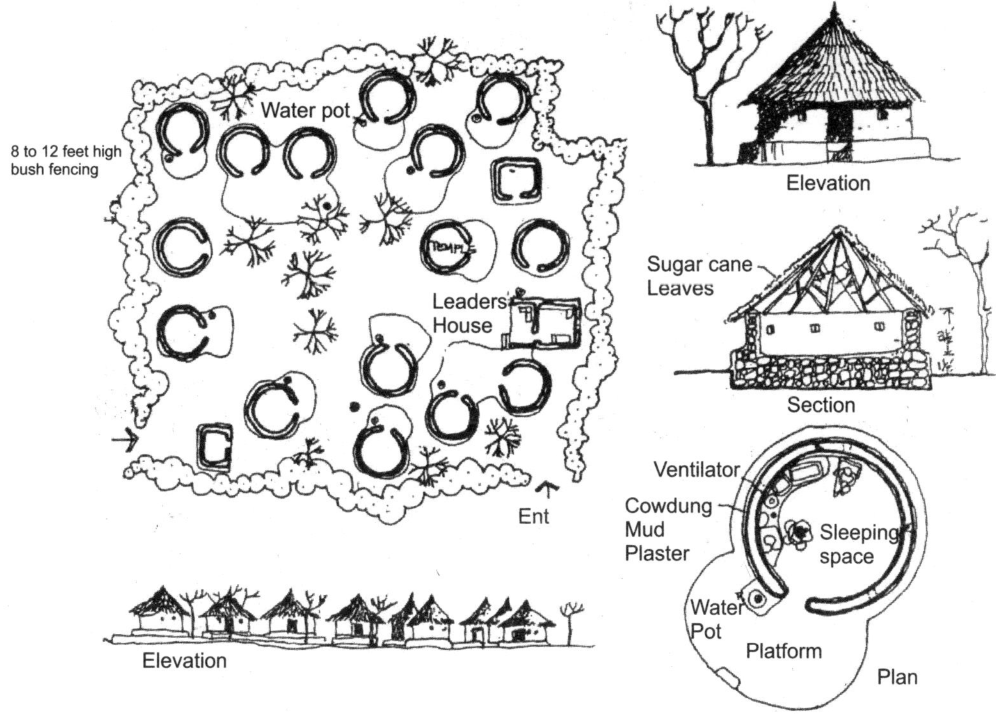


**Fig. 4.29 : Cluster houses in Plasva desert (Junagarh) facilitate joint family living with everyone's own space and privacy. The circular walls secure the family from hot winds and provide stability to the structure from storms and earthquake.**

industrial township of 40,000 to 50,000 population, each tied up by a string of mass transit system would allow mobility to the population. These townships should be planned on modular basis with about a kilometer of open agricultural belt separating them. This would enable the people to walk or cycle to work, schools, shopping etc., to adjacent township by public transport.

The layout, and services planning will vary according to the situation. The site should be laid out taking full account of local circumstances and socio-cultural factors. The physical layout of the settlement can have a significant impact on security, cultural activities and social cohesion. Although, layout plan arranged in a grid pattern may appear to ease some aspects of services management and the provision of access roads, such a pattern is not normally conductive to social cohesion. In planning the layout, start with a modular social unit, which may be the family and build up using the basic unit of several dwellings to form communities, village cluster and block.

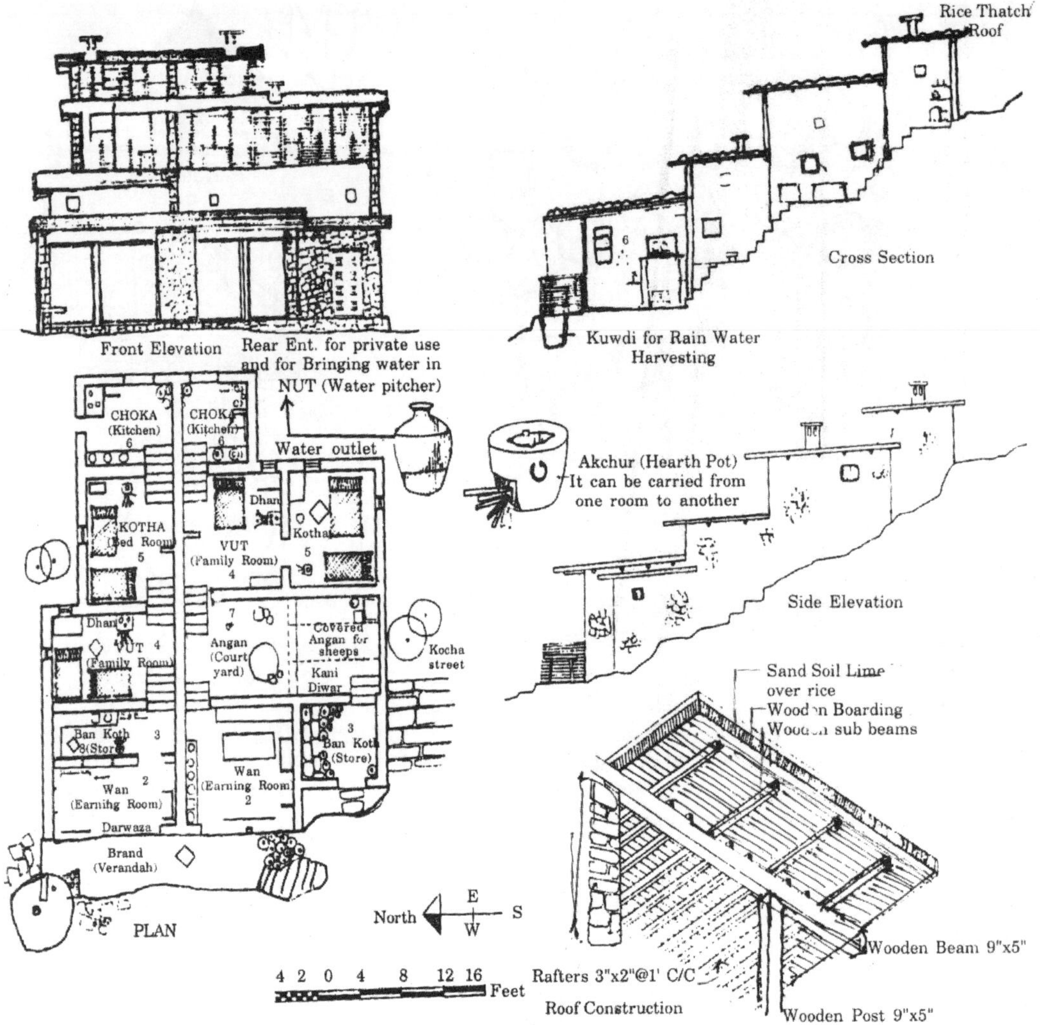


**Fig 4.30 : A Hillside House in Rural Kashmir.**

**Fig 4.31 : A tower house in a Himachal Pradesh village dominates the landscape. It provides a commanding view and is occupied by the village headman, who keeps an eye over a vast hinterland.**

**Table 4.6 : An Example of Planning Module**

| | | |
|---|---|---|
| 1 family | | = 4 to 6 people |
| 16 families | = 1 community | = 80 people |
| 32 communities | = 1 village | = 2500 people |
| 4 villages | = 1 cluster | = 10,000 people |
| 4 cluster | = 1 Block | = 40,000 people |

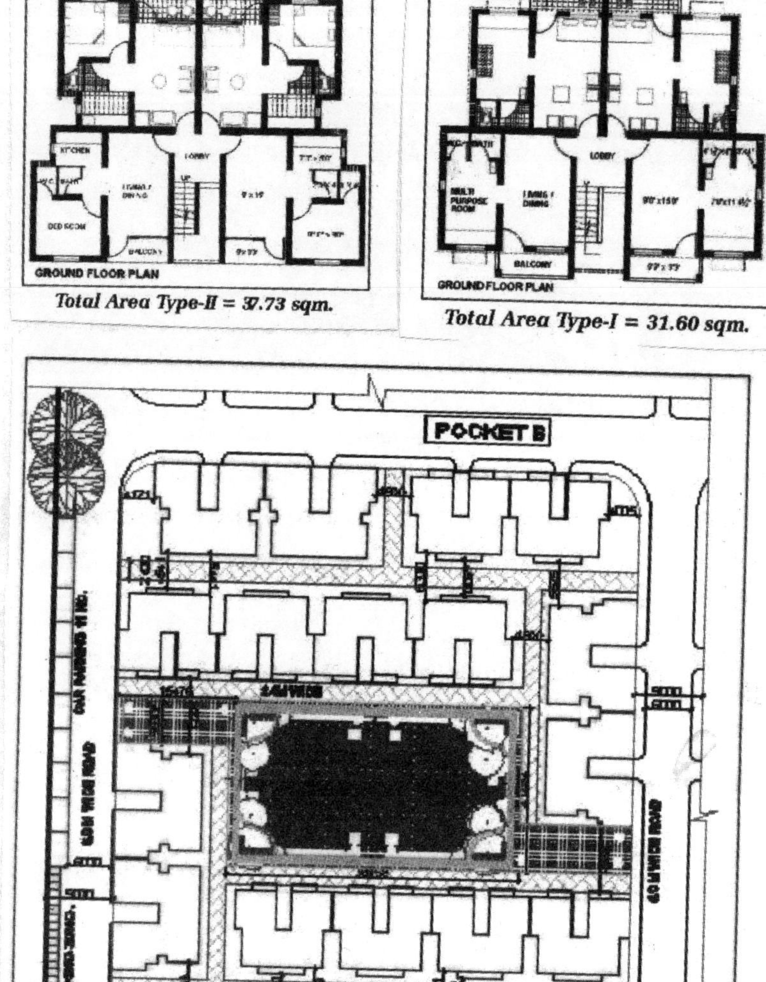


*Total Area Type-II = 37.73 sqm.*

*Total Area Type-I = 31.60 sqm.*

*A CLUSTER PLAN*

**Fig. 4.32 : The rural houses, even for the poor, need to be carefully planned with minimum 2 rooms, kitchen and toilets and common open space (or cluster courtyard) to preserve the traditional values of community living**

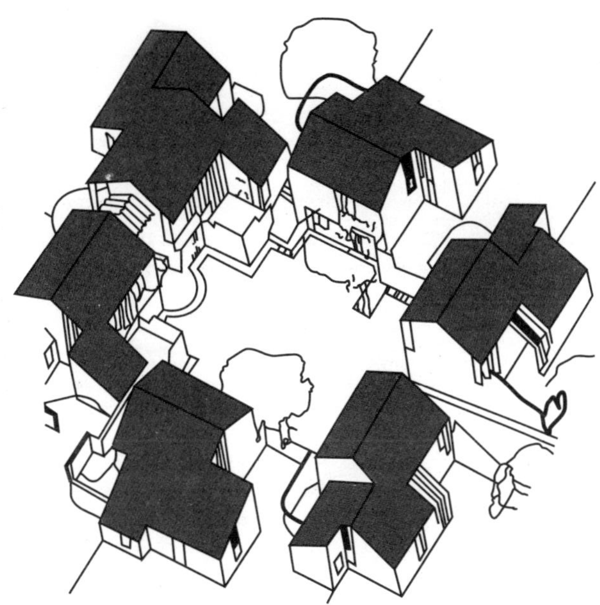

Fig. 4.33 : Common green enclosed by houses acts as a community courtyard

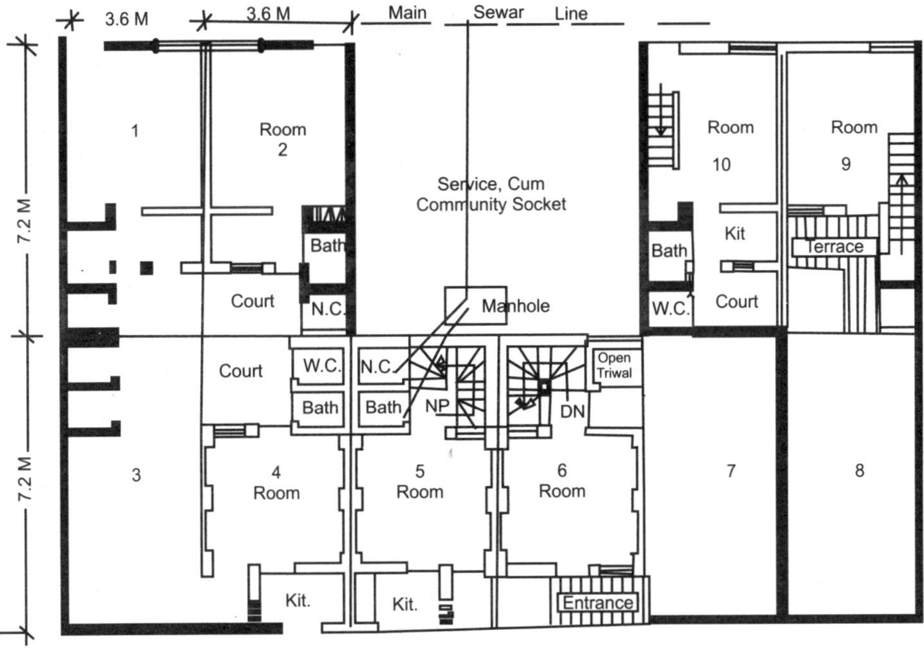


Fig. 4.34 : The houses for the poor, i.e. the people at the bottom of the pyramid, should facilitate living with dignity with independence and freedom should provide minimum sanitary, cooking and toilet facilities at individual level. The community socket is the common space for a cluster of 10-12 houses.

**Fig. 4.35 : Samaj Sadan-cum-Community Building at Sahabad-Daulatpur, New Delhi Most of the villages are normally deficient in community facilities and large buildings which are required for marriage ceremonies, etc. A community building/Samaj Sadan provides such space, together with accommodating village dispensary, bank counter, reading room-library, adult education and recreation hall.**

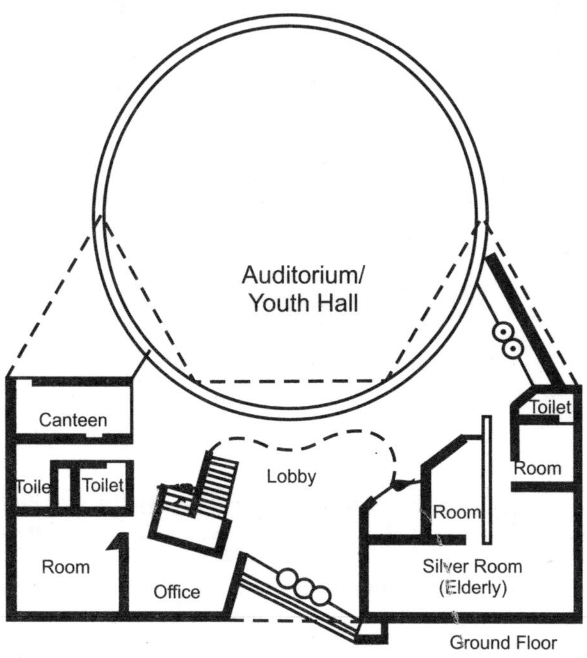

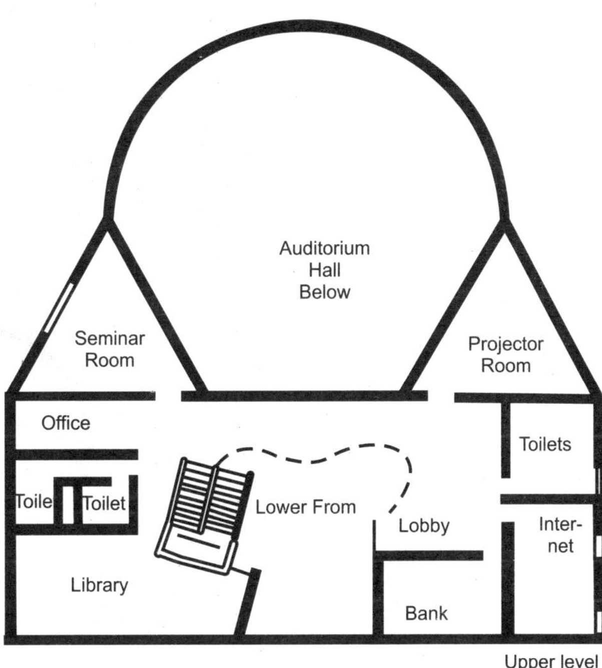


**Fig. 4.36 : Every village cluster should provide a community centre with a multipurpose hall for cultural performances, cinema, youth programmes, etc. It should also provide recreational, banking, library, health and computer facilities for in youth, women, aged, and the local population, enriching the lives of the rural people.**

The social structure and gender roles of the population should be reflected in the planning of the settlement and should take into account needs for markets, meeting places, recreational areas and so on. These facilities are essential in supporting the re-establishment of the displaced communities. Existing forms of social representation should be supported, given the importance of consultation with displaced people, particularly women, and their involvement in humanitarian interventions. The accessibility standards of various amenities should facilitate walkable distance to children and women for day to day activities, while higher level of facilities can be accessed by cycling or bus (Fig. 4.25)

It is necessary to provide rural housing integrated with employment opportunities. The layout of housing creates traditional values of community living. It is necessary to understand the local patterns of housing which responds to the ways of living, local climate and culture. (Fig. 4.26 to 4.34). The common denominators of village planning and housing should incorporate the following:

- Integrated development together with a composite community centre (Fig. 4.35 and 4.36).
- Ample green areas, parks, tot-lots play and sports field.

- Chowks and squares to recreate traditional community living.
- An attractive and cohesive street picture.
- Housing integrated with self-employment opportunities, artisan workshops and community sockets for every cluster.
- Modular system of housing development.
- Gradual augmentation of services and innovative systems of low cost sewerage, solid waste disposal and drainage.
- Building Center to develop traditional skills and to promote indigenous construction technology.

Chapter **5**

# Water, Floods, Drainage and Sanitation

*We have to tackle the triple malady which holds our villages fast in its grip; want of corporate sanitation, deficient diet and inertia.*

***—Mahatma Gandhi***

Water is the lifeline of rural India. It sustains irrigation, agriculture and livelihoods. The overall water resource scenario in India is alarming (Table 5.1):

India is criss-crossed by 14 major, 44 medium and 55 minor rivers, and the availability of water @2464 cu.m per capita. However, the availability of water, (both surface and ground) vary extremely in the various regions of the country. Rajasthan with 8% of the country's population has only 1% of the total water resources of the country, whereas Bihar with 10% of the country's population is endowed with 5% of water resources. Quantitatively it amounts to 562 cu.m per annum (1990) in Rajasthan, i.e., nearly at about absolute water scarcity level of 500 cu.m per capita per year as per World Bank indicator. The main source of replenishment of water is rainfall infiltration, which also exhibits large variations both temporally and spatially. About 90% of the rainfall is available only in 3-4 monsoon months. This too varies widely from 100 mm in western parts of the country to 11000 mm in Cherrapunji (Meghalaya). The annual rain and snowfall (average 114 cm) contribute to 4,000 cu km (bcm) of water annually. After evaporating and other losses, the water potential

**Table 5.1 : Water Resources Scenario in India**

| | |
|---|---|
| 1. Average annual precipitation | 4000 bcm |
| | 3000 bcm |
| | (During June-Sep) |
| 2. Average runoff in all the rivers | 1869 bcm |
| 3. Utilizable surface water | 1122 bcm |
| (*i*) By conventional means | 690 bcm |
| (*ii*) Replenishable groundwater | 432 bcm |
| 4. Present utilization | 605 bcm |
| 5. Future demand by | |
| AD 2025 | 1093 bcm |
| AD 2050 | 1447 bcm |
| 6. Possible additional water utilization through Inter Basin Water Transfer Scheme of GOI | 170–200 bcm |

**Source:** Mo WR (2003)

from surface flow is about 1870 cu km. Owing to topographical, hydrological and other constraints only 700 cu.km. surface water can be used. The annual replenishable resources of ground are assessed at 600 cu. km of which the annual utilizable resources will be about 450 cu. km. Thus, in spite of nature's bounty, drought is a major problem. There are a number of areas within the country that fall within the 'Dark' (extraction above 85% of the annual renewable ground water) and 'Grey' areas (annual renewable ground water extraction is 65 to 85%). This phenomenon is spread over 4500 blocks/taluks. The quality of surface water and ground water are closely linked to its circulatory phenomenon. Groundwater is brackish in the arid zone of Rajasthan close to coastal track of Saurashtra, some zones in east coast, pockets of Punjab and Haryana. Fluoride level is quite high in vast areas of Andhra Pradesh, Haryana, Rajasthan, and also parts of U.P., Punjab, Karnataka and Tamil Nadu. Iron content is higher than permissible in major parts of North-east India. Many parts of Bengal and Gujarat suffer from arsenic pollution of water.

Agriculture is a highly water intensive activity. Irrigation claims nearly 70 percent of water abstraction and over 90 percent in the arid and semi-arid tropics. The heaviest use of irrigation is in rice production. Irrigated-flooded rice typically consumes 5,000 to 20,000 cu.m/ha/cropping season or about 4 to 5 cu.m is needed to produce one kilo of paddy. The economic return per cubic metre of water used in rice production is usually low as compared with other crops.

The problem of water resource management is assuming critical dimensions due to the impact of climate change (Fig. 5.1). Further increasing population and urbanization are leading to indiscriminate expansion of urban footprints on the landscape of India. This is putting unbearable pressures on the ever-dwindling water resource. Sustainable development of water resource would chart the course for the future growth of the country. Therefore, it is imperative to not only initiate new projects and upgrade our present infrastructure, but also to promote water conservation through an integrated and a community driven model. The crisis of water in India has brought renewed focus on the urgent need for sustainable management of the water resources. This issue is intertwined with attitudinal, ethical, economic and social aspects.

India has to support 1/6th of the world's population besides $1/6^{th}$ of the world's cattle, with only $1/50^{th}$ of the world's land and $1/25^{th}$ of the world's water supply. Table 5.2 given the demand scenario for water in India in 2010, 2025 and 2050.

**Table 5.2 : Sector-wise Demand Scenario of Water in India**

| Sector | Water Demand (bcm) in the year | | |
|---|---|---|---|
| | 2010 | 2025 | 2050 |
| 1. Irrigation | 688 | 910 | 1072 |
| 2. Drinking (including livestock) | 56 | 73 | 102 |
| 3. Industrial | 12 | 23 | 63 |
| 4. Energy | 5 | 15 | 130 |
| 5. Others (Forestry, Pisciculture, Tourism, Navigation and so on) | 52 | 72 | 80 |
| **Total** | **813** | **1093** | **1447** |

**Sources :** Central Water Commission, 2003

The chronic water problem has resulted in conflicts, the most notable being the dispute between Karnataka and Tamil Nadu, the two riparian states over the Cauvery water. The Interstate Cauvery Water Authority as well as the Supreme Court are involved in resolving the dispute. Indiscriminate discharge of domestic and industrial wastes into rivers, lakes, wells, etc. have seriously polluted most water resources. Ground water is under continuous threat of over-exploitation as well as seepage of surface pollutants. As a result for reaching out to remote sources of water supply, dams and hydraulic structures are built at enormous ecological and financial costs.

For integrated development and management of water resources, a basin being the basic hydrologic unit, it is essential to know the water potential basin-wise. The country is having a large network of rivers, which have been divided into twenty river basins, comprising twelve major basins having drainage area exceeding 20,000 square kilometer (sq. km.), These are:

- Indus
- Ganga-Brahamputra-Meghna
- Godavari
- Krishna
- Cauvery
- Mahanadi
- Pennar
- Brahmani-Baitarni
- Sabarmati
- Mahi
- Narmada
- Tapi

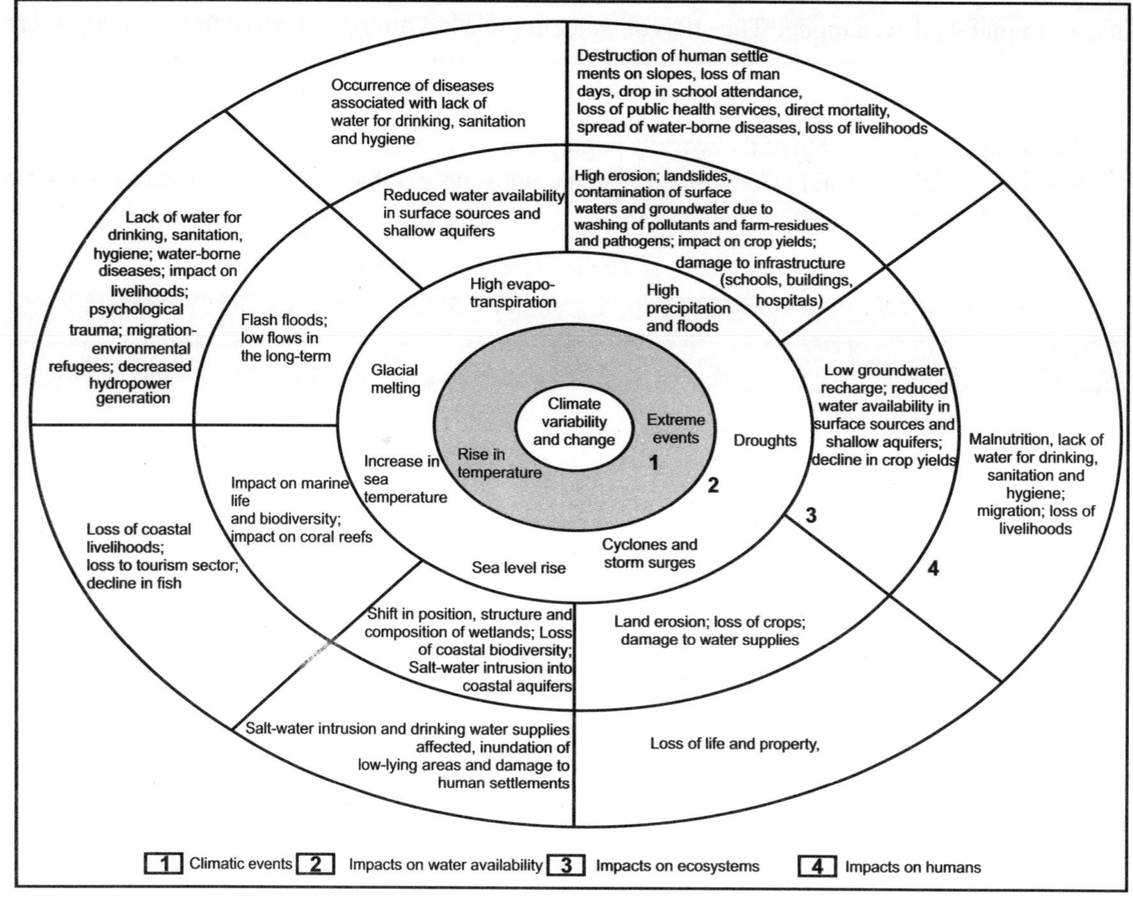


**Fig. 5.1 : Impacts of climate change on water availability**

**Source :** World Sustainable Development Forum Newsletter, January 2008.

The remaining medium rivers (with drainage area from 2000 to 20,000 sq. km) and minor rivers (with drainage area less than 2000 sq.km) are combined together to make eight composite river basins for the purpose of planning and development. These are:

- Subernarekha
- East flowing rivers between Kanyakumari
- West flowing rivers of Kutch Luni
- West flowing rivers from Tadri Kanyakumari
- East flowing rivers between Mahanadi and Pennar
- Area of inland drainage in Pennar and Rajasthan Desert
- West flowing rivers from Tapi to Tadri, and Saurashtra
- Minor rivers draining into Bangladesh and Myanmar.

The issue of river basins has been examined by National Commission for Integrated Water Resources Development (NCIWRD) and the Commission has considered 24 basins in the country for the purpose of assessment of water availability. Details are tabulated in Table 5.3.

## National Perspective Plan

The National Water Policy underlines the need for making water available to water-deficient areas by transfer from other areas including transfers from one river basin to another, based on a national perspective and after taking into account the requirements of the areas/basins. The Ministry of Water Resources had prepared of National Perspective Plan for development of country's water resources, disregarding political boundaries of States. The National Plan is in two parts, namely, (*i*) development of Peninsular Rivers which is entirely within the control of the Central and State Governments, and (*ii*) Himalayan Rivers. These two components are proposed to be linked by Mahanadi.

## The Himalayan Component

This envisages construction of dams, diversion works and canals to transfer water from surplus eastern rivers towards deficit central, western and southern regions. The National Water Development Agency (NWDA) took up eleven Himalayan links for study. These include Manas-Sankosh-Tista-Ganga link to transfer Brahmputra water to Eastern Ganga Basin. This link envisages high dams on Manas and Sankosh and very large canals running through densely forested as well as polluted areas cutting across major-drainages and the narrow strip of land north of Bangladesh. Other links proposed are Kosh-Ghagra. Gandak-Ganga, Ghargra-Yamuna and Sarda-Yamuna to supplement the supplies of Ganga and Yamuna and to further transfer water west to Rajasthan and Gujarat.

## The Penisular Component

The link from Mahanadi would require construction of Manibhadra Dam that would submerge 45,900 ha of agricultural land and displace 91,000 people. It is facing opposition from Orissa which, however, does not accept that there is surplus water in the Mahanadi. The Mahanadi-Godavari link would be 9,390 km long and cut across east-flowing drainages, though it involves no lift.

Godavari is joined by two major tributaries, Indravati and Penganga downstream of the major storage at Shri Ramsagar. Even after meeting downstream basin requirements, Godavari has surplus water in ths reach which can be stored in the available dam site of Incharmpalli. In spite of the displacement involved, the benefits, including to those to be rehabilitated from low yield unirrigated farming to high yield irrigated land, deserve an objective assessment and demand a high priority. After irrigating about 11.5 lakh hectares of dry land between Godavari and Krishna, there will still be about 3 lakh cubic metres of water available, which can be transferred to Cauvery Basin and relieve it from occasional shortages. It may also help to resolve the dispute between Tamil Nadu and Karnataka.

The Development Plan calls for cooperation among India, Nepal, Bangladesh and Bhutan. The Himalayan and Peninsular River Plans will add to the presently irrigation potential,

**Table 5.3 : Basin-wise Storage in India (in Billion Cubic Metre)**

| S.No. | Name of River Basin | Catchment Area (Sqkm) | Average Annual Flow (BCM) | Live Storage Capacity (BCM) | | |
|---|---|---|---|---|---|---|
| | | | | Completed Projects | Projects under Constru-ction | Projects under Consi-derarion |
| **A. MAJOR RIVER BASINS** | | | | | | |
| 1. | Indus | 3,21,289 | 73.31 | 13.83 | 2.45 | 0.27 |
| 2. | (*a*) Ganga | 8,61,452 | 525.02 | 36.84 | 17.12 | 29.56 |
| | (*b*) Brahmaputra & Barak | 2,36,136 | 585.60 | 1.09 | 2.40 | 63.35 |
| 3. | Brahmani & Baitarni | 51.822 | 28.48 | 4.76 | 0.24 | 8.72 |
| 4. | Mahanadi | 1,41,589 | 66.88 | 8.49 | 5.39 | 10.96 |
| 5. | Godavari | 3,12,812 | 110.54 | 19.51 | 10.65 | 8.28 |
| 6. | Krishna | 2,58,948 | 78.12 | 34.48 | 7.78 | 0.13 |
| 7. | Pennar | 55.213 | 6.32 | 0.38 | 2.12 | |
| 8. | Cauvery | 81,155 | 21.36 | 7.43 | 0.39 | 0.34 |
| 9. | Tapi | 65,145 | 14.88 | 8.53 | 1.01 | 1.99 |
| 10. | Narmada | 98,796 | 45.64 | 6.60 | 16.72 | 0.47 |
| 11. | Mahi | 34,842 | 11.02 | 4,75 | 0.36 | 0.02 |
| 12. | Sabarmati | 21,674 | 3.81 | 1.35 | 0.12 | 0.09 |
| **B. COMPOSITE RIVER BASINS** | | | | | | |
| 1. | Subernarekha | 29,196 | 12.37 | 0.66 | 1.65 | 1.59 |
| 2. | West flowing rivers of Kutch, Saurashtra including Luni | 3,21,851 | 15.10 | 4.31 | 0.58 | 3.15 |
| 3. | West flowing rivers from Tapi to Tadri | 55,940 | 87.41 | 7.10 | 2.66 | 0.84 |
| 4. | West flowing rivers from Tadri to Kanyakumari | 56,177 | 113.53 | 10.24 | 2.31 | 1.70 |
| 5. | East flowing rivers between Mahanadi & Pennar | 86,643 | 22.52 | 1.63 | 1.45 | 0.86 |
| 6. | East flowing rivers between Pennar & Kanyakumari | 1,00,139 | 16.46 | 1.42 | 0.02 | |
| 7. | Area of inland drainage in Rajasthan | 60,000 | Neg. | 0.00 | 0.00 | 0.00 |
| 8. | Minor river basins draining into Bangladesh & Myanmar | 36,202 | 31.00 | 0.31 | 0.00 | 0.00 |
| | **Total** | | **1869.35** | **173.73** | **75.42** | **132.32** |

***Note:***

1. Projects having a live storage capacity of 10 million cubic metre and above only are included.
2. An additional live storage capacity of 3 billion cubic metre (appx.) is estimated to be created through Medium Projects each having a capacity of less than 10 million cubic metre thus making a total live storage capacity of 177 billion cubic metre in completed projects.
3. Totals may not tally due to rounding off.

**Source:** National Commission for Integrated Water Resource Development (NCIWRD).

besides providing large quantum of hydro-power and flood control. Development and transfer of waters on inter-State and international rivers will require diplomatic, political and strategic initiatives by the Government in formulating an acceptable plan and its financing.

An most of the major rivers in India are inter-State in character having catchments/watersheds in two or more States, no integrated development on water resources is possible without inter-State co-operation. Even in those cases where the tribunals set up under the Inter-State Water Disputes Act, 1956 have given their final awards, implementation and operationalization of these awards become difficult if the participating States do not cooperate. Most of the arrangements for sharing river waters and co-operating on joint projects were mutually reached by the states themselves. Mediation by the Central Government was also sometimes necessary. There are currently 58 independent agreements 39 for joint projects and 19 for the sharing of river waters.

However, specific tribunals had to be set up under Section 3 of Inter-State Water Disputes Act, 1956 to resolve inter-State water disputes when the issues were highly contentious or water shortages serious enough that negotiation by the relevant parties, by itself, proved inadequate. So far, five river tribunals have been established and awards of three tribunals-Krishna (1976), Godavari (1979) and Narmada Water Disputes Tribunal (1979) have been finally delivered. Ravi-Beas Tribunal and Cauvery Water Disputes Tribunal are still continuing.

The project is facing several hurdles as given below:

- Absence of consensus among co-basin states to transfer of surplus waters.
- Construction of dams in India, Nepal and Bhutan requiring international agreements.
- Construction of dams involving environmental issues like submergence of forests.
- Land and Habitations. Manas-Sankosh-Tista-Ganga link passes through Manas, Raidak and Buxar Tiger Reserves and Gaburbasra Reserve Forest. Ministry of Environment and Forest, Government of India, has not granted permission for surveys and investigations.

Considering the availability of surplus flows in the Brahmaputra and its tributaries, the alternatives for transfer of surplus water from Brahmaputra to Ganga outlined in the National Perspective Plan, are as follows:

Option 1 : Jogighopa (Brahmaputra)-Farakka (Ganga) link through Assam, Bangladesh and West Bengal by gravity.

Option 2 : Brahmputra-Ganga link through Manas-Sankosh-Tista-Ganga (Farakka) by gravity

Option 3 : Brahamputra-Ganga link with lift from Jogighopa upto Tista and then by gravity upto Farakka (Jogighopa-Tista-Farakka link).

Option 1, that is, the proposed link canal from Jogighopa to Farakka via Bangladesh is the shortest compared to the other alternatives of National Perspective Plan being only 324 km. in length, while the others are 457 km and 440.53 km respectively. Further, entire flow will be through gravity. However, about 1/3$^{rd}$ of the link canal will pass through Bangladesh which requires consent and cooperation of Bangladesh Government. For working out option 1, diplomatic channels need to be opened up with Bangladesh, because this is the cheapest and best option which also provides flood control benefits in the Bangladesh portion of the Brahmputra valley. All the options, however, require the following :

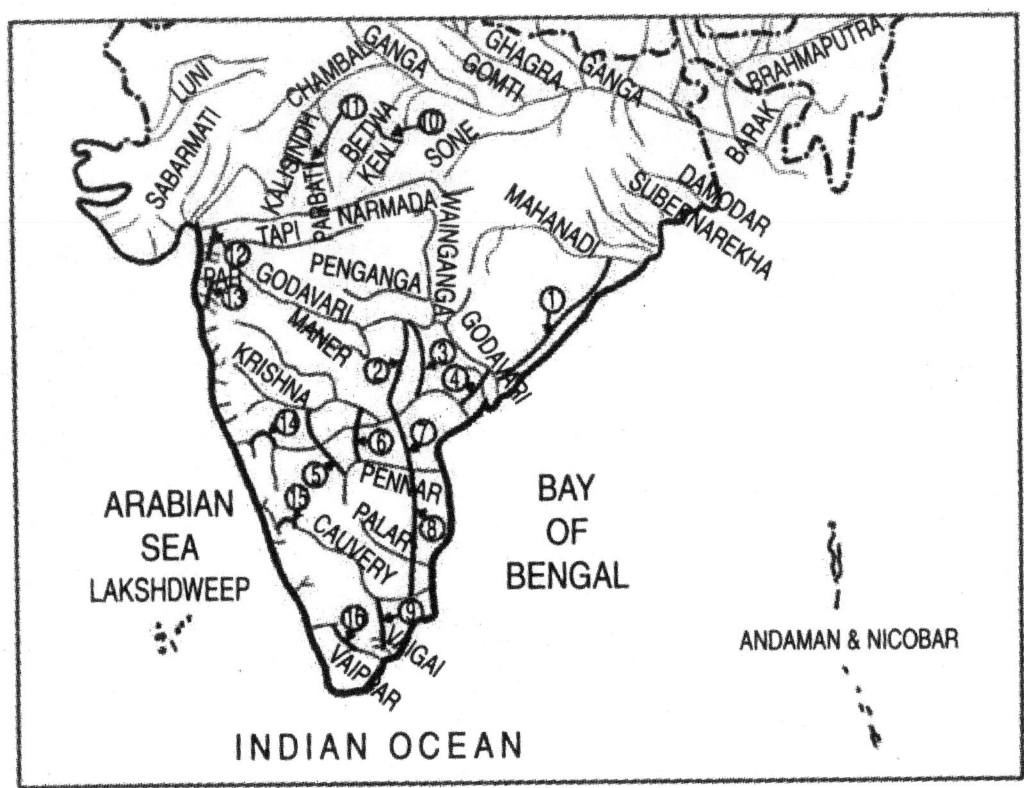


1. Mahandi (manibhadra)—Godavari (Dowlaiswaram)*
2. Godavari (Inchampalli)—Krishna (Nagarjunasagar)*
3. Godavari (Inchampalli)—Krishna (Pulichintala)*
4. Godavari (Polavaram)—Krishna (Vijayawada)*
5. Krishna (Almatti)—Pennar*
6. Krishna (Srisailam)—Pennar*
7. Krishna (Nagarjunasagar)—Pennar (Somasila)*
8. Pennar (Somasila)—Palar—Cauvery (Grand Anicut)*
9. Cauvery (Kattalai)—Vaigai—Gundar*
10. Ken—Betwa*
11. Parbati—Kalisindh—Chambal*
12. Par—Tapi—Narmada*
13. Damanganga—Pinjal*
14. Bedti—Varda
15. Netravati—Hemavati
16. Pamba—Achankovi—Vaippar*

**Fig. 5.2 : Proposed Inter Basin Water Transfer Links – Peninsular Component**

*FR completed
**Source:** http://www.nwda.gov.in

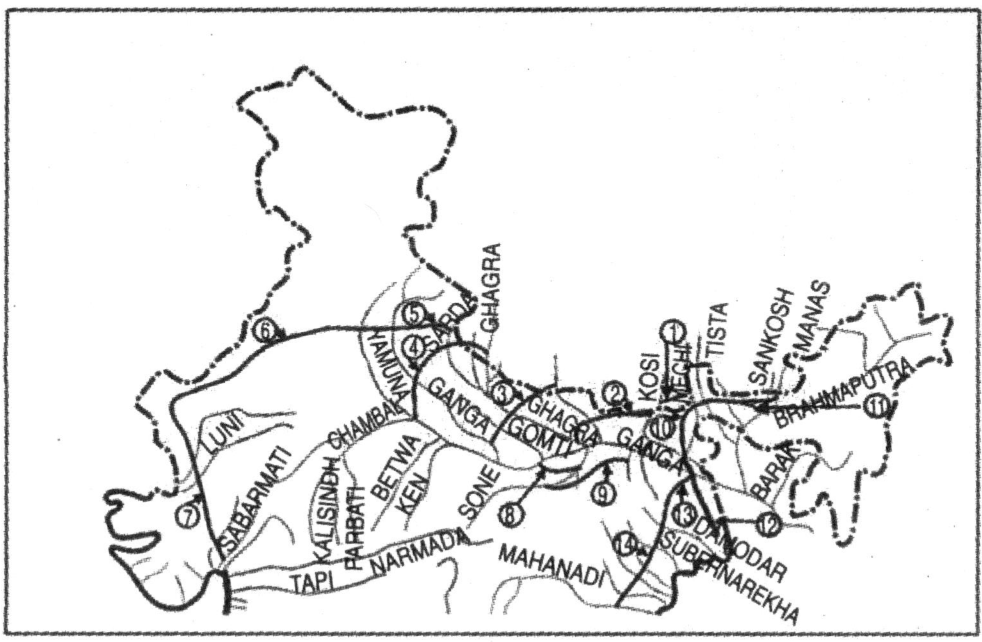


1. Kosi—Mechi
2. Kosi—Ghagra
3. Gandak—Ganga
4. Ghagra—Yamuna*
5. Sarda—Yamuna*
6. Yamuna—Rajasthan
7. Rajasthan—Sabarmati
8. Chunar—Sone Barrage
9. Sone Dam—Southern Tributaries of Ganga
10. Manas—Sankosh—Tista—Ganga
11. Jogighopa—Tista—Farakka (Alternate) to MSTG
12. Farakka—Sunderbans
13. Ganga (Farakka)—Damodar—Subemarekha
14. Subernarekha—Mahanadi

*FR Completed

**Fig. 5.3 : Proposed Inter Basin Water Transfer Links – Himalayan Component**

**Sources:** http:/www.nwda.gov.in

- To minimize displacement of people, transfer of water by tunnels should be explored to the maximum extent possible.
- Donor States should be helped in developing infrastructure, like small and big hydro-reservoirs.

The characteristics of the river link proposal are :

- Building dams for storage of water
- Construction of link canal systems
- Transfer of water mostly by gravity from surplus basins to basin/areas
- Pumping of water where necessary (confined to maximum depth of 120 M)

**Table 5.4 : Various aspects of Interlinking of Rivers (ILR) Projects**

| S.No. | Item | Size/Quantity |
|---|---|---|
| 1. | No. of Dams to be constructed | 33 |
| 2. | Length of the link canals (lined) | 9,629 km |
| 3. | Length of distribution network upto minors (lined) | 12,468 km |
| 4. | Size of link canals | Width varying from 3 m to 155 m and depth varing from 1.5 m to 10 m |
| 5. | Lining involved | 737 million square meters |
| 6. | No. of canal structures | 4,291 |
| 7. | Cement required | 56 million tones |
| 8. | Steel required | 2 million tones |
| 9. | Drinking water supply | 101 districts and Greater Mumbai, NCR of Delhi, Chennai, Kanpur, Lucknow, and other cities |
| 10. | Employment generation | 58 lakh man years |

**Source:** Pre-feasibility and feasibility studies of NHDA.

## Critical Issues

The pivotal issues are:

- Defining and calculating the normal average floods within and outside flood plain zoning areas to determine excess, unnatural flood waters for diversion.
- Water surplus/deficit studies of basins based on current usages and projected future usages.
- A definition of 'surplus' incorporating:

  (*a*) Basin capacity based on current, emerging and future use.

  (*b*) Basing capacity plus surplus monsoon runoff plus surplus monsoon spillover as floods.

  (*c*) Definition of minimum flow, average flow (non-monsoon and monsoon season)
- Integration of flood control, drought management and sustainable development
- Arranging availability of water on an equitable basis so that surplus of one area is used to cover the deficit of another.
- Demand side management through efficient management, planning, technology and institutional and legal frameworks.
- A combination of marco and micro scales of irrigation and water storage.
- A comprehensive water conservation strategy including financing and regulatory reforms

Table 5.5 indicates the impact matrix for various options of river basin development for water augmentation.

**Table 5.5 : Impact Matrix of River Basin Development**

| Development Option | Geographical Impact | Possible Effect |
|---|---|---|
| Dam Construction | • Soil erosion active<br>• Helocene/historical erosion<br>• Soil erosion controlled at source<br>• Seismic danger | Sedimentation in upland basins/ dams<br>Sedimentation from stores<br>Degradation of sediment stores<br>Submergence of forests & habitations<br>Ecological consequences |
| River regulation | • Dam above alluvial zone<br>• Dam with flood control/ hydropower<br>• Dam near coast | Channel change below dam<br>Habitat effects via floods/bed structure<br>Coastal erosion |
| Land-use development | • Land on slope/active tectonics<br>• Land on active/semi active stores<br>• Floodplain land<br>• Changes in water quality and pollution | Geological Impact, failure unless small scale<br>Changes in hydrology, release sediment<br>Loss of habitat/spontaneous regulation<br>Loss of potable water |
| River linking & Canal networking | • Buffer strips<br>• Re-vegetation of riparian zone<br>• Intercept existing drains<br>• Reduction in erosion<br>• Restoration of meanders, ripple, pool sequence<br>• Aquifer protection<br>• Rehabilitation of sub-merged settlements | Political/administrative disputes<br>Huge financial overheads<br>Need to conserve heritage<br>Acquisition of lands<br>Micro-climatic impacts<br>Morphological and environmental impacts |
| Water storage in Micro-structures | • Irrigation, flood management, drainage linked planning<br>• Restoration of local flora and fauna<br>• Aquifer protection | Drought relief at local level.<br>Seasonal/rain dependence<br>Small financial overheads<br>Participatory process and community control |

During the recent years, the environmental, social and human impacts of large artificial storage and changes in river hydrology and morphology have been the subjects of intense debates and disputes. It is essential to consider these aspects carefully during planning and management of river basins. Table 5.6 gives some broad guidelines.

**Table 5.6 : Guidelines for River Basin Management**

**1. Preservation or improvement of the spontaneous functions fulfilled by the river by :**

(*a*) Restoring erosion/sedimentation processes, through countering increased silt loads caused by upstream erosion (improvement of watershed management).

(*b*) Preserving genetic diversity through conserving natural areas and threatened species.

(*c*) Preserving the self-purifying capacity of the river through combating pollution (water-treatment plants at source, anti-pollution measures).

**2. Conservation of the natural values of the river basin by :**

(*a*) Preventing deterioration/destruction of natural resources by means of legislation (including compulsory environmental impact assessments) directed towards industrial development, impounding schemes and drainage activities.

(*b*) Establishing reserves in the most vulnerable ecosystems, with surrounding buffer areas.

(*c*) Establishing environmental education programmes.

(*d*) Initiating programmes to promote sound, durable exploitation of ecosystems (particularly fisheries, herding and forestry).

**3. Conservation of the river basins extensive exploitation functions by :**

(*a*) Guaranteeing the protection of productive zones, such as floodplains, estuaries and lakes, by allocating appropriate quantities of water and by means of sustainable development programmes.

(*b*) Implementing reforestations schemes for supply of firewood in relation to sound watershed management.

**4. Development of sustainable intensive exploitation functions by :**

(*a*) Drawing up a water allocation plan for the entire river basin, to achieve a better match between water demand and supply; this should give due consideration to the water requirements of the spontaneous functions, natural values and extensive exploitation functions.

(*b*) Develgping small-scale projects, e.g., irrigation, fishponds, forestry.

(*c*) Improving product processing, sales and marketing, e.g., by making better use of the river as a transport route.

(*d*) Ensuring that detailed plans for the above objectives are thoroughly checked within the framework of an environmental impact assessment procedure.

**5. Improvement of the overall health situation of the river basin by :**

(*a*) Combating water-borne diseases.

(*b*) Improving the flood control situation, both quantitatively and qualitatively.

(*c*) Establishing a drinking-water programme for rural areas, with the objective of making clean, healthy water available for the whole population.

(*d*) Ensuring that detailed plans for the above objectives are thoroughly checked within the framework of an environmental impact assessment procedure.

**6. Guiding principles of regional planning :**

(*a*) Work not against the environment.

(*b*) Start work from the existing situation, i.e., existing infrastructure, technical know-how, perceptions of subsistence security, cultural needs, etc.

(*c*) Protect the authentic evolution of local culture, institutions and know-how (*d*) Introducing social change, involving decision-making at the community level.

(*e*) Assess the carrying capacity of extensive agricultural and water-use systems, as well as their present value.

(*f*) Assess the required inputs for intensive systems of land and water use for growing number of people.

(*g*) Intensify or introduce intensive land and water-use systems at locations with the best soil and superior climatological and ecological conditions.

(*h*) Preserve, develop and utilize nature's spontaneous functions.

(*i*) When planning reserves for species or ecosystems, endeavour to make these as large, as varied and as interconnected as possible.

(*j*) Preserve rare species and ecosystems in their authentic ecological setting, giving due consideration to the long-term effects.

(*k*) Avoid land-use and water-use systems exhibiting irreversible dependence on a single crop or market.

## Flood Control

In the Indian sub-continent, a large number of natural drainage channels wind their way across settlements on their way to the rivers and sea. A few are in good shape whereas many are carriers of polluted water with certain stretches having become open lavatories. While the sewage water can be piped in a separate channel, other undersirable activities would be prevented with the provision of alternatives such as community toilets and fencing barriers. Frequent flash flooding during the monsoon season is another major problem, which needs attention.

Existing water channels (nallas) can be used to provide continuous on-channel recharge of groundwater, to transfer water from these channels to various storage sites and also to store water from the channels with the help of sluice gates. Continuous recharge would take place through deep holes on the channel floor. This would be a complex exercise that requires computer modeling of channel capacities, transfer mechanisms, storage capacities, flood prevention and systems operations.

The channels once filled with water thus could constitute urban waterways. Their cleanliness would be maintained with the use of root-zone system, mosquito weed, guppy fishes to consume mosquito larvae and for aeration. The channel would be shaped, landscaped and deepened to increase the water storing capacity wherever possible. While serving the primary function of on-channel groundwater recharge they would also modify the micro-climate. The use of groundwater together with on-channel recharge would also be possible. Their use for recreation, floaters, waterborne transport (with sluice gate barriers) should be integrated in the system. (Tables 5.7 and 5.8)

Ecological approach for controlling water logging, flooding and salinity, combined with recharging of ground water aquifer and plant physiology is by bio-drainage with the following basic principles:

- To reduce flooding, and ensure ability of existing primary and secondary drainage channels to handle storm run-off by defining drainage easements.

**Table 5.7 : Typology of Floods, characteristics and effects**

| Flood type | Characteristics of Flooding and effects |
|---|---|
| Type A | Localised flooding caused by inadequate drainage of storm water runoff, which can happen virtually every time it rains, where ihe provision of drainage infrastructure is poor. The main effects of these events are related to a deteriorating environmental health conditions, especially water-borne diseases. |
| Type B | Flood of this type occurs less frequently than type A floods, but affects larger areas. The effects may include temporary disruption of transportation systems and inconveniences to life. These events contribute to the propagation of water-borne diseases and can cause structural damage. |
| Type C | Large-scale inundation causing widespread disruption and damage affecting communities and businesses. These events are infrequent and often reach a dramatic scale of effects and structural damage. |

**Sources:** Adapted from Cairn Cross S. and K.A.R. Quano (1991), Surface Water Drainage for Low Income Communities, WHO/UNEP.

**Table 5.8 : Flooding problems and control strategies**

| **Flooding problems** | **Strategies** |
|---|---|
| Flood avoidance | Preventive responses to ensure that flood problems are avoided. |
| Flood mitigation | Immediate responses to flood warnings before a flood, and course of action to be taken during a floods to reduce risks. |
| Flood recovery | Action to be taken after a flood event to enable communities to recover from the impacts of a flood. |
| Solid waste management | Control of solid waste to avoid blockages (such as plastic bags, packaging) and reduction in hydraulic capacity of the drainage system. |
| Pollution mitigation | Reduction in the discharge of pollutants into the storm-water drainage system. |
| Vector control | Improved practices to reduce vector transmission of diseases releated to urban drainage and flooding. |
| **Stormwater management options** | |
| Natural catchments | Natural channels, Streams, Water courses. |
| Partly sewered | Man-made ditches, Open channels, Sewers |
| Combined sewer systems | Open channels, Combined sewers, Overflows, Treatment facilities. |
| Fully separated sewer system | Separate drainage/sewers and trunk Sewer treatment facilities, Outfalls |
| Advanced drainage systems | Separate drainage, Trunk sewers, Infiltration ponds and source control, storage basins, etc. |

**Source:** WHO

- These drainage easements will be determined by the 25 year floodplain (an area which had inundated anytime during last 25 years) but a minimum vegetation easement of undisturbed forest and undergrowth must be respected: 45 to 90 meters in for primary drainage channels and 20 to 30 m for secondary drainage channels.
- In order to minimize erosion and siltalion, there must be a legal and enforceable prohibition on clearing of ground cover, shrub undergrowth or trees within drainage easements.
- Existing channels should be enhanced where necessary with berms (side barriers) and create natural swales (water holding depressions) by introducing layered plantings of native vegetation. It is necessary to provide adequate storage of run-off in impoundments or temporary water storage ponds.
- In order to retard run-off and to enhance recharge, it is proposed to build check dams in swales over permeable soils to enhance recharge. Install trickle tubes in impound areas to permit even flow.

## Zero Run-off Concept

The concept of bio-drainage is based on the twin principles of segregation of rainwater from urban waste water disposal, so that it can be used for recharging of aquifers, etc. and, second, the principle of zero run-off drainage by way of complete retention of rainwater into the area by creating retention ponds, lakes and storage. This was the concept behind the creation of a network of lakes for flood/ rainwater discharge, which had been prevalent in the ancient India. The present method of draining of storm water through masonry drains entails huge costs and efforts, which also endanger the ground water aquifer. The age old system of having a pond in the low lying area not only solved the drainage problem, but also provided a multi-purpose source of water for recreation, cattle rearing, fishing and improving the microclimate.

The prevalent drainage system having open drains to direct the entire discharge of surplus water and rain water into the river (or sea) has created a serious problem of lowering of the underground water table, as it hardly allows and water to percolate down into the earth. With ever increasing number of tube wells being dug in the urban and rural areas, the water table is gradually going down. The increasing population channels become the first target. The system of zero run-off with small pondages not only results into huge financial savings, but also helps in maintaining the ecological balance and underground water reserve. This concept requires segregation of the storm water and waste water drainage network and landscape development of drainage channels as green corridors. In other words, blue network planning should synchronise with green network planning. A number of micro water management structure are more sustainable than few large projects.

A well planned system of lakes, balancing ponds, and porous paving can lead to avoidance of the construction of huge storm water drains, which offers the following advantages:

1. An efficient and effective drainage system which will add to the ecological sustainability.

2. Availability of self-sustaining greenery and water reserves for recreation, boating, fishing, etc.
3. The enrichment of the underground water-aquifer, thereby stabilizing and increasing the level of the underground water reserves.
4. A much quicker, economical and efficient process of drainage of the area;
5. A source of water for the lean periods, especially for horticulture and agriculture.
6. Saving in terms of the cost of construction medium and major drains and culverts;

The possible micro-water retention systems and their descriptions are given below:

1. **Low area drain:** Water collects at the lowest part of the site. It is generally designed as an extension of the lawn where the soil can become highly saturated during rain. After heavy rainfalls it can take up to three days for the water to drain away. Visually the area under drain functions like a lawn and can be used as a green trail.
2. **Ditches and swales:** These can also be grassed or planted with water-loving plants and laid out with rocks. The ecological value of ditches and swales is higher since they provide a habitat for animals. Ditches will form temporary water features after rainfall. They take up less space than a low area drain. They are permanent features and cannot be easily encroached upon. Swale can form part of a surface water collection network that feeds into a pond.
3. **Permanent retention ponds:** These are permanent water features that have a higher amenity value than the above options. Ponds require more space than ditches as water levels need to fluctuate and more water is permanently retained on site. Retention ponds can be well supplemented with reed-bed filtration systems prior to discharge into a local river.
4. **Underground collection cistern:** This is the most expensive option with the lowest environment rating and also limited capacity. Its strongest point is the minimal space required. Water is collected and slowly discharged into the groundwater through a sand and gravel pit. Filtration is therefore minimal and water quality inferior to that of the other systems.

The suitability and advantages of each system depends on the topography and the aims of the development in each case. The land-take necessary (the site area required for natural drainage systems) depends on the depth of the drain, which in turn depends on the local soil and slope. The approximate land-take is a percentage of the total site area to be drained and forms a rough guide to enable the planning of natural drainage system. The exact land-take for a natural drainage system relates to the actual quantity of scaled land on site and the degree of impermeability of materials used.

A geographic information system (GIS), computer mapping and simultation facility would provide baseline data and a correct picture of the deluge and the potential danger areas. GIS in recent years has emerged as a valuable forecasting tool, especially because of its ability to create complex digital maps with voluminous data. Accordingly, a detailed plan of all the waterways, with details of cross-sections, longitudinal profile, drainage basin and catchment areas of each of the gutters, creeks, drains and rivers should be produced.

## Reviving Indigenous Skills and Community Participation

Indians over centuries developed a range of techniques to harvest every possible form of water-rainwater, streams, rivers and flood water. They have tapped water from hill streams of springs known as kuhls ranging in lengths from one to 15 kms and carrying a discharge of 15-100 liters per second. In Meghlaya, a 200-year-old system of tapping stream and spring water for irrigating plants by using bamboos still exists. The "kundis" of Rajasthan are unique structures which look like huge saucers and are used for collecting rain water to meet the needs of local villagers and their animals. In Rajasthan, particularly Jodhpur, traditional water system still exists and village people maintain their traditional system even after they started getting piped water. Villages that neglected their traditional systems and relied solely on piped water sources faced scarcity under drought conditions, particularly when the canals dried up. A contrast in water management can be seen in Jaisalmer and Cherrapunji - Jaisalmer gets 100 mm of annual rainfall while Cherrapunji gets 15000 mm - yet Jaisalmer was able to collect enough water for itself until recent years, while Cherrapunji, the wettest place on earth faces a drinking water shortage. Societies must learn to perform their roles in water harvesting, and this is where the local administration must take responsibility and ensure that villagers are fully involved in such projects.

In the desert towns of Rajasthan roof top water harvesting was a common practice. The sloping roofs of the houses were used to collect the rain water which was taken through a pipe into underground tanks, sometimes as big as a room built in the main house or the courtyard. This would meet the drinking water needs of the household. Sometimes basement rooms would be built next to the tank, which used to be coolest in the summer. Another traditional rainwater harvesting systems in Rajasthan was the kund. It was a simple saucer shaped structure, having a circular depression, of about 15 mt. diameter, whose sides were plastered with lime and ash. As water would naturally flow down to the center along all the sides, a tank was built at the center to collect and store the water. A dome shaped cover was given on top known as "bhinda" made from phog plant and plastered with mud.

The kund had two or three openings from which rainwater could enter. The tanks and ponds were constructed in lowest terrains so as store rain water. Apart from the tanks, there were Augor or Agar which handled water. The Aav or Payatams were the channels that fed the reservoir. They were wide and shallow so that water velocity was low to avoid or reduce silting of the pond. Khurra or stone pieces placed strategically within the Aav reduced the velocity further. The tanks were stepped to receive the maximum water. The lower portions were known as Neshta and were constructed in lime and stone to withstand water pressure. This portion received the first rainfall. The shallower portions were encircled with soil embankment, sometimes reinforced and were referred to as 'Pal'. The embankments were constructed or repaired before the rainfall. The Neshta collected the initial water providing additional time for the Pal to consolidate.

Wells, baoli or Chuher were sometimes dug within the tanks or lakes to supplement the surface accumulation. The reservoir was planned and constructed taking into account the actual and projected demands of the community. Various sections of varying heights ensured supply throughout the year. Measuring rods with different codings indicated the quantum of water available at different points within the reservoir. Usually, the tanks were constructed 20 Basis or Purush deep, one Purush being roughly 1.8 mtrs. For large tanks small islands were created in the middle to absorb the wave energy and protect the mud embankments. Shrines were constructed on these islands to contribute to the waterbody's status and minimize its misuse. The catchment areas, the channels feeding the reservoir, the reserves and the outlets for irrigation or drainage were integral parts of the water societies created by electing members from the community who were responsible for its management together with that of arid agriculture. Special festival days were earmarked for repairs and desilting when the entire communities participated.

Particular communities having indigenous skills were engaged to plan and construct water systems. The Gajdhar was the key person who was responsible to estimate the quantum of water that could be awarded Saropas as recognition for his efforts. The Sirbhavs or the Jalsungha could 'smell' or identify locations where ground water was available and wells could be dug. The Sonkar or Matkut actually constructed the tank by producing the soil bricks required for the purpose. The Chunker or Lunias helped them in this. The Agaria manufactured and supplied the tools required to construct the tanks. The Odhya and Gond tribes (Orrisa) were famous for their skills in constructing such tanks and were much sought after.

Having forgotten the indigenous skills of water management, today there is almost a desperate situation in Gujarat, Rajasthan and elsewhere. The water table has dropped by 10 to 50 m. Groundnut and cotton crops in over 4 lakh ha in Gujarat were ruined (1999-2000) and a bucket of water was costing between Rs. 4 to Rs. 10. The fall in normal precipitation has reduced grain production by 60-70% and large number of families adversely affected due to depleting water table and excessive run-off. A study of Gujarat reveals that the areas where the water depth has gone below 10m increased from 3% in 1973 to 25% in 1990 and 46% by 1994. The gap between water use and sustainable yield of the aquifer in Punjab is alarming. It is feared that if water table goes below 15m all the tubewells will stop functioning.

In order to bring about the type of sustainable water management that is able to address poverty, employment creation, the role of women and the protection of the environment, there is a need to move beyond conventional approaches. Rediscovering the traditional water wisdom would enable sustainable community based management of water, small-scale irrigation and catchment management.

## Watershed Development

All along the history water has always been one of the basic determinants of human settlements-their location, growth and development. Today it is more so because of the impending water crisis, as well as the environmental threat, which our villages are facing. This calls for a review of the ongoing policies, concepts and strategies of rural development and evolving a new paradigm of land use planning, health, environment, legal framework and governance.

Often the land use plans propose the development of industries, sanitary landfill sites, power stations, housing, etc. along with wetlands, water bodies and rivers, which destroy the quantity and quality of water and make it unfit for human use. Indiscriminate urbanization and land use changes significantly alter the hydrology and quality of surface water. Incompatible land uses, together with encroachments along the water bodies are the built-in mechanism to kill the water bodies and no amount of effluent treatment or legislation can reverse the damage. Therefore, as a preventive measures, the land use pattern should be carefully worked and solid waste, disposal system to avoid hazards to water. It is a paradox that while on one hand we face the water crisis, on the other there is flooding in the same area, during the monsoons. This is largely due to lack of water based planning and development. Excessive hard paving of open areas, disturbing the natural drainage pattern, accumulation of high amount of solid waste in water channels and bodies and lack of greenery are largely responsible for such a situation. It is necessary to work out planning and development strategies, which should be based on a detailed analysis of hydrology, topography, aquifers, rainfall, flooding, drainage, vegetation cover, water harvesting potential, together with other technical and financial considerations. Local skills and community often prove to be valuable resources in evolving sustainable development strategies which should be identified and incorporated in the planning framework.

The starting point of planning should be to arrest the run-off, the conservation of natural valleys, water bodies and acquifers, where no roads or structures should be built. The natural drainage system should be meticulously studied and taken into consideration for allowing maximum ground water recharge. As shown in Figs. 5.4 to 5.10, watershed development, bio-drainage, conservation/ revival of village ponds, check dams, swales, gully control structures, contour bunding ridges and furrows, rain water harvesting, micro-irrigation, etc. are essential for sustainable water and drainage management and for rainwater harvesting in the natural or man-made catchment areas. The concept of zero run-off and bio-drainage with retention ponds, sediment traps and balancing lakes should be adopted for rainwater conservation and drainage, with a segregated wastewater disposal system so as not to pollute the rainwater. In this way blue network and wastewater drainage networks should be planned separately. A green network surrounding the blue network would protect the ecology of aquifers, as well as provide a pleasant environment. Simple methods of site planning, which incorporate porous/semi-permeable paving drop inlet/down pipe, sediment trap, storm sewer, retention ponds, etc. can immensely contribute in maintaining ground water table. In order to maintain an equilibrium between the elements of natural eco-system and human activities, the following are the necessary components of a blue network plan:

- Zero run-off drainage for rainwater harvesting
- Conservation of low lying lands for water harvesting, storage and channels

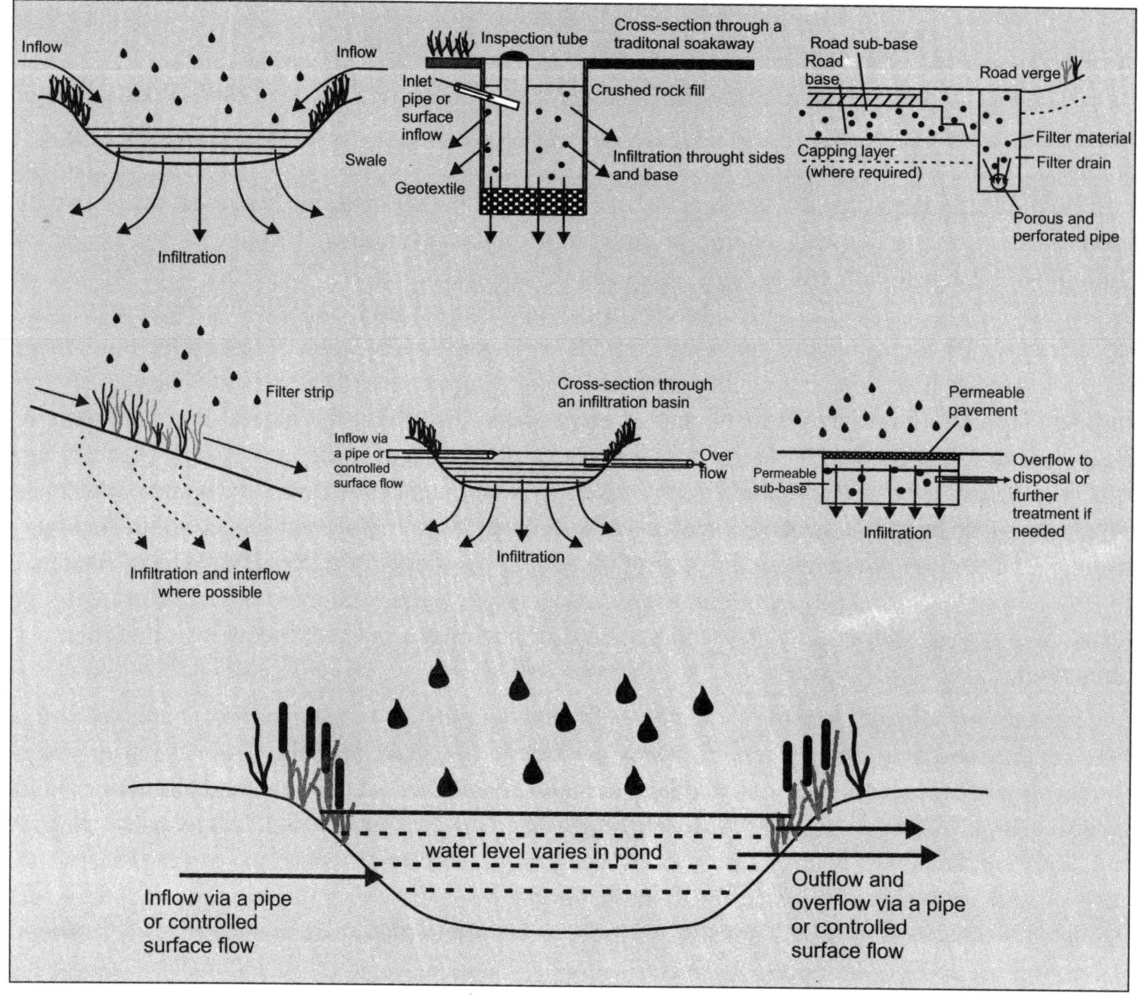


**Fig. 5.4 : Components of Sustainable Drainage System**

**Source:** www.environment-agency.gov.uk/suds

- Community participation
- Sustainable livelihood support system
- Decentralised planning
- Ridge to Valley treatment approach
- Adoption of bio-drainage

The basic principles of sound watershed management include the following basic considerations:

- Confine village/urban development to the uplands
- Protect the wet-lands, streams and water bodies by leaving adequate fringes of vegetation and giving them sacred or legal shield.

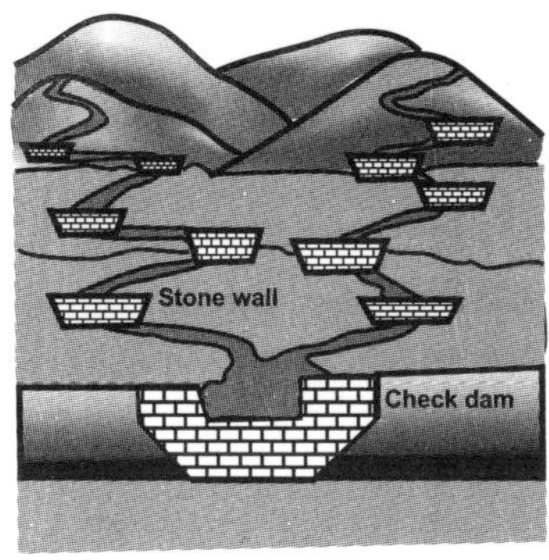


**Fig. 5.5 : Rainwater harvesting through watershed management**

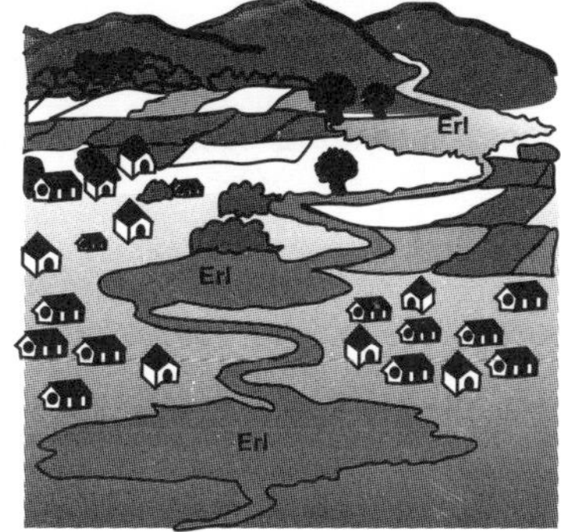


**Fig. 5.6 : Traditional water harvesting through eris (lakes)**

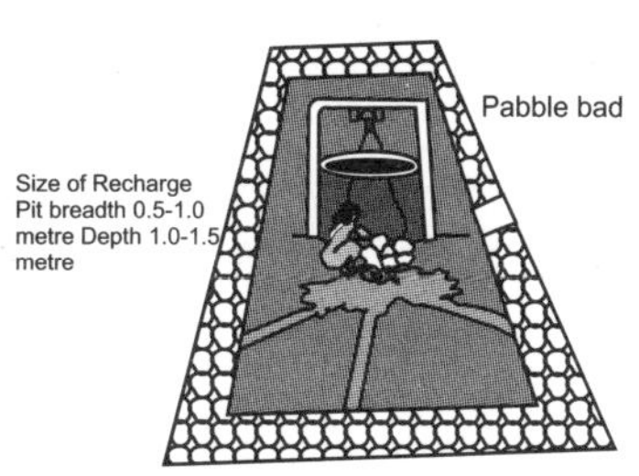


**Fig. 5.7 : Recharge ground water by pebble beds**

**Fig. 5.8 : Check dam and gully control structure**

**Fig. 5.9 : Contour bunding and trenching**

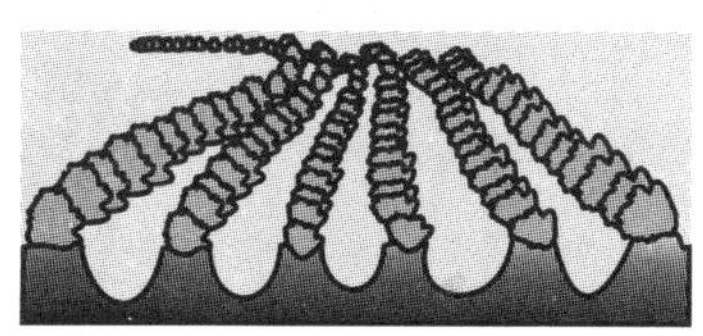

**Fig. 5.10 : Ridges and furrows**

- Preserve and utilize the natural drainways and maximize conservation of water by various methods, such as, underground rainwater storage, contour trenching, pits, deep hole wells, stepwells, tanks and baolis, ponds, balancing lakes, etc.
- Promote on-channel storage and groundwater recharge.
- To improve the quality of river water and to secure its continuous flow and encourage aquatic life.
- Installation of water purification facilities.
- Improvement of drainage, wastewater treatment and sewage.
- Adoption of porous paving for service roads, footpaths, plazas and parking areas; avoid pucca pavements and instead fill with pebbles and coarse sand to allow percolation.
- Leak detection and rectification works
- Rainwater harvesting, through in-situ tanks, check dams, etc.
- Controlling indiscriminate extraction of ground water

- Recharging of aquifers
- Meters to be installed along trunk mains and for bulk consumers
- System of roof-top rain water harvesting be made mandatory
- Recycling and reuse of wastewater
- Porous paving and percolation structures in open grounds, parking areas and footpaths/road side will help re-charge bore-wells and provide water for gardening, car washing, etc.

River and canals can give a sustainable form to the region through which they pass. With indiscriminate growth and dumping of wastes, the water bodies have become polluted and foul. This needs appropriate and strict pollution control measures and eco-sensitive river-edge land use controls.

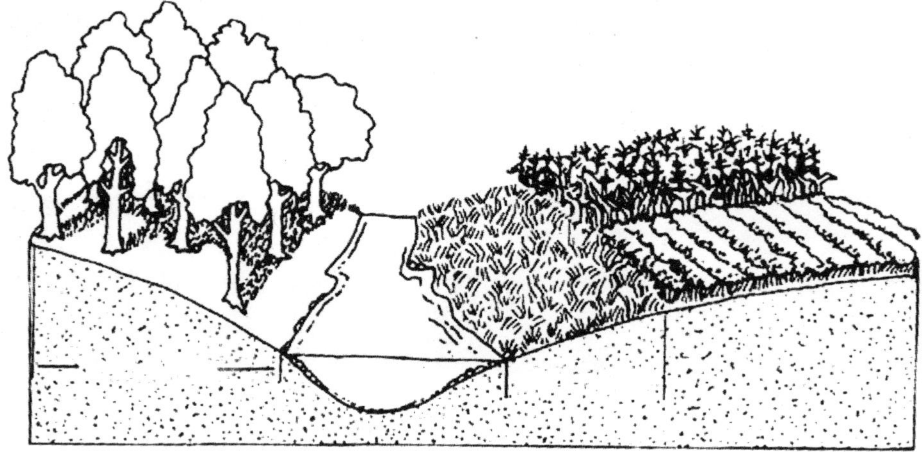

**Fig. 5.11 : Vegetation filter strip**

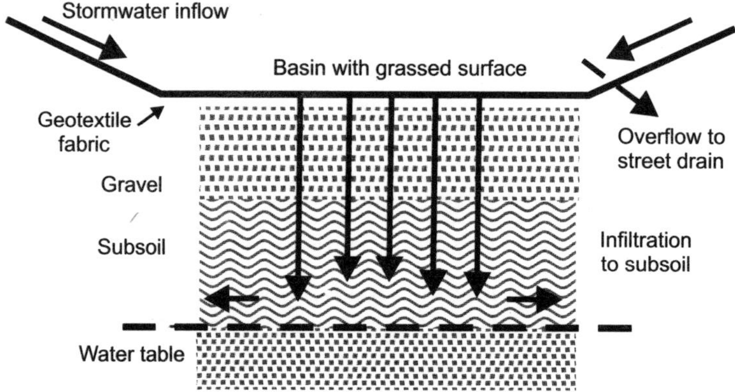


**Fig. 5.12 : Detail of a filter strip**

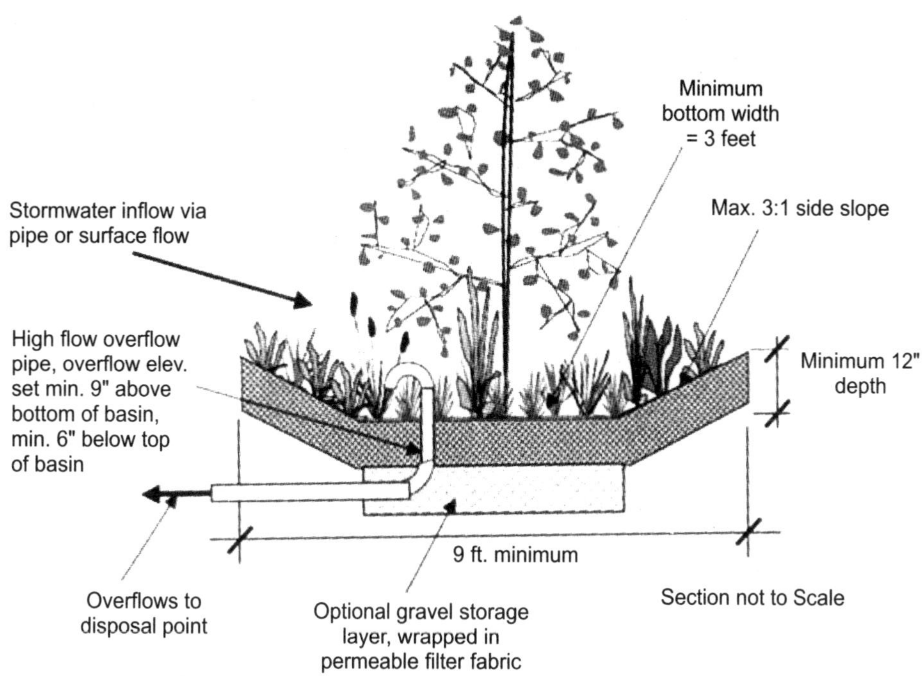


**Fig. 5.13 : Infiltration basin**

Water flow needs to be controlled at the tributaries and riverbanks should be stabilized and marked at each kilometer station. The valleys should be zoned so that the rivers are flanked with greenery, farmlands and forests, that provide to the village and city an attractive portal. The river basin should be administered by a joint authority, with uniform signals and regulations.

With the reduction in water in the water bodies, channels and ponds, these are continuously getting converted into urban uses. It is necessary to revive and rehabilitate the old canal systems. Some of the most delightful water-edge living is to be found where homes and shops are clustered along the edge of such man-made waterways. Many old canals, lakes and channels can be revived. One of the prime objectives development should be to improve the quality of river-water, to secure its continuous flow and to encourage the return of aquatic life. This needs installation of water purification facilities, improvement of drainage, wastewater treatment and pollution abatement by sewage treatment. This would lead to attractive and pleasant riverfront development besides improving the quality and quantity of water. The surplus water during the monsoons should be retained in swells or balancing ponds along the riverbed, rather than allowing to flood the downstream areas. Such ponds and reservoirs in the catchment zones in low-lying areas offer several advantages, such as a quicker, efficient and economical process of drainage, continuous replenishment and enrichment of underground water table, availability of rolling greens and recreational areas, linking the population with the waterfront, improving the micro-climate, and interconnected parkways. There is no need for elaborate gardening of the greenways, but these wild, simple and natural stretch would be ecologically important. Such trails could be one of the cheapest form of drainage and recreation.

No matter how littered or foul the stream, preserve the edges for public greens, together with restoration of water quality. Seal off the discharge of existing mines which are no longer working. Control by regulating the flow of acid and other wastes from active mining operations. Uniform laws and enforcement are needed to reduce the economic disadvantage of certain localities. Since the costs of corrective programs are usually too heavy to be borne wholly by districts plagued with abandoned strip and deepmine workings, state and federal funds will be required.

## Conserving Groundwater

85% of the drinking water needs are met from ground water and although only 5% of total groundwater extraction is needed for domestic water supply, irrigation accounts for 90% of all groundwater extraction and industry takes the remainder. The rapid development in groundwater based irrigation and its overexploitation has caused ground water depletion, because of which the life of drinking water supply source becomes short. Highly subsidized irrigation electricity tariffs have led to an indiscriminate and disproportionate level of groundwater extraction. Although significant areas in States, such as Punjab, Haryana, Gujarat, Karnataka, Maharashtra, Rajasthan, Tamil Nadu and Uttar Pradesh (in all 144 districts in 10 States) have been declared 'Dark' and 'Grey' zones, there has been no let up in the depletion of ground water aquifers. In many cases, ground water depletion has aggravated water quality problems due to excess fluoride, arsenic and brackishness. In certain areas, Public Health Engineering Departments were forced to abandon low-cost hand pump based systems and to undertake costly and complicated piped water supply schemes. The need for regulating the extracting of groundwater arises from the following considerations:

- Protection of water resource against over exploitation (particularly for irrigation).
- Protection against quality degradation
- To ensure social equity and to guarantee minimum provision to all sections of the society.

A number of steps need to be taken urgently in order to manage groundwater in a more scientific manner, especially in dark and grey zones. There must be legislation against subsidies on electricity tariffs for irrigation. Although the World Bank approved a drinking water project in principle for Punjab, further processing was withheld by the World Bank because of the Punjab Government's policy of providing free electricity and power for irrigation sector. In fact farmers do not stand to benefit from this due to undependable power supply and consequent disruptions in the supply of water. Many of them are forced to operate diesel pumps. It is a fact that charging a power tariff with an assured power supply is more beneficial and acceptable to the community. The Model Bill framed by the Government of India and circulated to the States in 1996 should be adopted by the States and implement it seriously. Also the user groups should be formed on the lines of Joint Forest Management Groups, who should do ground water monitoring and ensure that it is managed as a common resource, rather than allowing it to be overexploited as an open access resource.

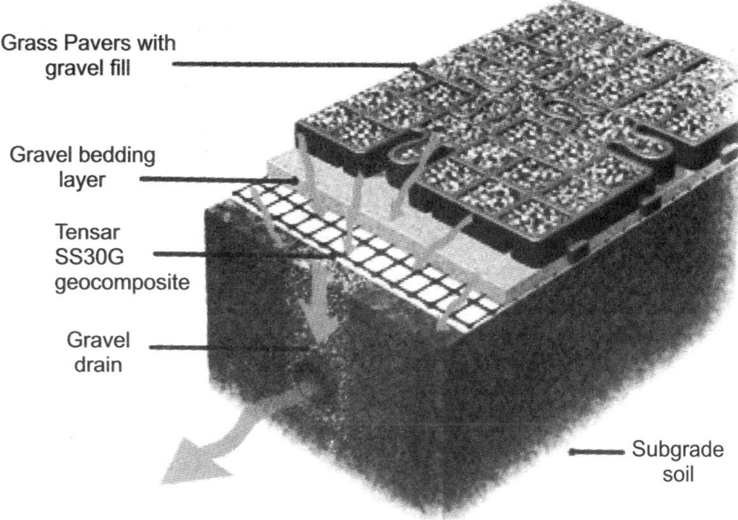


**Fig. 5.14 : Water on-site retention (Porous Paving)**

**Fig. 5.15 : Rainwater harvesting in a park by an infiltration trench**

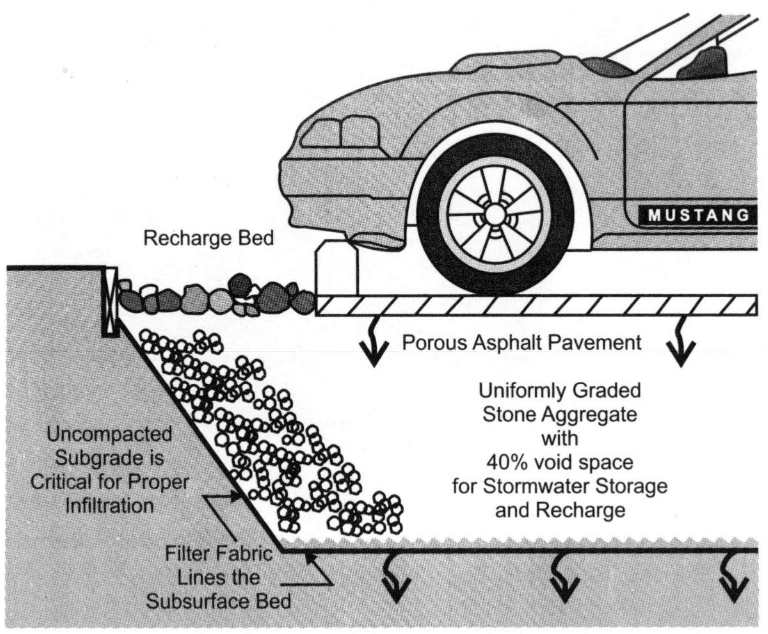


**Fig. 5.16 : Roadside pavement and Parking Recharge Bed for Infiltration**

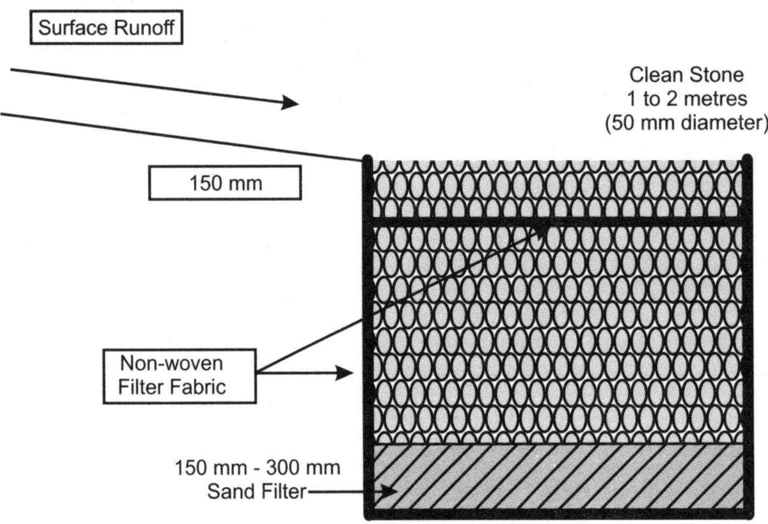


**Fig. 5.17 : Section of infiltration trench**

A two pronged strategy comprising of regulating indiscriminate groundwater withdrawal and to adopt appropriate measures for augmenting its recharge is adopted through spreading techniques in alluvial areas, check dams and percolation tanks besides direct injection methods, utilizing abandoned structures. Their suitability for receiving recharge and also the quality of source water should be thoroughly examined to confirm the technical feasibility. Rainwater harvesting is another attractive feasible option for conservation of water. Besides, ground water recharge can be suitably dovetailed with watershed development programs aimed at soil and water conservation by arresting the run-off.

## Rainwater Harvesting

To enhance underground percolation of rainwater, it is advisable to keep about one third of the abadi area under soft landscape and 2 to 3 percent of area for water harvesting. Porous paving should be used to encourage ground water recharge. Pre-cast perforated concrete slabs are now widely available which can be used for hard paving of pedestrian paths as well as for parking areas. To discourage mosquito breeding in stagnant water, the options like providing small fountains and cascades, are inexpensive and practical. The revival of the concept of rooftop rainwater harvesting can substantively resolve the urban water crisis. This requires awareness and mandatory provisions in the building bye-laws. The building plans should indicate the system of storm water drain, points of collection of rainwater in surface reservoirs or recharge well and dual piping system. While one piping system will feed the rainwater for washing, water coolers and garden taps, the second for supplying potable water. All non-residential buildings having a discharge of over 10,000 litres a day should incorporate a wastewater recycling, which may be used for horticulture purpose. For conservation of urban water supply, building should have twin or triple water systems- one for drinking water, which comes from public utilities, and one for the rest. Water for second system will be obtained from the rain supplemented with the drinking water when necessary. This will be used for washing, showering, etc. The ideal house will also have separate taps for treatment of grey water (GW). Grey water is the waste water from the washings, shower and washbasins. This water passes through a treatment cycle set up for one or more houses together. The sewerage system will also have a twin drainage system which separates heavily polluted water from slightly polluted water.

Underground rainwater storage can be a paragmatic initiative from which rooftop water tank can be filled by a motor. By solar energy, the condensed water can be passed through a filter or coal, sand and marble chips to provide clean water. Although the best way to save water is to use it sparingly, another option is to treat wastewater and reuse it for various purposes. Recycled water can be used to irrigated the grass in parks and along embankments. Increasingly areas with chronic water shortage are installing recycling systems. The flushing cistern capacity should also be reduced to a maximum of five litres.

Excavated and natural underground depression and depleted mines can be used for bulk water storage. An indigenous plan can be worked out whereby the outfall from the combined storm and sanitary/sewage system could be dropped through shafts into deep underground storage tunnels drilled for this purpose. In these subterranean chambers the first stage of sedimentation and water treatment can take place. The energy of the falling wastewater in the drop shafts will be able to generate electrical power to meet peak-load power requirements. In off-peak hours the surplus power can be used to pump the water to the surface for further treatment and purification. The problems of sewage disposal will thus be relieved and freshwater reserves would be replenished.

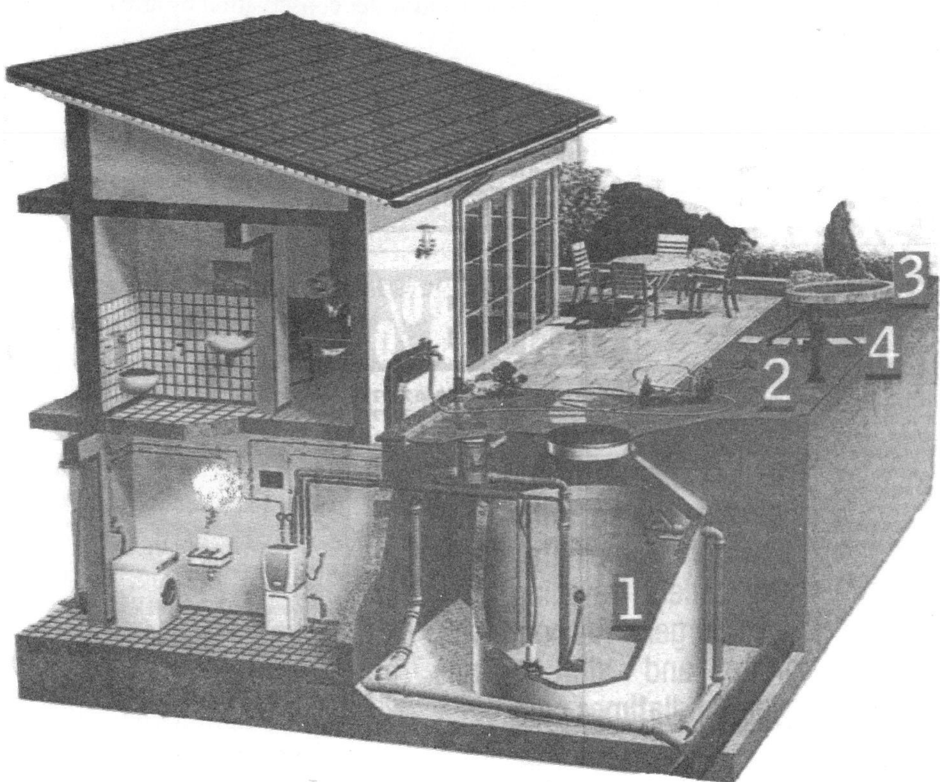


**1. Recharge PIT**

Dig a deep pit. After excavation, fill the pit with pebbles and boulders. Direct rainwater collected on the roof and other places to the recharge pit. Make sure that water is silt-free. Clean the pit regularly.

**2. Recharge Well**

Rainwater is channelled from roof to a well which recharges due to gravity. It is suitable where land availability is limited. Though a bit expensive, this method recharges groundwater quickly and effectively.

**3. Hand Pump Method**

Same as abandoned well method, here a running or abandoned hand pump is used instead of a well. It is suitable for smaller buildings. Very cost effective and water can be used for household purposes.

**4. Abandoned Well**

Most popular method and yields good results. A dry or unused well is used as recharge structure. Recharge water is guided through a pipe to the bottom of well. Add chlorine periodically to avoid contamination.

**Fig. 5.18 : Rainwater harvesting and greywater recycling. In most of the regions in India, water is a critical problem. By rainwater harvesting, wastewater recycling, primary treatment and checking of leakages, the problem can be mitigated to a great extent.**

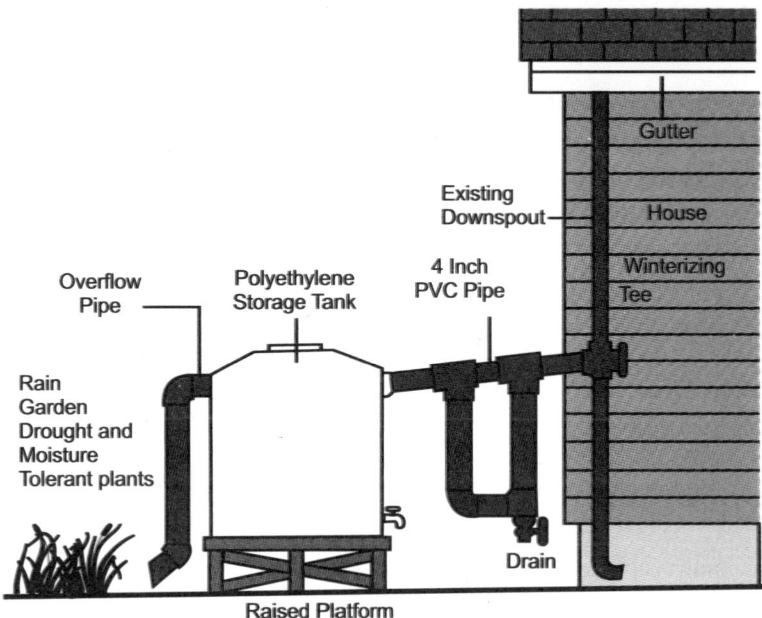


**Fig. 5.19 : Rainwater storage tank detail**

The rapid runoff of precipitation and groundwater is wasteful, for it prevents natural percolation into the earth and water tables where it might otherwise have been stored. In addition to checking the surface drainage, other means must be found by which the underground water reserves may be replenished. Such water-management procedures will include the collection and pumping of surface runoff into natural wetlands or into man-made holding ponds or percolating basins. Treated sanitary waste may be used and disposed of in this manner and for irrigation, for even raw sanitary sewage can be converted to a quality fit for human consumption.

## Water Recycling

Conserving the scarce water and recycling of used water is a major challenge for India. For this, a new technology, known as root zone cleaning system is feasible. It consists of a receiving tank into which the toilet, kitchen and bath water flows by gravity; a mud area where suitable reeds, rushes and other plants are grown; and an outlet tank in which the water cleaned by the natural process is accumulated. The processed water is clean and without any smell. Fish and amphibians living and growing within it show that the water is clean and the system is successful. Chlorination, which removes germs and bacteria, leaves chemical residues that are unfavourable for human consumption.

Removal of forest cover and the addition of impervious surfaces increasing the frequency of flooding and change stream characteristics. However, the use of a natural drainage system increases water-table recharge and increases lag time for run-off entering streams. Protection of flood plains and drainage swales is imperative for flood control, for regulating stream control and for maintaining water quality.

Indian Vedic knowledge prescribes locating a city along a serpentine bend of a river and towards its west so that the morning sun rays and breeze purify the homes (which should have lower height and vegetation towards the north and east). The reason for choosing site along the curving river are its drainage potential as well as self purification of river water by oxidation and the gradient. The research at Banaras Hindu University reveals that the speed of the flow of the water along the concave bank of Varanasi (that is the city and the ghats) is much slower than the speed of the river along the opposite bank. The level of the opposite bank is much lower than on the side of the ghats. The sandy bed on the opposite side has a far greater capacity to absorb the effluents than is possible on the city side. The gradients and the basic asymmetries that nature has provided to cleanse the effluents generated by the city as the velocity of the river is markedly higher along the opposite (convex) bank. The capacity of the river to dilute, diffuse, disperse and digest the effluents and organic water matter is much higher than on the city side of the river.

The time has come when the unlimited use of water can no longer be permitted. In many areas its use for irrigation or as an industrial coolant, may have to be reduced or even banned. In some cases these functions may be served as well by treated or even untreated fluid wastes. Otherwise, if new sources of fresh water cannot be tapped, the bulk consumers may have to relocate to other areas where suitable water is in adequate supply. In any event, it is incumbent upon planning authorities to run a check upon the quantity needs and uses of all existing or potential consumers together with water demand management.

## Drinking Water

The stipulated norms of drinking supply in rural areas is 40 Ipcd, which should be available within a walking distance of 1.6 km or elevation difference of 100 metres in hilly areas, to be relaxed as per field conditions in arid, semi-arid and hilly areas. At least one handpump/spot source for every 250 persons is to be provided. Additional water is to be provided in the Desert Development Programme (DDP) areas for cattle, based on the cattle population. The water requirements for cattle need not necessarily be met through piped water supply and could be made through rain water harvesting structures/spot sources.

According to Central Public Health Environmental Engineering Organisation (CPHEEO) estimates, the average water availability is dwindling. A major concern is depletion of ground water that supplies to 80% of rural water and 50% of urban and industrial usage. Death tolls have increased recently to 1.5 million children every year by drinking contaminated water in rural area. 1.51 lakh people suffered from water quality problem such as excess arsenic, fluoride, salinity and iron.

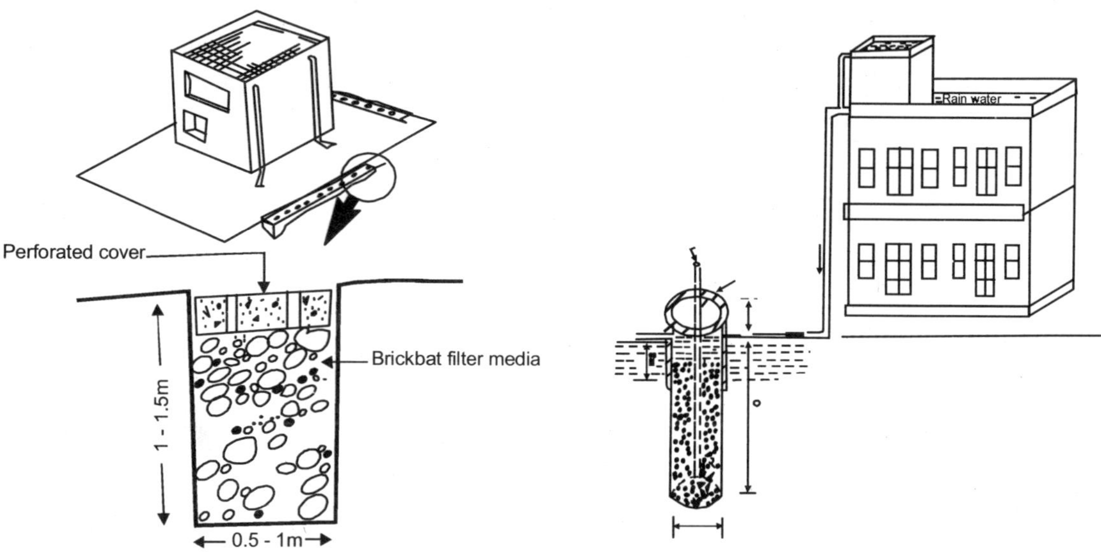


**Fig. 5.19.** Recharge Trench

**Fig. 5.20.** Rainwater Harvesting Pit

**Source :** *CSE*

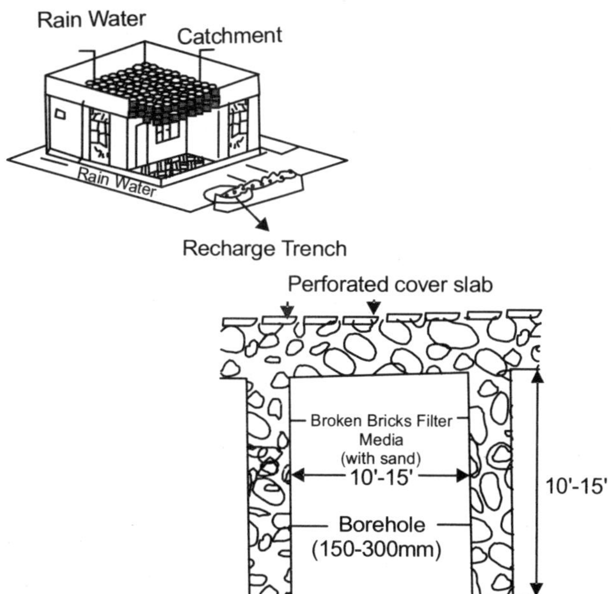


**Fig. 5.21.** Recharge Trench with Bore Method

State Governments have the responsibility to provide safe drinking water and sanitation in the rural areas. Government of India supports and supplements efforts of the State Governments. Programme for Drinking Water Supply and Sanitation have been under implementation ever since inception of the first Five-year Plan. The Accelerated Rural Water Supply Programme (ARWSP) was introduced by the Government of India in 1972-73. A Technology Mission on Drinking Water called the National Drinking Water Mission (NDWM) was launched in 1986, which subsequently was renamed as the Rajiv Gandhi National Drinking Water Mission (RGNDWM) in 1991. Upto end of November 2001, 87.89% habitations in the country is having access to adequate water (fully covered) with 40 litres per capita per day (Ipcd). About 10.85% are partially covered and remaining about 20,000 habitations are still not covered. States are also being supported, under the rural drinking water component of Prime Minister's Gramodaya Yojana (PMGY-RDW). Sector Reforms have been introduced in selected 63 districts in the country on a pilot basis on demand driven, community participation, and cost sharing approach by the user groups. Other support programme like social mobilization, capacity building, Human Resource Development (HRD) and MIS, etc. supplement the main ASWSP and PMGY (RDW).

## Protecting the Quality of Water

Since rivers and their tributary streams are the potential respositories and carries of pollution, they must be guarded from contamination at all points and from all sources. The major pollutants are present to some degree in almost every river system. Treating the incoming waste through a series of carefully engineered process is called the Advanced Integrated Wastewater Pond System, (AIWPS) which uses bacterial and oxygen-releasing micro algae to remove parasites, heavy metals, bacterial and viral pathogens from waste water. This has been experimented in cleaning of Ganga at Varanasi. Ganga water will meet World Health Organisation standards for the flood crop irrigation water.

While pond systems are generally more efficient and less costly than mechanical treatment facilities, they require more land and more time. For this reason, larger municipalities generally favour mechanical systems. The ponds use the ability of bacteria and algae to decompose and oxidize sewage. It greatly diminishes the dependency on electricity to treat the water. Sewage is stored from 20 to 45 days as compared to mechanical facility where sewage is stored only for one day. Methane produced from waste is captured at the site and used to meet the meager energy requirements of the AIWPS systems.

Arsenic in water is proving to be a colossal problem in India and Bangladesh. All one requires is merely 3 litres per capita per day of good potable water with the essential minerals provided by nature. It is to mother nature and traditional wisdom that one must turn to when all else seems to fail. Be it the holy waters of the Ganga and Jamuna, it is where passes through limestone belts that you get the best waters. If they contain other minerals such as traces of silver, etc., these waters are literally worshiped. These waters are stored in copper vessels, so that they remain pure. Water is best purified by storing in a silver or gold vessel, which have the status of noble metals. Excessive intake of these metals in no way harms the body but only gives the skin a very pale blue colour and therefore the term "Blue Blooded" in royalty. Coconut shell charcoal is one of the finest filters to remove e-coli and suspended impurities. One can use copper vessels with a small hole at the bottom to slow down the rate of water passage. The first has water, the next contains coconut shell charcoal. The third contains white marble chips, the fourth contains white sand and the fifth vessel is for water collection and contains a silver coin or chain and has a small tap to drain out water.

Arsenic is a heavy toxic metal and ingestion of amounts beyond 0.05 milligram per litre of water can pose a serious health hazard, where aquifers are the main source of drinking water. Currently experiments are being undertaken with a number of arsenic mitigation technologies. The basic methods involve oxidation-coagulation-flocculation—sedimentation-filtration. The bucket treatment method is simple and cost effective. Based on the chemical behaviour of arsenic in water, the bucket-type chemical treatment was designed to remove arsenic from water. The method uses a ratio of chlorine or potassium permanganate and alum to treat ground water for arsenic removal. The water is collected in a bucket and the chemicals are mixed and rigorously stirred. The arsenic-free water is then drained out from the top. Another method is water filter which uses activated alumna in a nylon bag to filter water and makes it free from arsenic.

Along the rivers and coastlines an increasing threat is being posed by the infiltration of waste water, sewage and sea water into the aquifers. As the hydrostatic pressure of the landward water table is reduced by drawdown, the normal flow to the oceans is reversed. Preventive techniques include the construction of extensive system of efficient treatment plants, filters, dams and barricades, coupled with the regulation of freshwater consumption within the limits of adequate supply.

Most villages in India suffer from severe water scarcity while the little water that is available is often unfit for consumption. To meet the needs of rural India in terms of appropriateness, cost, operation and maintenance, technology should be backed by community support and awareness programmes.

## Village Water and Sanitation Committees (VWSCs)

The village water and sanitation committee is a formal body, with legal status as a sub-committee of the statutory gram panchayat. The committee consists of 7 to 12 elected representatives, with at least 20 per cent representation from the socially and economically backward sections of the community. At least 30 per cent of the members are women. Unlike the gram panchayat, which is responsible for multi-sectoral development in the village, the water and sanitation committee is a user association set up specifically for the project. Each committee has a Chairperson and Treasurer who jointly operate the bank account. While all the elected members work in an honorary capacity, the village committee usually employs a local technician, who is known as village maintenance worker to operate and maintain the water supply scheme after construction is completed.

**Table 5.8. Community Contracting Models in Water Supply and Sanitation Works**

| Works | Average Value Contract | Type of Contractor | Type of Process | Selection |
|---|---|---|---|---|
| Mechanized borewell with Overhead tank, Distribution network | Rs. 12-15 lakh (mid-size scheme) | Written | Private/public sector | Bidding/market survey by VWSC/SO |
| Boreholes with hand pumps (8 hand pumps per Village on an average) | Rs. 1.5 to 2 lakh | Verbal | Private/government | Market survey |
| Hand dug wells | Rs. 1.5 to 2 lakh | Verbal | Private/government | Market survey by VWSC/SO |
| Gravity-flow system | Rs. 80 to 1.20 lakh | Verbal | Community technician | Community Consensus |
| Individual household latrines | Rs. 4000-5000 | Verbal | Local mason | Household chooses |
| Drainage soakpit | Rs. 2000 to 2500 | Verbal | Community technician | Household chooses |

The following priorities had been set for achieving the objective of providing safe drinking water supply to all rural habitations :

(*i*) Highest priority to be given to ensuring that the 'not covered' habitations are provided with sustainable and stipulated supply of drinking water.

(*ii*) It will be equally important to ensure that all the 'partially covered' habitations having a supply level of less than 10 litres per capita per day (Ipcd) and those habitations facing a severe water quality problem are fully covered with safe drinking water facilities on a sustainable basis.

(*iii*) Thereafter, other 'partially covered' and 'quality affected' habitations are to be covered.

(*iv*) Once drinking water supply facility is provided to all rural habitations, the funds should be utilized for consolidation. This will involve covering newly emerged habitations and those which have slipped back to 'partially covered' or 'not covered' status due to a variety of reasons.

(*v*) Simultaneous action is needed to identify and tackle habitations where water quality problems have emerged recently.

(*vi*) It should be ensured that scheduled caste/scheduled tribe (SC/ST) population and other poor and weaker sections are covered fully on a priority basis. A systematic survey of all such identified habitations will be undertaken.

**Table 5.9. Trigger for Disbursing Investment Funds in the Swajal Project**

| Fund Release in Implementation Phase | Activities/Triggers |
|---|---|
| Installment 1 (50%) | (*i*) IPTA signing<br>(*ii*) Market survey<br>(*iii*) Rates, quality and quantity endorsed<br>(*iv*) Proforma invoice obtained and submitted to PMU<br>(*v*) Rate, quality and quality verified |
| Installment 2 (40%) | (*i*) 80% utilization of Installment 1 funds<br>(*ii*) Achievement of construction and community development milestones as per IPTA<br>(*iii*) Physical and financial audit |
| Installment 3 (10%) | (*i*) Physical and financial audit compliance report<br>(*ii*) Implementation/Completion Report |

**Source:** Govt. of India, Ministry of Rural Development

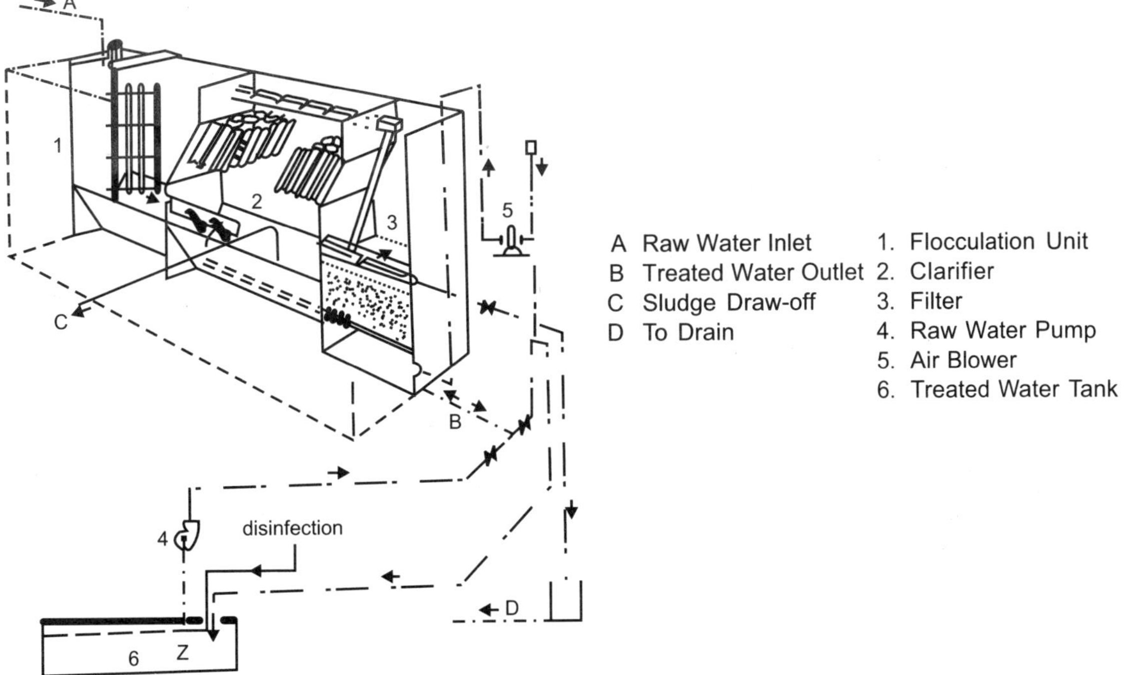


**Fig. 5.22 : A Compact Water Treatment Unit for Villages**

## Sanitation and Environmental Engineering

A major problem of the rural area is insanitation, lack of individual toilets, cattle dung scattered all over and lack of solid waste disposal system, resulting in serious health hazard, pollution of surface and underground sources of water and germination of mosquitoes, flies and harmful vermins. In the words of Nobel laurate V.S. Naipaul. “Indians defecate everywhere. They defecate mostly beside the railway track. But they also defecate on the beaches; they defecate on the hills; they defecate on the river banks; they defecate on the streets; they never look for cover. Muslims, with their tradition of purdah, can at times be secretive. But this is a religious act of self-denial, for it is said that the peasant, Muslim or Hindu, suffers from claustrophobia if he has to use an enclosed latrine.”

Today, we have a unique opportunity to use a whole new range of environment friendly technologies in our settlements. The adoption of eco-technology for sanitation infrastructure services is essential for improving the living condition as well as for environmental sustainability. The development of simple, small eco-technologies integrated with bio-architecture, which facilitate community and self-management and adopt recycling, provide environmentally sustainable alternatives to the present sanitation crisis and pollution caused by it. These are crucial for the sustainability of the rural settlements.

## Local Sanitation and Latrines

In most of the Indian villages, where municipal sewages does not exist, local on-site sanitation systems have been adopted. The most popular ‘on-site’ system is the age-old septic tank and its various versions. The septic tank comprises an underground concrete or brick tank separated by a suspended baffle wall. The system is basically a horizontal continuous flow sedimentation tank in which sewage moves very slowly so as to be retained for a period sufficient to permit most of the suspended matter to settle in the form of sludge at the bottom of the tank. Some of the lighter solids including grease and fat rise to the surface of the sewage to form a floating scum. The scum and the sludge so formed are retained with the sewage in the tank for a period of several months during which they are decomposed anaerobically to form gases and liquids through the process of sludge digestion. This also reduces the volume of the sludge. The septic tank effluent is generally disposed of in a soak/seepage pit normally filled with brick or stone aggregate. Methane gas produced in the tank is removed through a vent pipe which releases the gas, high enough so as to avoid nuisance from smell.

The septic tank suffers from a number of problems. Periodically the tanks have to be desludged. Although the cost of construction is generally low but because of spatial and financial constraints the soakage pit is usually not constructed and the highly septic effluent is allowed to flow into storm water drains or in open land. To function properly sufficient water supply is necessary.

A serious flaw is that if any crack occurs in the floor or wall of the tank then the hydraulic pressure inside leaks the liquid contents to the surrounding soil creating a no-flow situation in the tank which stops its functioning. Another factor is that when septic tanks are cleaned manually, they expose the cleaner to grave risks. The disposal of the tank contents in insanitary manner contaminates subsoil water (Fig. 5.23).

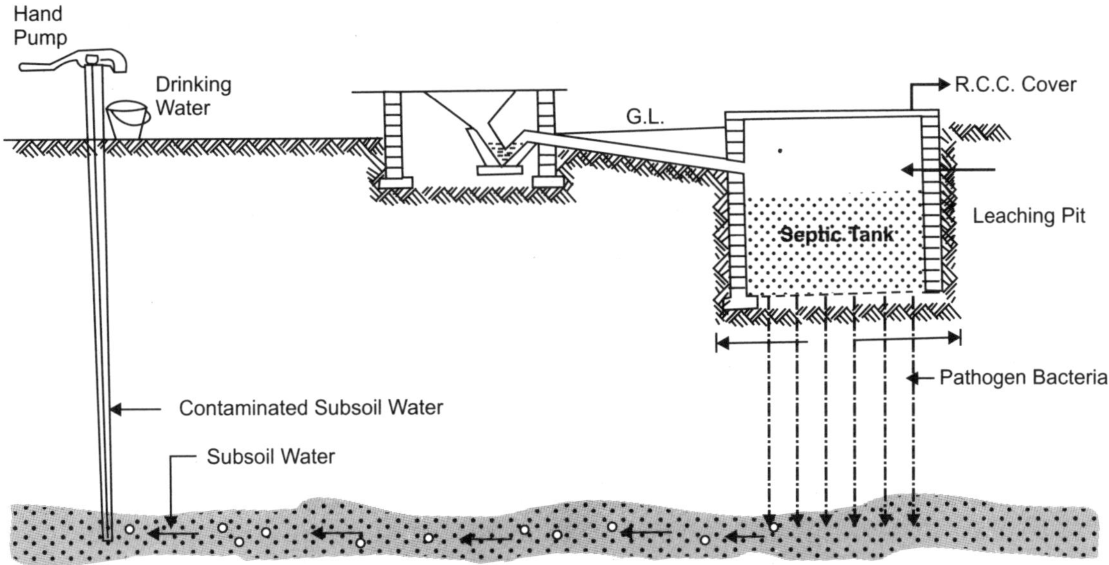


**Fig. 5.23 : Contamination of Sub-Soil water due to a leaking Septic Tank**

When the septic tank pit is filled, it is either excavated or a new pit is dug. The existing superstructure is either moved over to the new pit or a new superstructure is constructed. In cases where the pit is to be reused, pit contents are disposed of in nearby low-lying areas. Otherwise the old pit is simply covered over with soil. The liquids leach into the soil by way of the unlined pit while the solids are retained. When the pit is filled the top slab is moved to a newly dug pit and the old one covered over with soil. The main problem with all single pit latrines is that when full there is dislocation of latrine use for some time which may extend to a number of days. The single pit contents endanger the health of the scavenger and final disposal of sludge is an environmental hazard.

The two-pit pour flush (TPPF) waterfall latrine provides an alternative and intermediate on-site sanitation system. It is comparatively easy to construct, operate and maintain and is economical in quantity of water required. The system consists of a squatting pan connected to a junction box outside the latrine, further leading to two underground leaching pits. The pan has a steep bottom slope of 30 degree to the horizontal, a narrow neck of 70 mm and a 20 mm waterfall trap set into the floor of the latrine. This makes it amenable to complete flushing with only two litres of water. The junction box has a Y-junction so that flow can be directed to one pit at a time by blocking on branch of the Y-junction. It has a removable cover to facilitate easy inspection. The junction box is connected through a pipe or drain to two brick-lined leaching pits with the bricks laid in a honeycomb pattern. The pit bottom is left unlined. The pit can be square or circular and are fitted with reinforced concrete top slab (Fig.5.24)

When the latrine is flushed, the excreta passes to the pit. The liquids percolate out into the surrounding soil through the honeycomb openings and down through the open pit bottom while any gases produced are absorbed into the soil. Only the solids accumulate in the pit. Each pit is designed to last for about three years before it gets filled. When this happens the connection in the junction box is switched so that excreta can pass to the second pit while the first one is taken out of use. The filled pit is left untouched for 14-18 months during which time all the pathogens die out and the contents turn into a rich organic humus which is safe to handle. The pit is then opened during any dry period and the dry contents can be easily removed. With its established high fertilizing value, it can be used as manure. The empty pit is then ready to be back into use.

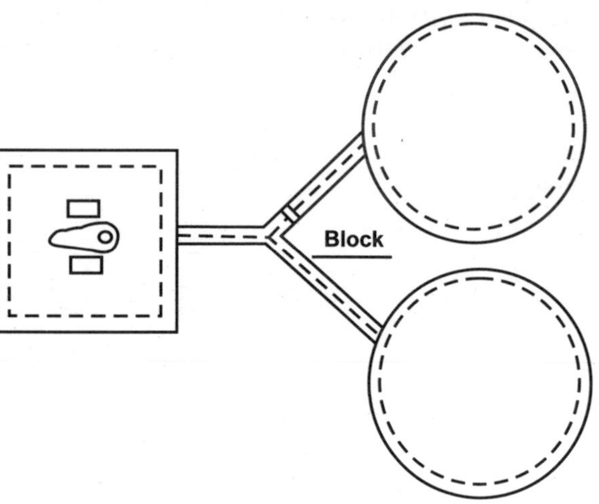


**Fig. 5.24 : A Typical two pit pour flush Latrine**

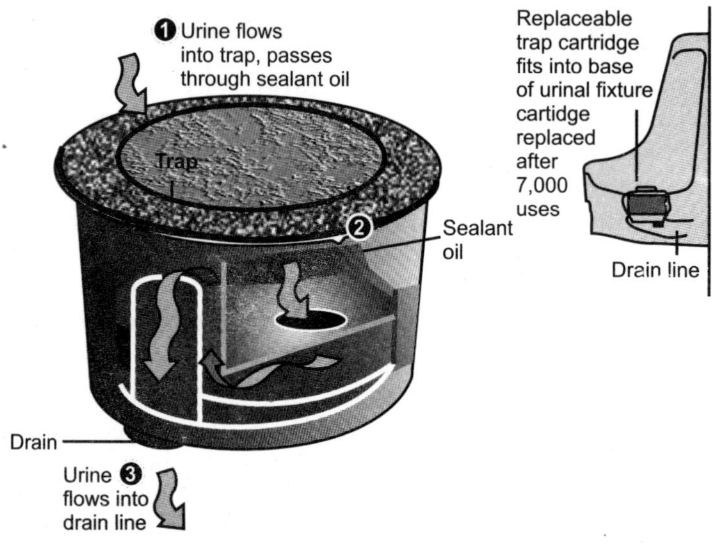


**Fig. 5.25 : Waterless (Cartridge) Urinal for Saving Water**
**Saves upto 40,000 gallons (152,000 liters) yearly; water savings can offset cost. However, maintenance requires knowledgeable staff with regular replacement of costly parts.**

## Bio-Gas

The bio-gas plants work on animal/human excreta which is fermented in semi-liquid form. It is fed at one end and the fermented spent slurry is extracted at the other end periodically without disturbing the whole system. The combustible gas can be used for cooking, lighting, etc., while the digested sludge is available as organic manure.

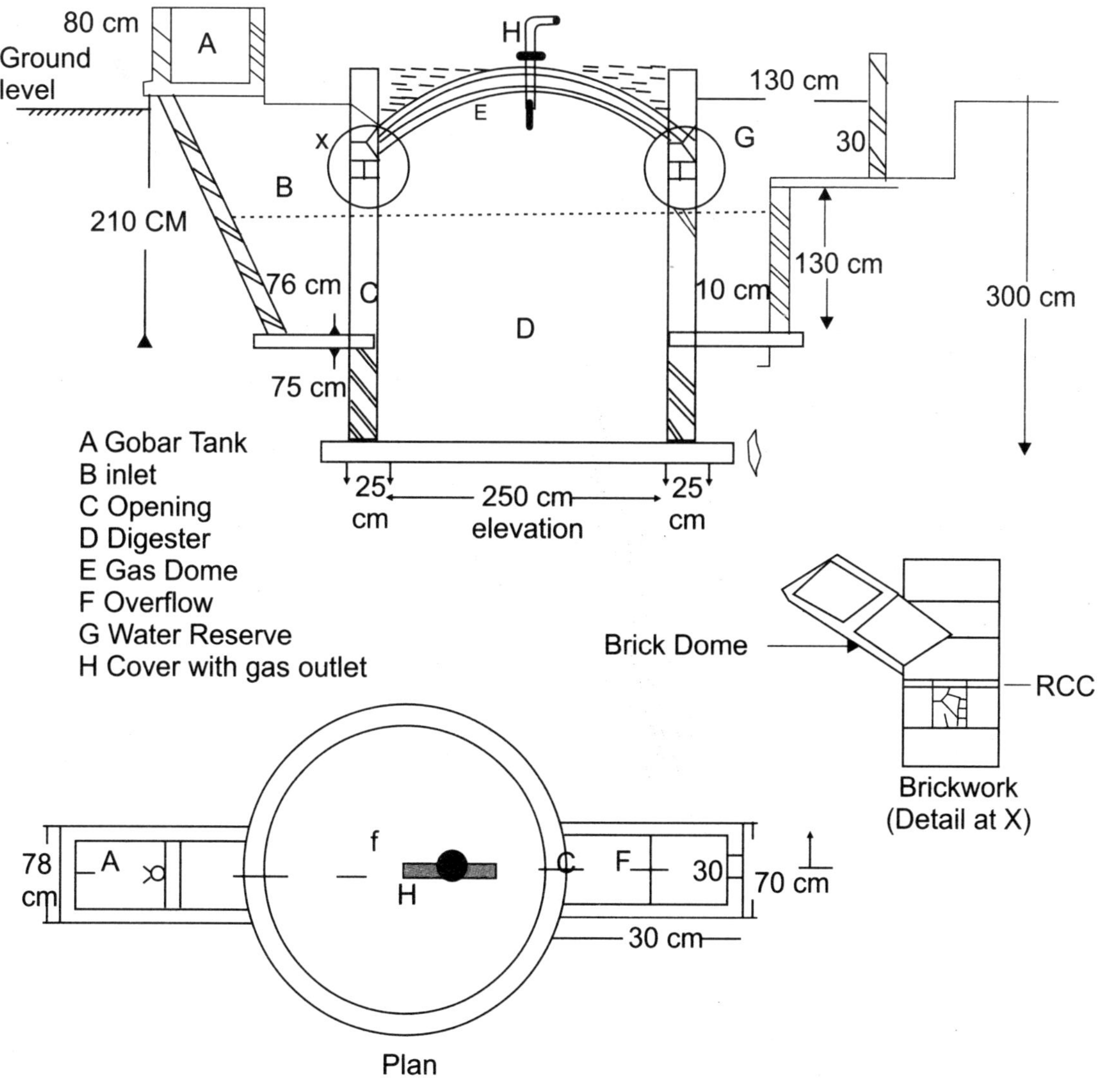


**Fig. 5.26 :A Bio-gas Plant**

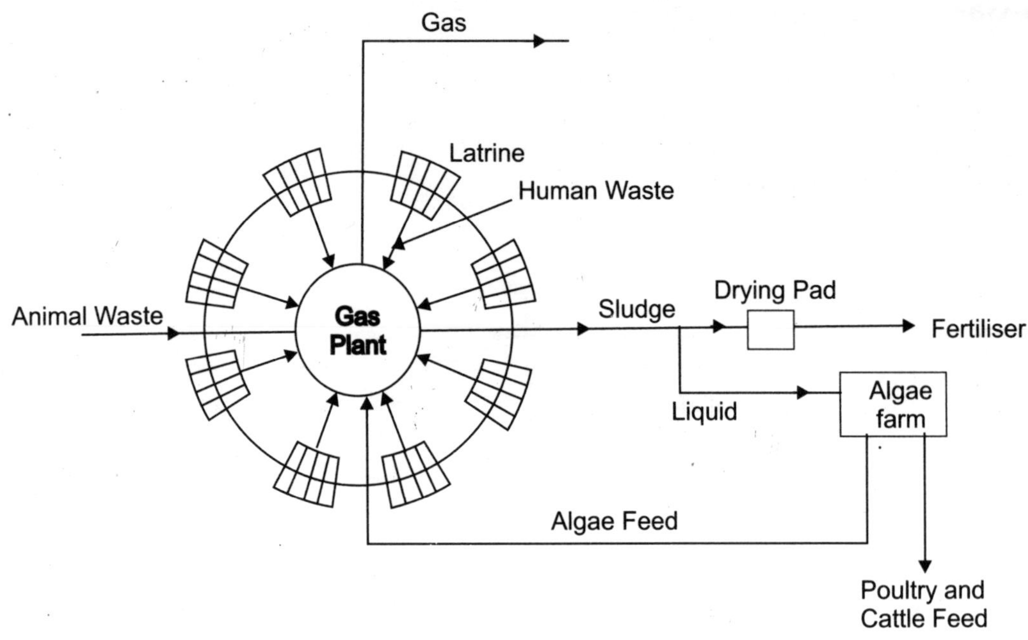


**Fig. 5.26 : A centralised, composite Bio-gas Plant**

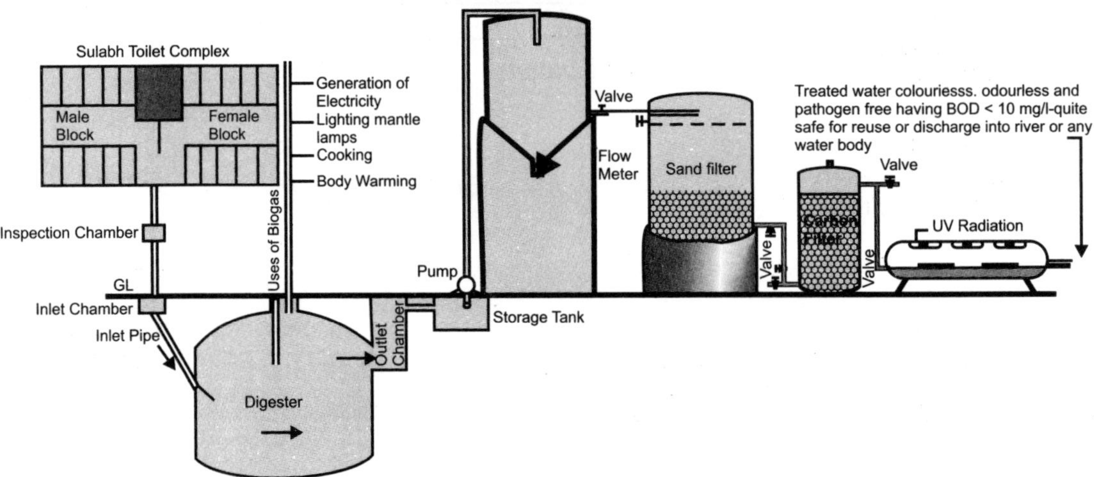


**Fig. 5.27 : Bio-gas plant with S ET technology: Costs on collection sewage and operation and maintenance of the system are minimal, and no manual handling of human excreta is required. Bio-gas is used for different purposes, treated effluent is safe for reuse in agriculture, gardening or discharge into a water body.**

**Source:** Sulabh International, New Delhi.

Bio-gas plant is a composite unit of a digester and a gas holder. The gas holder floats on the top of digester, wherein gas is collected and delivered at a constant pressure to the gas appliance through the pipe-line. The underground digester made of brick, is covered by a reinforced masonry dome. While the bio-gas plants working only on the night soil are not very successful, mixing of night soil with the cow, dung producing bio-gas given encouraging results. Such plants can be integrated with community latrines where WCs are without flushing tanks and connected directly to the digester. Small quantity of cow dung and other organic wastes are mixed for increasing the production of bio-gas, which can meet most of fuel requirement of a kitchen (Figs. 5.25, 5.26 & 5.27).

## Root Zone System

Developed in the sixties in Germany, the Root Zone Process has been emerging as an economical and efficient method totreat industrial and domestic effluents. Bio-diversity is the key to the Root Zone process. More than 2000 types of bacteria and tens of thousands of fungi exist in the reed bed. These microbial organisms oxidize impurities in the waste water. Since the process occurs underground, aerobic and anaerobic zones exist side by side, inducing different types of chemical reactions and balancing bacterial growth, thus decomposing the contaminants to their basic form.

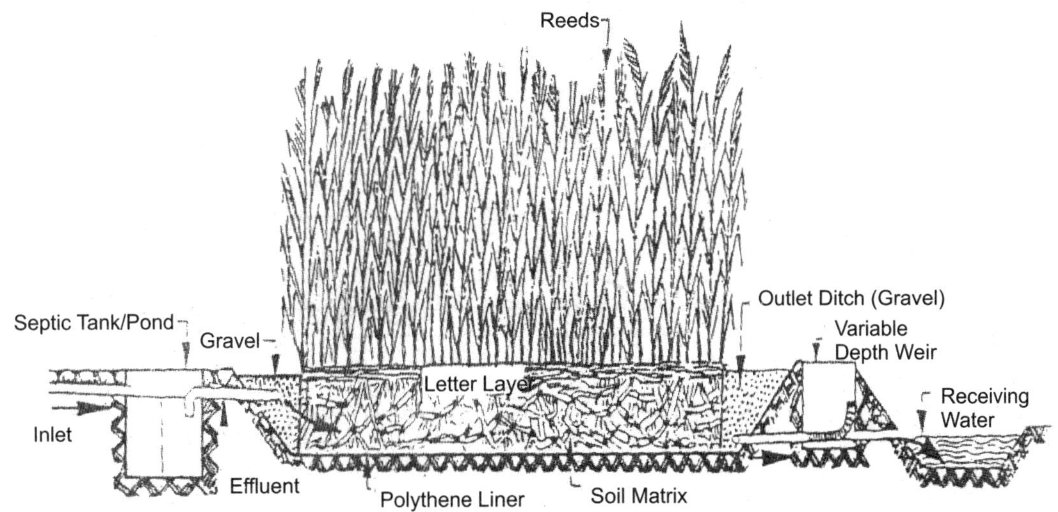


**Fig. 5.28 : Root Zone System**

Three integrated components are essential to the system-the reeds, the reed bed and the microbial organisms. The system involves running contaminated water through the root zones of specially designed reed beds. The reeds and the reed bed together provide efficient effluent treatment, and the released water is environmentally acceptable (Figs. 5.28, 5.29). Phosphates, sulphur compounds and nitrogenous materials reduce their elemental forms, while BOD and COD are drastically brought down. Heavy metals precipitate from solution and are bound into the soil matrix. What comes out of this constructed marsh is treated waste water which is not only environmentally acceptable but much cleaner than possible with any other technique.

The capital cost of the Root Zone system is roughly half that of conventional systems while operation and maintenance costs are around one fifth. The technology has the potential to reduce treatment costs considerably and therefore may gain wide application.

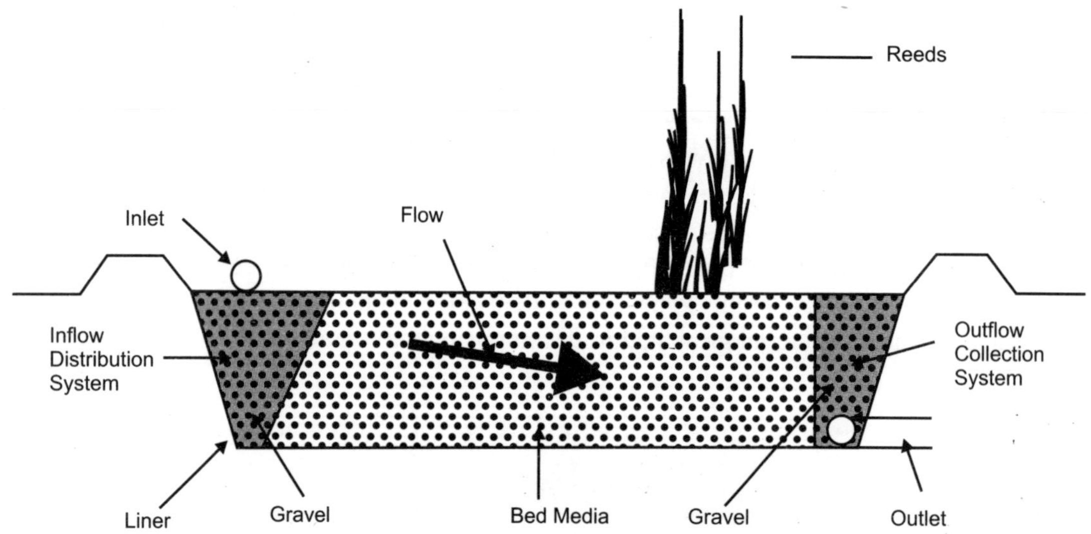


**Fig. 5.29 : Root Zone Treatment Systems (RZTS) are artificially prepared wetlands comprising of clay or plastic lined excavation and emergent vegetation growing on gravel/sand mixtures and is also known as constructed wetland. This method combines mechanical filtration, chemical precipitation and biological degradation in one step for the treatment of wastewater. Seemingly, low operating cost, less energy requirement and ease of maintenance are some of the attributes that make RZT system an attractive alternative for wastewater management.**

## Biological Composting System

The micro-organism process using oxygen in the air sludge and organic wastes into carbon-dioxide, water, and energy. The energy thus produced enables the microbial cells to divide, to move and utilize yet more sludge and waste. This is a natural process by which fallen leaves get converted into humus and revitalize the nutrition of the soil. Based on the principle, continuous bio-reactor composting system is a second generation technology for treatment of the sludge and organic waste. It has been in use in Europe since 1972. The digesters use the anaerobic bacteria to stabilize the sludge, whereas bio-reactors use aerobic bacteria for the same process. The aerobic bacteria is faster, thus the process is more efficient and also the capital cost is reduced. The heat is generated in a vessel or a tunned by bacterial action, raising the temperature to 70 degree C, which kills all the pathogens.

Thus, the bio-reactors convert the sludge into hygienically pollution and germs free material, which is not possible in the digestion process.

A common problem in cities and villages is ever-increasing shortage of the land. Conventional sludge beds use large areas and create foul smell. An alternative of the open beds is flocculation and dehydration of sludge by mechanical means. By filteration, shearing and de-watering of the sludge, its volume is greatly reduced. After that sludge can be compost and converted into humus-like product. The system uses very little space as compared to the conventional sludge drying beds.

The reaction chamber, which can be constructed in masonry or concrete, is comprised of two main components. The first is the compaction chamber with delivery hopper to feed the material, a pusher plate pushes the water/sludge into the compression chamber. The reactor is closed on all the sides having smooth surface on the inner walls. Ventilation ducts or channels in the floor supply air to dry the sludge. The compressed material is then delivered to the maturating chamber, where micro-organisms process the sludge. Heat produced by composting process, or if necessary, by artificial heating to 60° to 70° C ensures a pathogen free end-product. The final product can be used for local parks, agriculture or for treatment of wastelands. The reactors can be designed and installed in standard modules of batteries. This system eliminates pathogen contained leachate. As such, there is no danger to pollution and contamination of sub-soil water.

For treatment of sanitation/sewage wastes and sludge, methanisation and aerobic biological treatment are appropriate methods which can reduce the sludge formation by one-third, as compared to conventional methods. Bubble diffusion process, flotation, anaerobic reactors, root zone cleaning system and other forms of biological, tertiary and physiochemical methods can be adopted for treatment of sanitary effluents.

## Activated Sludge Technology

It involves production of an activated mass ofmicro-organisms which is kept under suspension by mixing. This does not contain any filter media for bacterial growth. It is commonly used for treatment of municipal sewage and other industrial liquid wastes containing organic matters. The stablisation of organic matter takes place in a suspension form.

## Solar Aquatics Septage Treatment System

In a typical septage treatment plant (Fig. 5.30), effluent is discharged into a headwork consisting of a receiving station and degritter. Then it flows by gravity into in-ground tanks where the effluent is blended to compensate for variations in loads and is preconditioned. Following equalization and preconditioning, effluent is pumped to a clarifier. From here sludge is pumped to the sludge stabilization tank where it is aerobically stabilized. It then flows to the reed bed for passive composting. Underflow from the reed bed is recycled by pumping it back into the equalization tank for further treatment.

Liquid from the clarifier enters a series of solar silos that contain the plants and worms involved in the clean-up operation. After moving through the silos by gravity flow, the liquid enters a second clarifier. Solids from this clarifier are recycled back to the equalization tank, where they re-enter the system, reseeding microbes as they travel. Next, the liquid moves through a gravel-filled de-nitrifying marsh planted with grasses and is then sterilizd with ultraviolet light before being discharged. Depending on total suspended solids limits, a sand filter may also be required at this point in the system for final polishing before purified water is discharged.

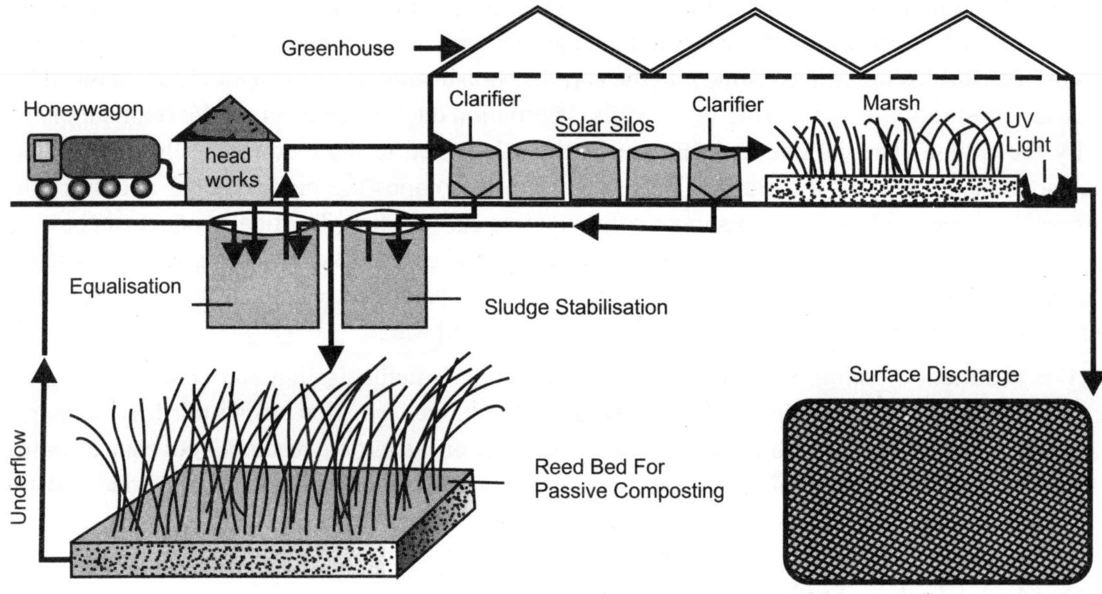


**Fig. 5.30 : Solar Aquatic Septage Treatment System**

**Source:** Ecological Engineering Associates, Marion, USA.

## Extended Aeration Technique

An innovative system of sewage treatment is extended aeration technique. The processing unit can be designed in the form of a compact, modular and a self-contained system. It can be installed independent of the overall system and is suitable for sewerage needs of remote areas. The process is based upon the phenomenon of self-oxidation by the bacteria. When the bacterial cells reach their ageing stage, the consumption of organic matter is maximized. The bacterial cells draw their own oxygen for additional energy which they require. The process of self-oxidation leads to stabilization of sludge and purification of the effluents. A sequence of the treatment processes, viz., screening, aeration, setting and thickening take place within the package unit. Thus, open land can be saved from spillover of sullage and waste. The unit can be installed underground and the site can be landscaped from above. It is cathodically protected against electrical currents and corrosion. The unit can also be constructed in the masonry/concrete over the ground (Fig. 5.31). For scattered villages, and suburbs which often lack the availability of sewerage system, the concept of package unit has been developed. The package unit contains the compartments required for the treatment process in one metallic parallel piped shaped casing:

- Screening unit
- Aeration zone
- Settling zone
- Thickening zone

The package unit is attached with an adjacent motor to lift the sewage water to the inlet of the unit. Generally, the unit is buried and does not affect the appearance of the site where it is installed. Earthwork is usually started a few days before delivery of the package unit so as to limit any risk of flooding.

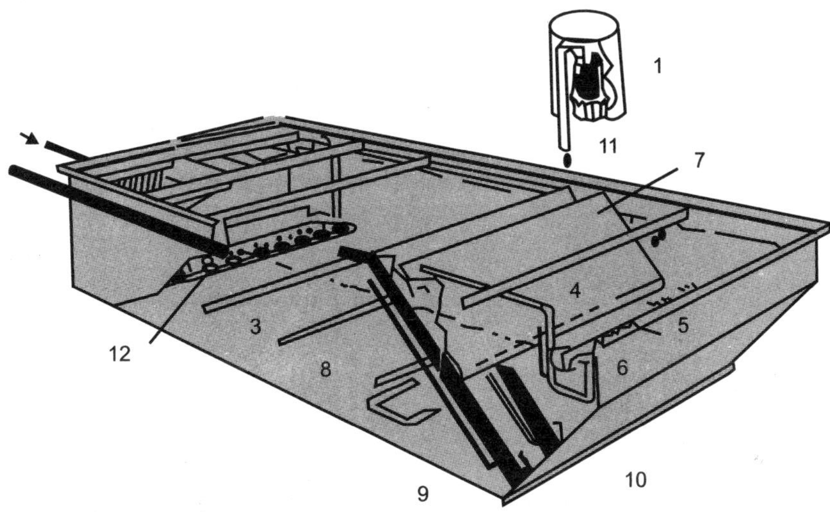


1. Electric Blower Set
2. Raw Water Inlet
3. Extended Aeration
4. Calcification
5. Treated Water Collection
6. Scum Collection
7. Baffle
8. Communication Port
9. Sludge Recirculation
10. Scum Pumping (Optional)
11. Air Feed
12. Air Diffuser

**Fig. 5.31 : Extended Aeration Technique**

## Vermicomposting for Solid Waste

Composting of bio-degradable waste by earthworms, including human excreta, is gaining popularity. Organic waste is allowed to be decomposed by micro-organisms already present in the waste. The process can be accomplished either in presence or in absence of oxygen known as aerobic or decomposition respectively. During aerobic decomposition, organic compound gets oxidized to oxides of carbon and nitrogen and temperature of the mass rises to 70°C.

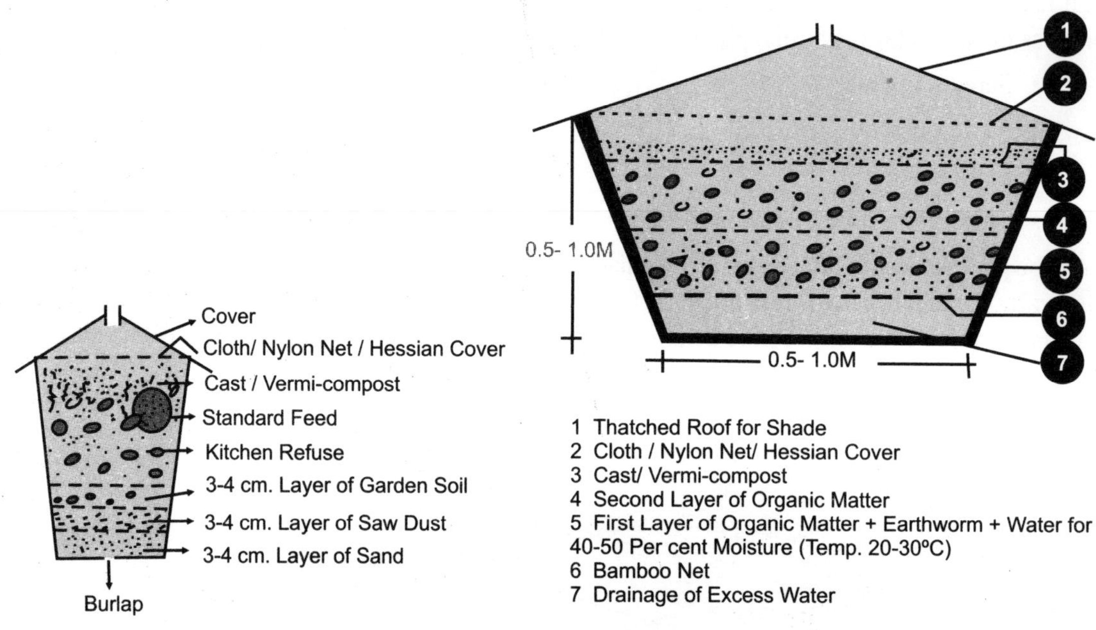


**Fig. 5.32 : Vermiculture and Vermicomposting**

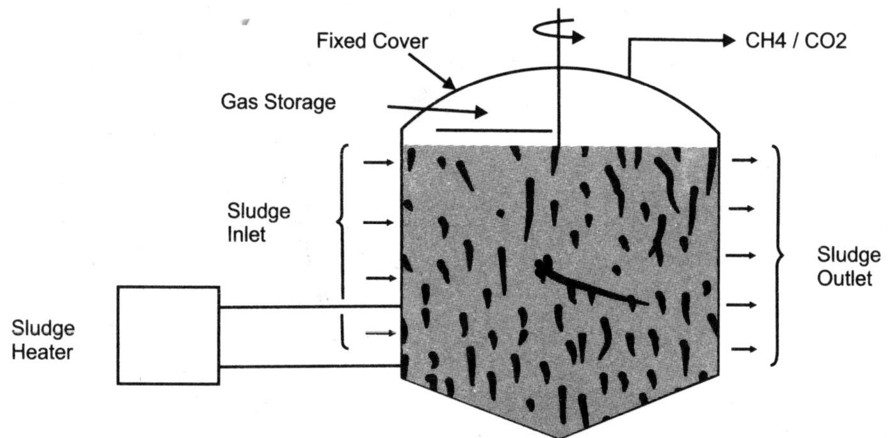


**Fig. 5.33 : Activated Sludge Technology**

The destruction of common pathogens and parasites takes place during this period. The presence of oxygen ensures elimination of foul smelling gases like hydrogen sulfide and methane. Absence of oxygen during the process generates methane in addition to other gases. The mixture of methane and carbon dioxide is known as biogas which is a useful source of energy. This process requires controlled environment and closed reactor to reduce odour problem, eliminate files and for effective collection of gas.

Vermicomposting is the process in which earthworm species are used for the conversion of organic waste into compost (Fig. 5.32). Selection of appropriate species of earthworms for vermicomposting in India is limited to a few. The best choice for vermicomposting are two species i.e. Eudrilus eugeniae and Eisenia foetida. Eudrilus eugeniae, popularly known as African Night Crawler, is found to be the best for vermicomposting. It has excellent growth and high conversion ratio.

Earthworms degrade the organic waste by both physical and chemical breakdown in their gut. The gut of an earthworm acts as a bio-reactor providing ideal conditions for temperature. PH and oxygen concentration for speedy growth of aerobic bacteria which outcompete pathogens resulting in pathogens destruction. These micro-organisms produce useful compounds like antibiotics, vitamins and plant growth hormones. Worms use about 5 to 10 per cent of the organic material for their growth and excrete the rest in the form of granular cast which is known as vermicompost. The granular loose vermicast provides oxygen rich, nutrient rich media for aerobic microbes which further promote decomposition process. About 2,000 worms are required for a volume of $1 \times 1 \times 0.5$ m. On an average, 5 kg of waste is partially digested by 1,000 worms in a day.

Chapter 6

# Praxis for Inclusive and Sustainable Development

*To forget how to dig the earth and to tend the soil is to forget ourselves.*

***—Mahatma Gandhi***

The Mahatma Gandhi National Rural Employment Guarantee Act (MG NREGA) had been in implementation since 2005-06 in Kokrajhar which is one of the twenty-three districts of Assam. Kokrajhar is the gateway to the north-eastern region of India. Both road and rail touch this district at Srirampur before they go on to other districts in Assam and the other northeast states (Fig. 6.1). Kokrajhar district is located on the north bank of the river Brahmputra that slices the state of Assam into two, identified as north and south banks. The district lies roughly between 89.46′ E to 90.38′ E longitude and 26.19′ N to 26.54′ N latitude. The district is bounded on the north by the Himalayan kingdom of Bhutan, by Dhubri district on the south, Bongaigaon district on the east and the state of West Bengal on the west. Brahmaputra flows from east to west far from the southern boundary of Kokrajhar district (Fig. 6.2). The important rivers of the district that flow from north to south are Champamati, Gaurang, Tipkai and Sonkosh. There are other rivulets like Bhur and

Laopani. All the rivers and rivulets flowing through the district have their origins in the Bhutan hills.

Kokrajhar District (Bodoland area) covers 3538 sq. km of area of which 3520 sq km is rural and forest area comprising of 1082 villages and 11 blocks. It has 1623 sq. km of area under forests, 1408 sq. km under agriculture and only 18 sq. km is urban area. District has a population of 9.3 lakh of which 8.4 lakh (1.70 lac families) are rural. During 2008-09 about Rs. 200 crore during 2009-10 about Rs. 157 crore were spent under Mahatma Gandhi National Rural Employment Guarantee Act (MG NREGA) schemes, which generated about 1.70 lakh mandays of employment.

Most of the NREGA Schemes in the District cover small works, like connecting a village by paved road, construction of culvert, construction of fishery ponds, construction of rainwater reservoir, construction of drain along a road, social forestry, horticulture, irrigation canals, etc, except a mega scheme of construction of flood protection bunds (14 km long) and deflectors (80 nos) along the river Saralbhanga costing Rs. 46 crore. (Fig. 6.7)

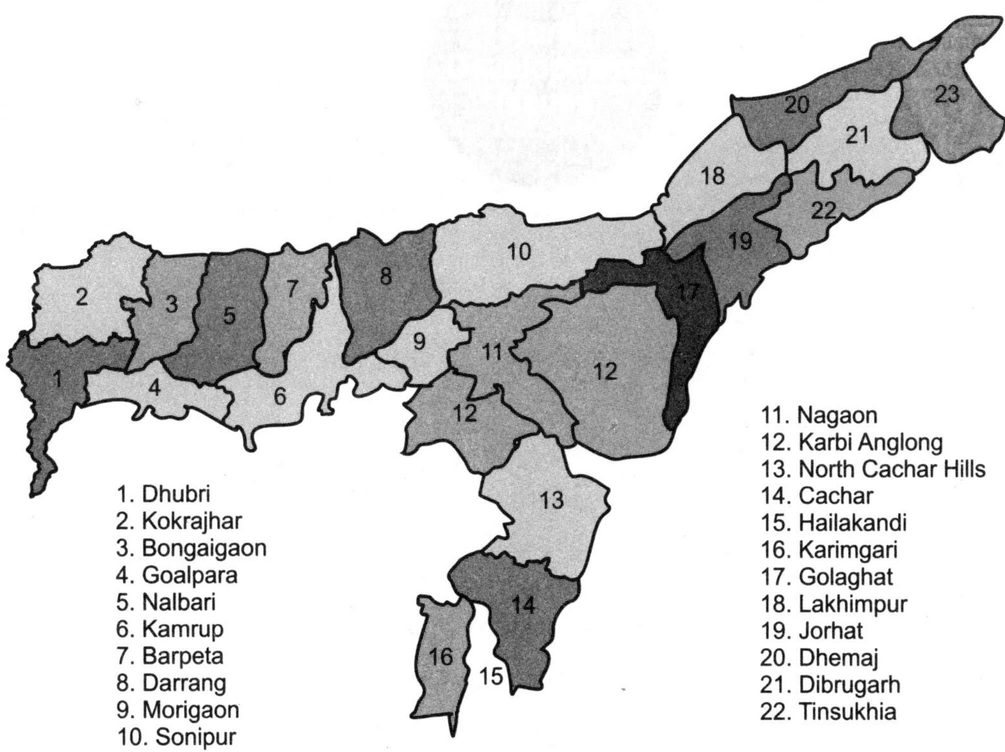


**Fig. 6.1 : Assam Districts (2001)**

The Bodoland Territorial Council is incharge of the District Administration which was established under the BTC Accord of February 2003. For development of rural areas, a hierarchy of Blocks and Village Council Development Committees (VCDC) (instead of Gram Panchayat) have been constituted each for a cluster of 6-10 villages. In Kokrajhar District 11 Development Blocks and 130 VCD exist for 1082 villages. The annual growth of economy of BTC area ranges between 5 to 7 per cent for which. 37 departments are engaged with their headquarters at Kokrajhar. An outlay of Rs. 2888.37 crore for district has been made in the State Plan for 11th Five Year Plan (2007-12) The Annual Plan for 2009-10 provided an outlay of Rs. 418 crore for BTC area.

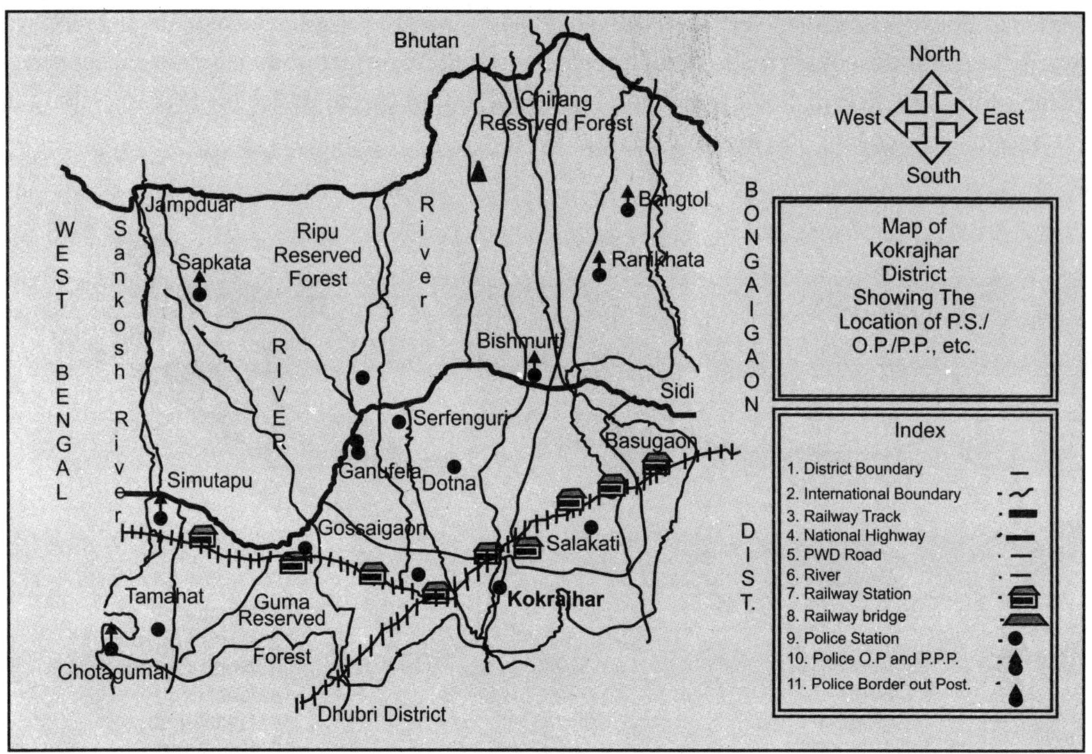


**Fig. 6.2 : Map of Kokrajhar District**

A unique feature of the MG NREGA scheme is that it is 'rights based' and not a dole or charity. The government recognizes the fundamental rights of the citizens-such as education, employment and information, which empower the poor people, leading to inclusive development. When people are given rights by legal instrument the role of cunning politician and officials diminishes who sometimes try to thrive on poverty and people's difficulties. In Kokrajhar District an estimated per family investment of Rs. 50,000 had been made during last four years, which is unprecedented and is reflected by new prosperity. There is no visible poverty-people wear good clothes and eat adequately, no beggars seen, no child labour, very few hutments, almost all children attending schools and there is a spurt in private vehicles-cycles, mobikes and even few cars in rural areas. There is no sign of distress migration to the cities from rural areas of the district.

A striking feature of MG NREGA projects has been 'value for money'. It is observed that small investments, such as a construction of a drain, retaining wall for flood protection, small culvert, retrofitting a bridge on a local stream/drains, construction of half kilometer road, where the expenditure is around Rs. 1 to 5 lakh, have given immense relief to the rural population in their day to day life.

The ownership of the job card has given a sense of pride and self respect to the rural poor, apart from a better livelihood. As per the reports about 40 to 45% of the job card holders are women. The district looks green and clean. During discussions with about 50 villagers and officials, the following were mentioned as the major challenges of MG NREGA schemes being implemented in the District (Fig. 6.3).

## Officials

Lack of overall Development Plan and Block Plans, lack of staff, lack of convergence, too much paperwork and overlapping in monitoring, lack of autonomy and defined powers, non-banking villages, notified wage (Rs. 100/-) less than market wage resulting in difficulty in getting local labour, maintaining the momentum of past three years is a major challenge for next years.

## Villagers

- Low wages and inflation
- Delay in payment of wages, expenditure and loss of 1 day in wage collection in non-banking areas.
- Corruption
- poor roads, shortages of power, sewage and sanitation
- Lack of dispensaries/healthcare facilities, doctors, veterinary hospitals, community marriage halls

- Frequent accidents and deaths of cattle on highways
- Lack of public transport
- Lack of farmers' markets, warehousing, cold storage, fish market, milk chilling and marketing facilities, etc.
- Expensive fertilizers, obsolete irrigation facilities and agricultural tools, etc.

The prevailing per day wage is Rs. 100. There are frequent complaints that the present wage is below market rate and there are delays in the payment which is mainly due to non-availability of local bank or post office. This point out towards a need to take the bank or post office to the doorstep of villages/NREGA site and proactivate the banks/post office officials to put up regular camps for making the wage payment, wherever necessary. Providing accommodation at R.G. Seva Kendra, VCDC/Block office will facilitate decentralized functioning of the bank and post offices. Lessons can be learnt from success stories, such as Rae Bareli District where business correspondents provide banking facility and NREGA payments are made at the doorstep of the villagers.

One of the issues is concerning the corruption and leakage of public funds. According to the officials most of such complaints are frivolous and stem from political/public rivalries which should not camouflage the 'success' and 'achievements'. The issue of corruption in civil works needs to be tackled first at the 'systemic' levels, for which following actions are necessary :

- The order to reduce ad hoc decision making, unintended investments and diversion of NREGA funds, the preparation of District Development Plan and Block Plans are essential.
- This should be complimented by prescribing Standard Operating Procedures and defining the roles.
- A system of checks and balances should be put in place by defining powers to approve the scheme/finances, norms and standards, specifications, issuing regular public bulletins, notices, etc.
- By using computer, internet, website, press briefings, handouts, etc. information should be shared with the public, apart from the implementation of the RTI Act.
- Define the powers, responsibilities and accountability at various levels.
- Asset management and adoption of GIS based Computerised Land Record (CLR)

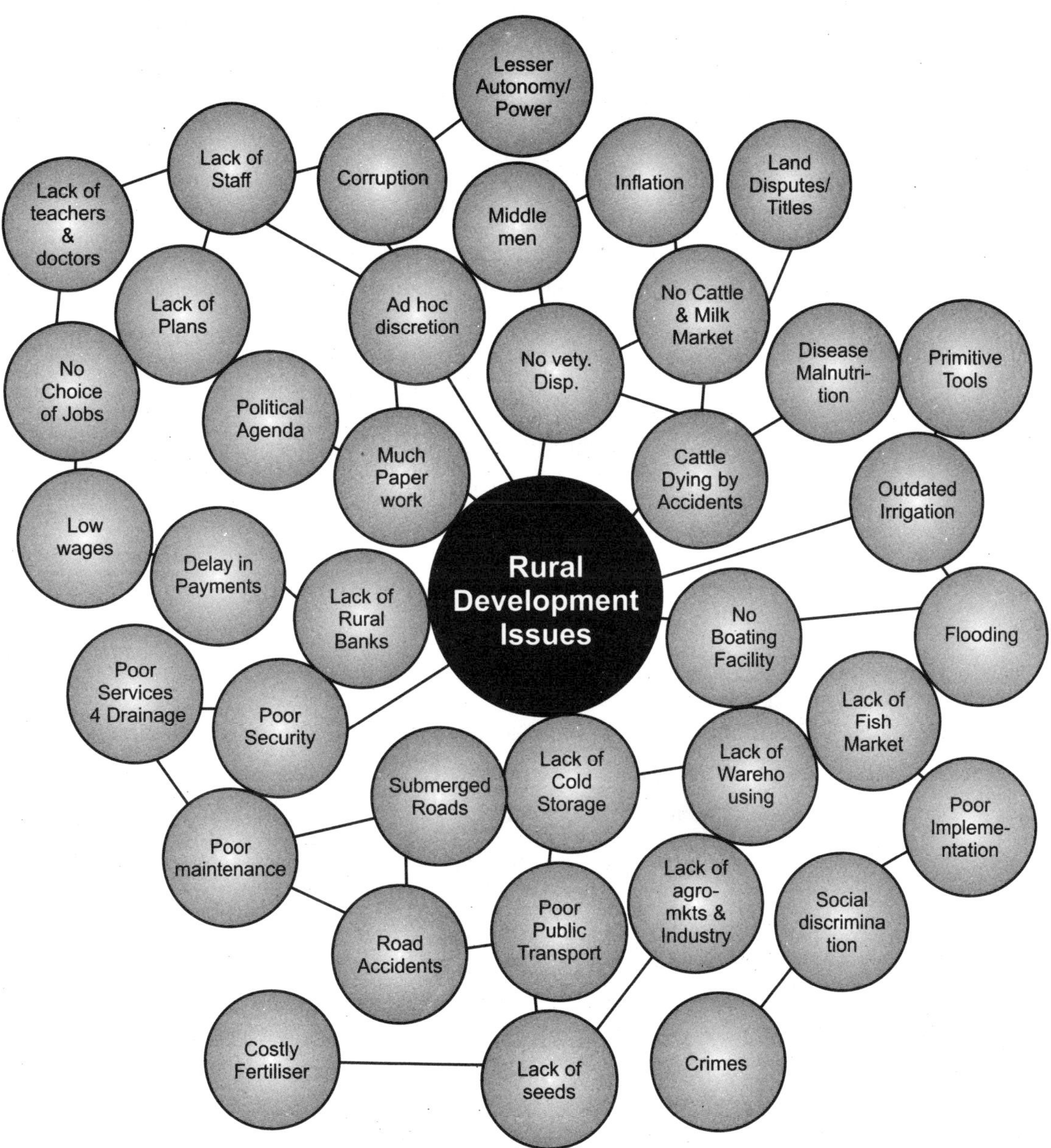


**Fig. 6.3 : Major issues and challenges of NREGA/Rural Development as learnt from 50 villagers and officials in Kokrajhar District, Assam (June 2010)**

The MG NREGA Scheme after 4 years of implementation in the Kokrajhar District should now embrace an enlarged paradigm. Moving from the traditional model of projects, programmes and financial allocations, it should combine the wider dimensions of sustainability, spatial integration and people's rights. (Fig. 6.4).

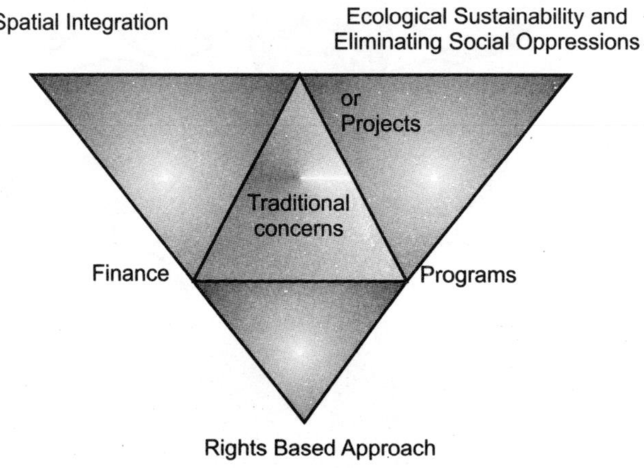


**Fig. 6.4 : New Enlarged Paradigm**

It should harmonise with the emerging aspirations of the rural folks and embrace the third generation reforms, such as transparency guarantee, self-governance, local autonomy and new technology, such as solar energy, bio-gas production, wastewater recycling, systems building, etc. (Fig. 6.5).

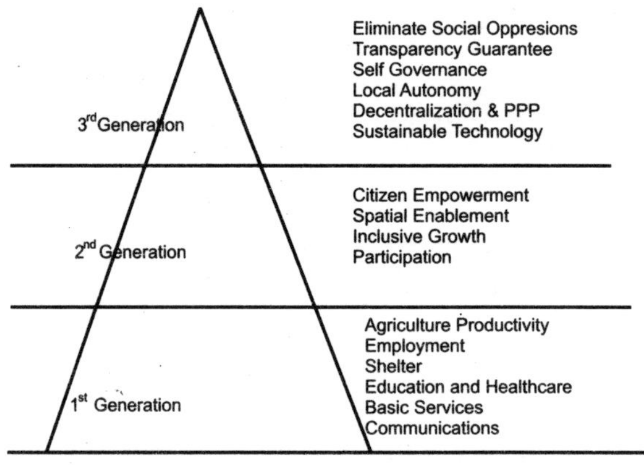


**Fig. 6.5 : Aspirations Pyramid**

The NREGA schemes can play a major role in breaking the barriers such as societal operessions, lack of spatial integration, lack of transparency and lack of convergence in the praxis of rural development (Fig. 6.6)

**Fig. 6.6 : Breaking the Barriers of Rural Development**

At present the entire NREGA and rural development are government driven and publically financed. In the long run, it is necessary to incentivise the private sector/industry to invest in Kokrajhar District, which is quite rich in natural resources, skills and manpower and provides new opportunities to the entrepreneurs. To facilitate, incentivise and to adopt a business friendly approach, it would be worthwhile to consider creating a 'Rural Employment Generation and Infrastructure Corporation', a corporate entity on the lines of REC. To start with, the Corporation could be established for NE states whereby about 50 per cent of the central government funds for rural development could be channelized for PPP mega projects under NREGA and other MORD schemes, while the remaining 50 per cent can be utilized through the state government/rural development department funds. It is time to widen the base and scope of rural employment, which involves the expansion of non-farm sector, development of Rural Business Hubs, Public-Private Partnerships and social entrepreneurship development.

Fig. 6.7 : Training of River Saral Bhanga under NREGA

Fig. 6.8 : Pride of Owning a Job Card

**Fig. 6.9 : Village Road Developed Under NREGA**

**Fig. 6.10 : Basic Information Hoarding at Titaguri, Kokrajhar Development Block**

## INNOVATIVE WAGE PAYMENT UNDER NREGA

**BOX**

Kalavati, a widow and NREGA labourer, is learning the joys of banking. "Earlier, I had to leave my children alone at home and spend nearly Rs. 50 to Rs. 60 a day to get my money from the bank and even stand in long queues. But now, I can do that at home. Today, I withdrew Rs. 500 from the bank but since I had managed to save Rs. 50, I also deposited it in my account," says Kalavati.

In Rai Bareli district, the business correspondent scheme is managed by Integra Microsystems Pvt. Limited. Integra not only appoints business correspondents, but also provides the biometric machines and the smart cards. The battery-operated machine runs for four hours on a single charge and Integra supplies the batteries and the paper for the receipts. Correspondents are paid on commission basis, depending on the transactions they carry out every month.

Ashish Kumar Verma of Integra says unemployed graduates from the villages were chosen to be business correspondents. "We asked the villagers to give us options and then we chose the business correspondents. Since the villagers recognize the correspondents and have a level of trust, it is easier for them to handle the work."

The gram pradhans too are happy with the system. "One of the allegations against gram pradhans is that we withdqaw NREGA money from others accounts. But now, since the machine can only identify the customer's finger impression, there is no charge of forgery. And now, no one is complaining. In fact, both my wife ad I handle our accounts through this system." Says Kamlesh Kumar Yadav, gram pradhan of Delha.

Bank of Baroda GM (UP and Uttarakhand), Subhash C. Ahuja, calls this system another step to bring banking services closer to the rural masses. "As per the guidelines of the Reserve Bank of India, banks have to take steps to make rural banking easier. Since the banks can not open their branches in every village, the rural business correspondents are a good step". The next step, he says, is to "introduce mobile banking where vans will go door to door, and also a shoppers' debit card in villages."

**Source:** The Indian Express, 30 May 2010

Fig. 6.11 : A Flood Protection Bund

Fig. 6.12 : Village Road Developed Under NREGA.

## Widening Rural Employment Spectrum

All over India, the annual growth of non-farm rural employment is continuously exceeding the average annual growth rate of work force, (Table 6.1). The average annual growth in employment for the years 1998-2005 was 2.5 per cent as compared to the rate of 1.7 per cent between 1990 and 1998. It is important to continue with the thrust on rural employment, through the wide spectrum of employment programmes devised by the central government and also to increase the value added component of non-farm rural enterprises so as to make them sustainable. The expansion of the non-farm sector is essential to absorb the surplus labour. It should maintain a balance and supplement the growth of agricultural incomes. Rural enterprises can, become both an engine of growth as well as a major contributor to the reduction of rural poverty. Commercialization of agriculture could catalyse growth by diversifying into dairying, animal husbandry, fisheries, floriculture, horticulture and other areas. This would spur the growth of agro-processing industries in rural areas to meet domestic as well as export demand. Contract farming facilitates the integration of small farms with agro-processing companies, which extend technical expertise and financial support to the farmers to grow high value crops.

The concept of Rural Business Hubs (RBH), Agro-Service centre, Amenity Village and PURA for a cluster of villages aim at diversification of rural incomes and value addition of farm production through off-farm rural enterprises. The need is to realise the potential of rights' and enablement of the rural populatin in development praxis. The widening of the rural employment base and development need a series of intertwined, coordinated actions, particularly in the following areas :

- Financial and Institutional Enablement,
- Spatial Enablement,
- Social Enablement,
- Technology Enablement.

**Table 6.1 : Growth of Employment in Rural Enterprises**

| State/Union Territories | Annual growth Rate in non-farm Rural employment | Annual growth rate of rural workforce |
|---|---|---|
| Andhra Pradesh | 5.37 | 3.05 |
| Arunachal Pradesh | 3.65 | 3.07 |
| Assam | 6.62 | 2.08 |
| Bihar | 4.50 | 1.79 |
| Chhattisgarh | 3.24 | 3.82 |
| Goa | 1.75 | 2.99 |
| Gujarat | 3.11 | 1.27 |
| Haryana | 9.68 | 8.80 |

...(*Contd.*)

| State/Union Territories | Annual growth Rate in non-farm Rural employment | Annual growth rate of rural workforce |
|---|---|---|
| Himachal Pradesh | 2.73 | 2.54 |
| Jammu and Kashmir | 7.64 | 7.65 |
| Jharkhand | 3.44 | 0.66 |
| Karnataka | 4.78 | 2.69 |
| Kerala | 7.93 | 4.21 |
| Madhya Pradesh | 1.74 | 1.69 |
| Maharashtra | 4.95 | 3.29 |
| Manipur | 4.46 | 3.24 |
| Meghalaya | 6.48 | 5.05 |
| Mizoram | 8.40 | 4.96 |
| Nagaland | 6.05 | 1.95 |
| Orissa | 3.02 | 2.54 |
| Punjab | 7.34 | 5.19 |
| Rajasthan | 4.15 | 3.44 |
| Sikkim | 8.39 | 6.41 |
| Tamil Nadu | 9.66 | 5.43 |
| Tripura | 9.85 | 5.84 |
| Uttar Pradesh | 7.07 | 4.98 |
| Uttaranchal | 7.72 | 7.06 |
| West Bengal | 4.77 | 1.70 |
| Andaman and Nicobar Islands | -6.16 | -3.90 |
| Chandigarh | 15.57 | 12.11 |
| Dadra and Nagar Haveli | 8.65 | 7.56 |
| Daman and Diu | 13.64 | 15.32 |
| Delhi | -0.91 | -2.26 |
| Lakshadweep | 1.70 | 3.53 |
| Pondicherry | 3.37 | 3.83 |
| India | 5.53 | 3.33 |

**Source:** Fifth Economic Census (2005).

## Financial and Institutional Enablement

The basic idea of financial and institutional enablement is to facilitate the rural poor and farmers towards commercial and employment opportunities by diversifying their activities, obtaining a fair wage/price and development of self-managed markets, business hubs and Service Centres. The concept of Rural Business Hub is based on the object of the transaction and transformation of rural areas, and seeks to reduce the Urban-Rural divide by bringing prosperity. It acts as a platform to:

- Procure crop surplus,
- Retail goods and services,
- Capacity-building through PPP,
- CSR initiatives

The Key Result Areas would be the following :

- Improve dairy and farm productivity through knowledge dissemination transfer of technology and better infrastructure, roads, communications, irrigation, water, transport, drainage, power, fuel, etc.
- Empowering the rural population with banking facility, micro-loans, etc.
- Provide essential services like health, education, women and childcare, entertainment, sports facilities, etc.
- Capacity building to create livelihoods and skilled jobs

Rural Business Hub (RHB) could be developed as 'Rurban growth centre' for a cluster of villages. These could be identified in the District Development Plan on Hub and Spoke model. Each RBH is supported by spokes around it. While an RBH may be located in the vicinity of the existing mandi, its spokes may be situated inside or around the villages. A spoke would cater to a radius of 5 km around it.

The Rural Business Hub and Services Centre provide a systemic network of infrastructure utilities, facilities and services for a cluster of villages, which include warehousing, markets, milk chilling centre, cold storage, food processing industry, fuel station, entertainment, sports and youth complex, banks, IT centre, educational, and healthcare facilities, etc. This can be developed in a public-private and community partnership mode where the role of the government is to leverage the entrepreneurship by providing land and basic infrastructure (roads, water, power, etc).

A major requirement of financial enablement is the rural infrastructure and its financing. The Government of India has several schemes of which Rural Infrastructure Development Fund is the lead scheme.

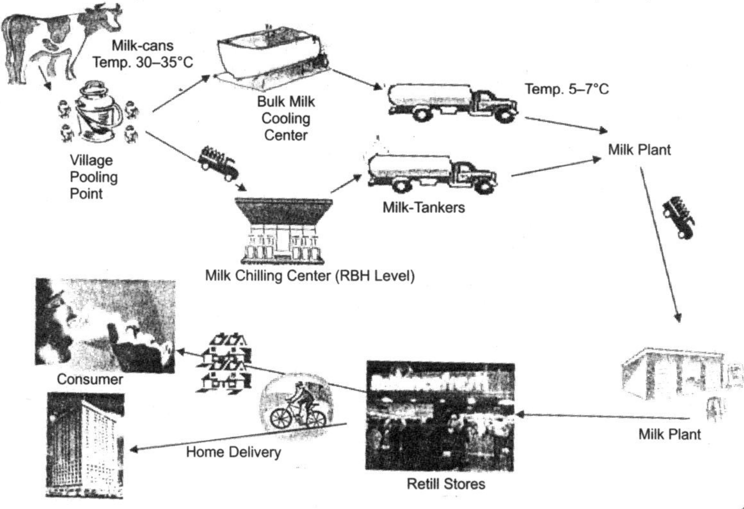


**Fig. 6.13 : Dairy Business Value Chain**

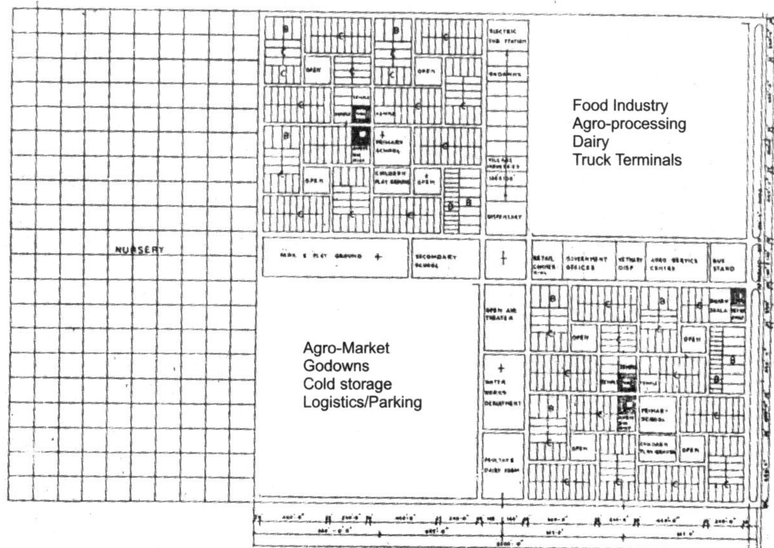


**Fig. 6.14 : Development Plan for Amenity Village (Agro Service Centre)**

| Land use Analysis | Area in Acres | Precentage |
|---|---|---|
| Residential | 132.08 | 52.03 |
| Commercial | 7.51 | 2.86 |
| Offices/IT centre | 2.31 | 0.90 |
| Village Industries/Godowns | 6.43 | 2.57 |
| Community Facilities/Service Centre | 30.50 | 1208 |
| Parks & Open Space | 25.00 | 10.00 |
| Roads/Truck Terminal/Bus Stand | 46.17 | 10.68 |
| **Total** | **250.00** | **100.00** |

## Rural Infrastructure Development Fund

The GOI in 1995-96 established the Rural Infrastructure Development Fund (RIDF) which was set up within NABARD by way of deposits from Scheduled Commercial Banks operating in India, to the extent of shortfall in their agricultural lending subject to a maximum of 1.5 per cent of the Net Bank Credit. The scheme has been continued with substantial allocations in the successive Union Budgets and NABARD has partnered various State Governments in the creation of rural infrastructure. Initially, the mandate under the Fund was to support projects in the irrigation sector where substantial investments had been made but which could not be completed owning to resource constraints of the State Governments. Over the years, the coverage under RIDF has been made more broad based in each tranche and at present a wide range of 31 sectors under RIDF XII are being financed.

**Table 6.2 : Eligible Activities under RIDF XII**

1. Rural Roads;
2. Rural Bridges;
3. Minor Irrigation Projects/Micro Irrigation;
4. Soil Conservation;
5. Flood Protection;
6. Watershed Development/Reclamation of waterlogged areas;
7. Drainage;
8. Forest Development;
9. Market Yard/Godown, Apna Mandi, rural haats and other marketing infrastructure;
10. Cold storage, Public or Joint sector cold storage at various exit points;
11. Seed/Agriculture/Horticulture Farms;
12. Plantation and Horticulture;
13. Grading and certifying mechanisms such as testing and certifying laboratories, etc;
14. Community irrigation wells for the village;
15. Fishing harbour/jetties;
16. Riverine Fisheries;
17. Animal Husbandry;
18. Modern Abattoir;
19. Medium Irrigation Projects;
20. Mini Hydel Projects;

21. Drinking Water;
22. Infrastructure for Rural Education Institutions;
23. Public Health Institutions, including mobile health clinics;
24. Construction of toilet blocks in existing schools, specially for girl students;
25. 'Pay & Use toilets in rural areas;
26. Major Irrigation Project (only those projects already sanctioned and under execution);
27. Village Knowledge Centres;
28. Desalination plants in coastal areas;
29. Small Hydel Projects (upto 10 MW);
30. Infrastructure for Information Technology in rural areas; and
31. Construction of Anganwadi Centres.

The annual allocation of funds has gradually increased every year from Rs. 2000 crore in 1995-6 (RIDF I) to Rs. 10,000 crore for 2006-7 (RIDF XII). The aggregate allocations have reached the level of Rs. 60,000 crore. Further, a separate window under RIDF has been created with a corpus of Rs. 4000 crore for partly funding the rural road and bridges component of the Bharat Nirman Programme.

## Spatial Enablement

The development often suffers, as it ignores the spatial dimension and availability of land and lack of land information data often leads to expropriation of rural lands and perpetuating the 'Jamindari' traditions. Sound land governance is the key to achieve sustainable rural/regional development. Land governance is about the policies, processes and institutions by which land, property and natural resources are managed. This includes decisions on access to land, land rights, land use and land development. Land governance and spatial enablement are basically about determining and implementing sustainable land policies. Spatial enablement is the process to leverage employment generation, rural development and marketing. In India this had always been an important tool to trigger development by way of land ownership rights, land tenure, land markets, land taxation, land-use control, land development and management. Land administration systems therefore need high-level political support and recognition. Right to land also includes the right of use. This right may be limited through public land use regulations and restrictions, sectoral land use provisions, and also various kind of private land use regulations, such as easements, covenants, etc. Many land use rights are therefore in fact restrictions that control the possible future use of the land. Land use planning and restrictions are becoming increasingly important as means to ensure effective management of land, provide infrastructure and services, protect and improve the urban and rural environment, prevent pollution, and pursue sustainable development. Planning and regulation of land activities cross-cut tenures and the land rights they support. In the rural areas, many schemes do not take off due to lack of land. Right from village roads, agriculture produce markets to warehousing, bus terminal, rural business hub, parks, schools, playgrounds, community halls, weekly markets, etc. land is a basic requirement. Often the government/Village Panchayat/Gaon Sabha lands get encroached upon. The traditional system of 'Jamindari' (land lords) continues to prevail and control most of the land holdings that excludes the poor, low caste, farm labour from property ownership. The absence of computerized land records, delays in transfer and lack of transparency in rural land market add to spatial disablement.

## Land Use Conversions

A curse for the Indian villages had been the custom of Jamindari, that is the unscruplous land owner who exploited the farmers and labour employed on the land. The system was abolished after the independence of the country (1947) and by the Constitution of India (1950). However, during the last decades, a new form of Jamindari has emerged, much to the detriment of the principles of equitable and inclusive growth. This is in the form of widespread government sponsored land use conversions which has brought in the outside developers and others in the garb of economic development, employment generation and modernization of rural areas. As result today the private real estate and infrastructure developers, information and communication technology (ICT) companies, SEZ developers, multinational, etc. are holding the prime rural greenfields.

With increasing urbanization together with economic development the rural lands are undergoing rapid transformation. The governments have encouraged the private sector to take up various schemes, such as residential and industrial township development, special economic zone (SEZ), Infotech/Software Technology Parks, Food Parks, Hi-tech townships, Railways and Highways corridor development, etc. There is a booming real estate market, which is taking up urbanization of rural areas. The state government and local authorities have framed their own policies and regulations for land use conversion of rural lands. Apart from formal land use conversion, the informal markets are also thriving in this business.

The State Government of Uttar Pradesh has a policy to promote private sector participation in developing hi-tech townships in and around large cities of State, viz. Kanpur, Lucknow, Varanasi,

Agra, Ghaziabad, Meerut and other cities which have high growth potential. The development of Hi-tech township involves private developers to assemble a land area of 1500 acres or more and minimum investment of Rs. 750 crores with a project period of 5 years. Development of Hi-tech townships in the private sector is intended to achieve economic development and bring in private investments. Similar township schemes, Special Economic Zones (SEZ), etc. are being promoted by almost every state government.

In Haryana the Haryana Urban Development Authority (HUDA) issues licenses and allows the acquisition of land by the private developers from the farmers directly at negotiated market prices. The private colonizer takes up the development of area, which is often rural, by paying conversion charges. In Gujarat large scale rural lands, especially along highways and large cities are converted into townships, under the 'Town Planning Scheme'. This also covers regularisation and land the conversion. Average size of the scheme varies between 22 Ha to 400 ha. The model is most attractive to the property dealers/real estate developers who get back 54% or more of the land. An equal portion of land is deducted from every agricultural plot as contribution of land for physical and social infrastructure, and to raise resources. Remaining land is reconstituted in regular shaped plots with roads and services.

The Guided Urban Development Model of Chennai Metropolitan Development Authority (CMDA) encourages the participation of private sector on a minimum area of 4 hectares located outside the Chennai urban area, and the use of agricultural land is changed to urban activity.

In Rajasthan, ad hoc conversion of use of agricultural land for urban activities is allowed legally. To encourage private sector investments and Foreign Direct Investment (FDI) in real estate sector the Government of Rajasthan issued policy guidelines in January 2002, which were revised in August 2005 under section 297 of the Rajasthan Municipal Act, 1959, section 90 of the Jaipur Development Authority Act, 1982, section 60 of the Rajasthan Housing Board Act, 1970 and rule 31 of the Rajasthan Urban Improvement (Disposal of Urban Lands) Rules, 1974. These provide for approval of Township Schemes by Private Developers in minimum area of 100 acres in Jaipur, 50 acres in other Divisional Headquarters and 25 acres in other municipal towns. The local authority helps in procurement and consolidation of lands. Chunks of lands available with the government/local authorities can be transferred for development under the joint venture. The developer is encouraged to come up with a scheme and the local authority facilitates land consolidation in cases where the developer owns substantial land parcel. Under Section 90B of Land Revenue Act the conversion of land use is processed against the payment of the conversion charges. From Agriculture to residential and Instititutional use the charges vary from Rs. 60 to Rs. 100 per sq m, while for commercial use, it varies from Rs. 240 to Rs. 400 per sq m. The charges for external development are calculated on the basis of actuals which include construction of roads, drainage, sewerage, water supply and power, etc. An F.D.I. project in real estate/housing is approved as per the Ministry of Commerce & Industry G.O.I. Circular No. 5 (6) 2000 FC dated 03.03.2005, land use conversion is allowed and conversion charges are levied.

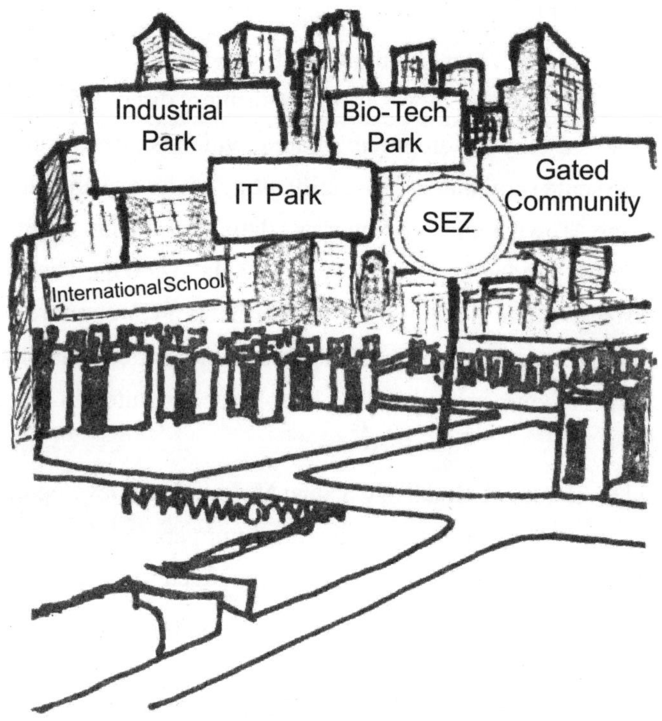


**Fig. 6.15 : The Global Village or new colonialisation, in the villages around a metropolis or along highways-agricultural lands are often converted into real estate high end projects**

Land use conversion of rural lands through revenue/town planning acts or other state acts has given tremendous power to local politicians and revenue officials, who tend to form a nexus with the developers in land transactions-both in formal/official way, as well as in the informal ways. There is a huge underground land market operating in the rural areas, usually in proximity to rail-heads, highways and large cities. Someone remarked that this is the real PURA, that is, 'Privatisation and Urbanization of Rural Areas'. The gram pradhan, councilor and other local leaders have discovered their powerful position in the process of informal or formal land use conversions. They feel that it is no more necessary to indulge in the traditional ways of making money-like working as contractors, bus owners, transporters and material suppliers, fabricating muster rolls, taking cuts from the payments and so on.

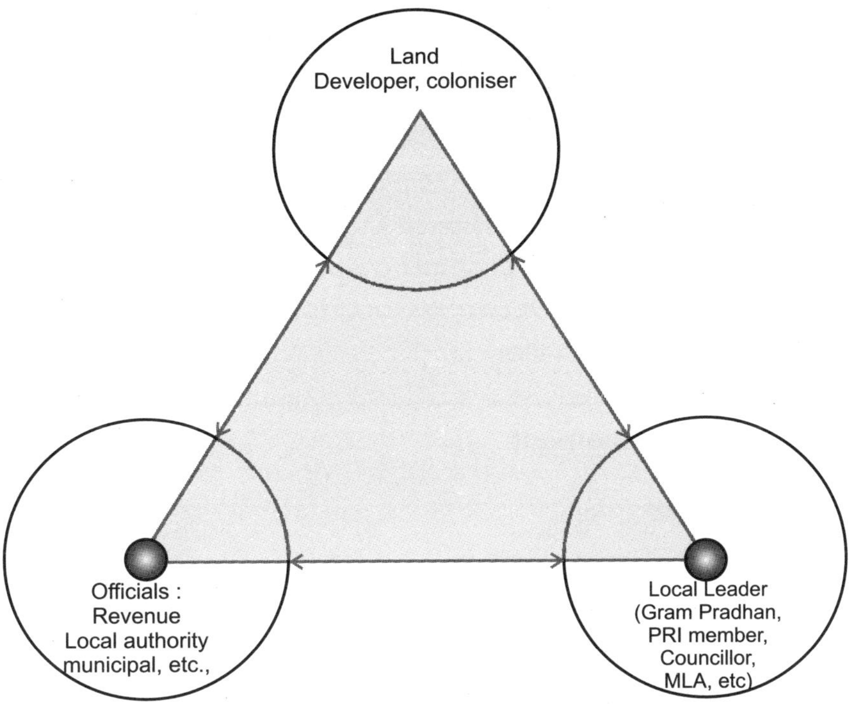


**Fig. 6.16 : Rural Land Conversion Nexus**

According to Peruvian activist and economist, Hernando de Soto, people are poor because they usually lack formal title to the little property that they own. Without a legal right they cannot use their property as collateral. They cannot go to the bank and get a loan in order to start business. Their potential is locked up in “dead capital”. De Soto calculates that the dead capital locked in unititled assets held by the world’s poor is around $9.3 trillion. Hernando de Soto observes in his book, The Other Path, the most businesses in Peru lacked titles, and it took them 289 days working full time plus Rs. 55,400 in bribes and expenses to get all the approvals they needed from 11 deaprtments. To build housing, it takes about seven years plus, Rs. one lakh per person to get all the bureaucratic clearances. To get a pushcart licence to sell fruit on the street in Lima took 43 days plus Rs. 26,550. This goes against the basic constitutional and human right to live and work.

In the last two decades, over 90 per cent of India’s new jobs have been created in the unorganized sector. It generates about 60 per cent of the country’s GDP and accounts for two-thirds of total savings. The term informal sector’ is taken to represent low productivity activities. The ILO report refers to the following set of critera in characterizing the informal sector: (*i*) condition of free entry into the product market; (*ii*) dependence on traditional resources; (*iii*) family ownership of enterprises;

(*iv*) small-scale of operation; (*v*) adoption of labour intensive technology; (*vi*) skills acquired outside the formal school system; and (*vii*) unregulated and competitive markets.

Spatial enablement is necessary to boost rural employment and entry of the informal sector in the formal markets. It enables the change management in terms of the development of organized rural industry, warehousing, agriculture market, dairy, transport, provision of social, healthcare and education infrastructure, development of transport and circulation networks, provision of better utilities and services, etc. The process of spatial enablement is contingent upon institutional/organizational set up, technology (GIS SDI, computerisation of land records/CLR), and the participation of the people, including the private sector.

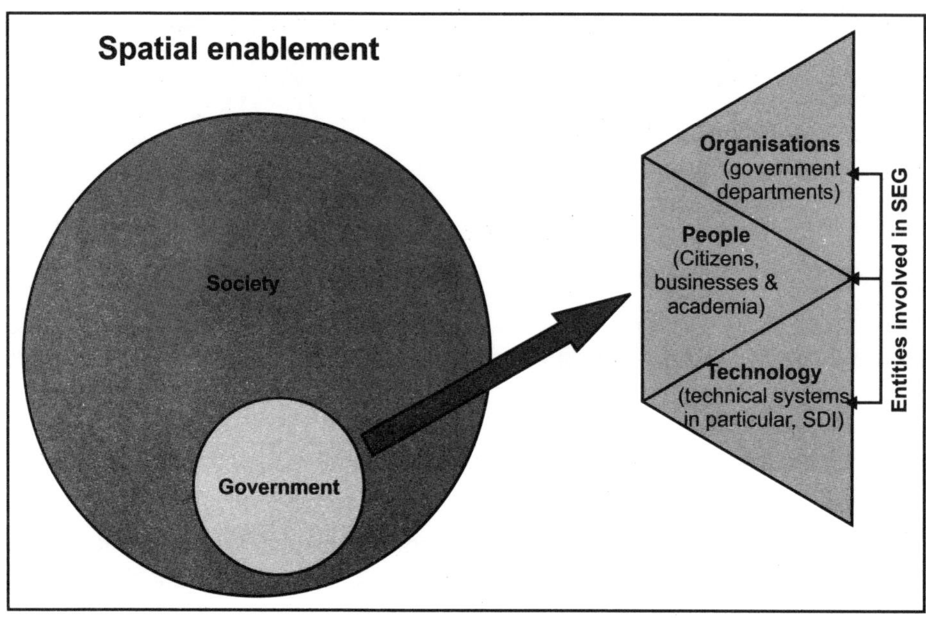


**Fig. 6.17 : Spatial Enablement is a synergy of government and society through the entities of organization, people and technology**

## Social Enablement

Social enablement means access of the rural poor to their own cultures, religions, land, resources, and traditional industries. A social enterprise is a business with primarily social objectives whose surpluses are reinvested for that purpose rather than being driven by the need to maximize profit for shareholders and owners. The main characteristics of social enterprise are:

*Trading*—they have to be viable business through trading activity

*Social Purpose*—they have defined social purpose such as job creation, training and/or the provision of local services and goods

*Social Ownership*—they are owned and run by the communities, especially the working labour class. Profits are distributed either by profit sharing to their members or used for the benefit of the community. The examples include the following:

- Employees owned business, such as village shop, marriage hall, dispensary, maternity centre, etc.
- Credit Unions, micro-banking
- Co-operatives of farmers, workers, fruit and vegetable growers, agro-food producers, etc.
- Development Trusts
- Community Businesses/Contracting (e.g., tubewell, sanitation, water supply, etc.)
- Social Firms
- Intermediate labour market
- Trading arms of charities

*Employee-owned businesses* range from the small, niche 'lifestyle' co-operatives to medium-sized or large social enterprises that combine social goals with strong economic performance. The common feature of all successful employee owned business is an ownership culture.

*Credit Unions* are financial co-operatives established to help people save and borrow money. Members of a Credit Union save in a common fund.

*Co-operatives* include ratailing, banking, insurance, travel and funeral services. These also include housing co-operatives, care co-operatives, workers' co-operatives and new generation agriculture co-operatives.

*Development Trusts* operate as umbrella organizations under which different activities take place. Their boards include representatives of key stakeholders, e.g. local community representatives, local business people, and representatives of community organizations.

*Community Business* are trading organizations owned and controlled by the local community, which aim to be a focus for local development and create self-supporting jobs for local people.

*Social Firms* are business created for the employment of people with a disability or other disadvantaged in the labour market. It is a business which uses its market-oriented production of goods and services to pursue its social mission.

*Intermediate Labour Market Projects (ILM) projects* provide training and work experience for the long-term unemployed. Some ILMs are independent companies, others are projects incorporated into the structure of other organizations, such as Development Trusts. The aim is to assist the long-term unemployed to re-enter the labour market. The heart of an ILM is the provision of paid work together with high quality training, human resource development and active job seeking.

*Community Development Finance Initiatives (CDFIs)* lend money to those who are unable to access mainstream finance and often concentrate on lending to organizations that are enterprise oriented and aim to create jobs. They are independent financial institutions with funding for the loans coming from a variety of sources. These also include micro-savings and micro-credits through micro-banking.

Social enterprises can meet many social and economic challenges across a range of sectors for the economically disadvantaged sections:

- For entrepreneurs it offers an innovative and dynamic way to think about creating and running socially driven businesses.
- For the voluntary sector it enables some financial autonomy through the introduction of income generating activities,
- For the public sector it provides a way of improving service quality which involves employees, service users and the wider community.
- For the private sector it presents an opportunity to deliver a corporate social responsibility strategy and to engage in socially responsible investment activity.
- Social enterprises help in creating job opportunities in economically deprived areas, generating local wealth and empowering local people.

People generally identify social entrepreneurship with non-profit business. Many social enterprises that are well known are not really known for their income strategies. In fact, these social entrepreneurs are masterful at attracting philanthropic donations. What makes them entrepreneurial is that each of them has pioneered creative ways of addressing social problems and marshaled the resources to support their work. Some follow the view that social entrepreneurship is about innovation and impact, not income. Good examples of social entrepreurship among the rural poor are found all over India, while Gujarat had been a leading State. What is required is to institutionalize such efforts and provide leveraging supports by the government and corporate sector. Many of the government schemes can promote local community contracting and social enablement by way of certain incentives and priorities in the rural areas.

## Technology Enablement

Technology and innovation are the powerful tools to catalyse process development that add value to the produce from primary agriculture and by-products from agro-industry. Innovative applications of technology to farm produce can enhance income from agriculture by 2 to 3 folds. A good part of this share can come by manufacturing high value products from surplus produce, agro industry by products and agri-waste. Examples include high value oil from rice bran, protein from cotton seeds, chemicals and cellulos fibres from biomass, bioactive molecules from peels and processing industry by-products. With the information and communications Technology (ICT), the villages are no more the islands of deprivation and backwardness. The ICT is being employed to bring state of the art technology, services and participatory governance of the rural areas. This is a powerful tool of rural transformation and in bridging the rural-urban divide. New technology in necessary for sustainable development in all the fields, such as agriculture, industry, construction, energy, transport, infrastructure services, pollution control, healthcare, etc. Sustainable development envisages socially equitable growth and supports economic progress. The issues include:

- the costs and environmental impact of current patterns of transport, industry, agriculture, etc.
- the future of distressed areas excluded from the economy at large.
- the character and potential for sustainable rural development.
- the future of the village in the context of globalization of economic activity.

Ecological sustainability demands reducing the impacts of industrial/agriculture production and consumption on the integrity and health of the region and its carrying capacity. This needs a long-term consideration between the development objectivies, dynamics of environmental resources and the demands exerted over them. Reducing the greenhouse gas and carbon emissions and climate impact are becoming crucial issues along with increasing energy-efficiency, promoting renewables and reducing the need to travel. India's present per capita annual carbon emission is around 1.2 tonnes. Two decades from now, India's per capita GHG carbon emissions will be around 2.8 tonnes, which would still be well below the 2005 global average of 4.3 tonnes. Nevertheless, India has to play its part in contributing to the global effort to combat climate change. India has already drawn up a National Action Plan on Climate Change. There are eight national missions, viz., Jawaharalal Nehru National Mission for Sustaining the Himalayan Ecosystem, National Mission for a Green India, National Mission for Sustainable Agriculture, National Mission on Strategic Knowledge of Climate Change, NM on Enhanced Energy Efficiency, N M on Sustainable Habitat and NM on water. Planning Commission has constituted an Expert Group to recommend how India could move towards a low carbon economy to combat climate change threats.

The relationship between development and carban emissions/climate change should be the strating point of rural planning and governance. This requires the adoption of the following principles:

- Organic methods of farming, production and seeds, fertlisers and food processing.
- Adopt micro-irrigation, drip irrigation, pollution abatement of water bodies/rivers, etc., reduce water consumption by cropping pattern.
- Reduce the need for travel and consumption of fossil fuels,
- Conservre water and natural resources, adopt zero-runoff drainage, porous paving and rainwater harvesting.
- Promote zero-pollutting industry,
- Reduce the demand for energy, promote development of renewable energy sources
- Provide toilets, sanitation, and solid waste management to every village/house.
- Recycle wastes, waste-water, reduce packaging and use of paper.
- Develop green buildings, use environment friendy recycled building materials, design passive climate compatible buildings.
- Use intelligent/bionic controls for services, lighting, services maintenance, etc. and adopt clean development mechanism (CDM).
- Adopt Environment Impact Assessment (EIA)
- Reduce leakages, transmission losses and wastages in energy, water and other infrastructure delivery.
- Upgrade technology, adopt computerisation, MIS, e-governance, etc.
- Decentralise and localize rural development, use micro-systems at community and household level.
- Adopt circular metabolism that demands recycling of wastes and creates the loops that minimize waste generation.

**Fig. 6.18 : The indiscriminate development of rural areas in urban fringes for industries and power plants have led to heavy pollution of land, water and air.**

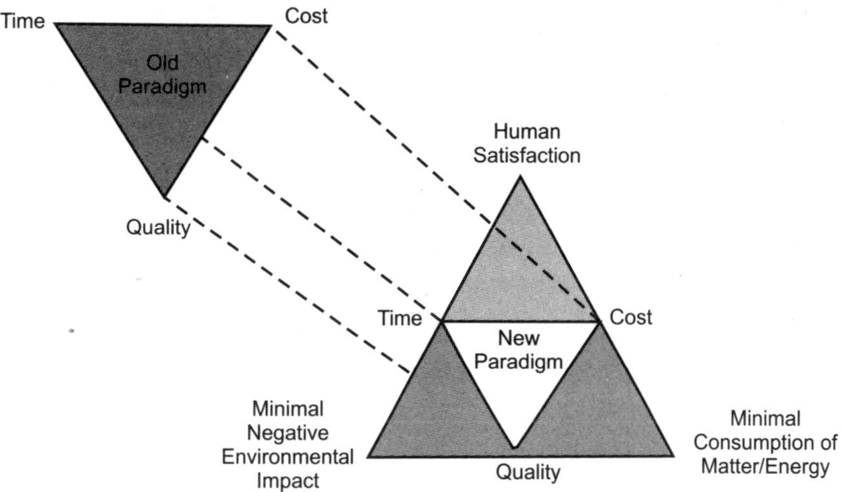


**Fig. 6.19 : Old and New Paradigms–the new paradigm enlarges the scope of development to environment impact, energy and resources efficiency and human satisfaction.**

## Renewable Sources of Energy

Wind, earth and water are the primary energy sources of the world. It is the solar energy, conserved through billions of years that we are now enjoying as fossil fuels. The energy crisis of the 1970s jolted the world into greater awareness for alternative energy developments. We have to realize that it is the solar energy that is the only source of our past and future energy, it is the sun that converts water into water vapours and makes it back on the land surface. It is this fall-back on the photosynthetic conversion of the solar energy that enables the vegetation to grow and survive on the earth surface. It is again the sun that helps to generate oxygen and enables the survival of the entire life in this world.

**Table 6.3 : Renewable Energy Sources Potential**

| Source/Technology | Unit | Potential/Availability |
|---|---|---|
| Bio-Gas Plant | Million | 12 |
| Bio-mass based Power | MW | 19,500 |
| Efficient wood stoves | Million | 120 |
| Solar energy | MW | 20 |
| Small hydro plant | MW | 15,000 |
| Wind enegy | MW | 45,000 |
| Energy recovery from waste | MW | 1,700 |

**Source:** Planning Commission.

The harnessing of renewable energy aims not only increasing energy generation, but also helping restore a pollution-free environment. It is estimated that India has a potential of generating more than 1,00,000 MW from non-conventional sources of energy. The concept of Renewable Energy Vision 2010 targets for an installed renewable energy capacity of 3000 MW and disbursement of Rs. 13880 crores in the form of financial assistance. The potential of Renewable Energy Resources is shown in Table 6.3. The estimates of potential contribution of renewable energy sources by 2030 towards energy needs are listed below :

**Table 6.4 : Potential contribution of Renewable Energy Options**

| Energy Source | Potential Contribution |
|---|---|
| Solar water heaters | Could provide half the world's hot water |
| Solar cells | Could supply 10% of grid electricity by 2030 |
| Solar power plants | Can provide 7,000 gigawatts of solar generating capacity |
| Wind power | Could provide 20 percent of world's electricity |
| Biomass | One billion tons could be available for energy conversion by 2030, replacing one-third of current oil use |
| Geothermal heat | Could provide 100 gigawatts of generating capacity |
| Wave and ocean thermal energy | Long-run contribution could be of same magnitude as current world energy use |

In the Indian context, energy efficiency and alternative energy sources offer the biggest scope of cutting carbon emissions. The two missions, Solar Mission and Enhanced Energy Efficiency Mission, are therefore timely. Some of the energy options which are relevant for rural development are given below.

## Integrated/Roof-top Photovoltaic Systems

- SPV modules form part of building material in BiPV systems
- Used for roof construction, wall paneling or replacement of glass windows
- Available with leak proof designs and offer good acoustic/thermal insulation
- System custom designed for site requirement can be installed on roof
- Works as independent unit, can be useful in areas having long power cuts/high electricity tariffs
- Meets total power requirement of building, excess exported to the grid.

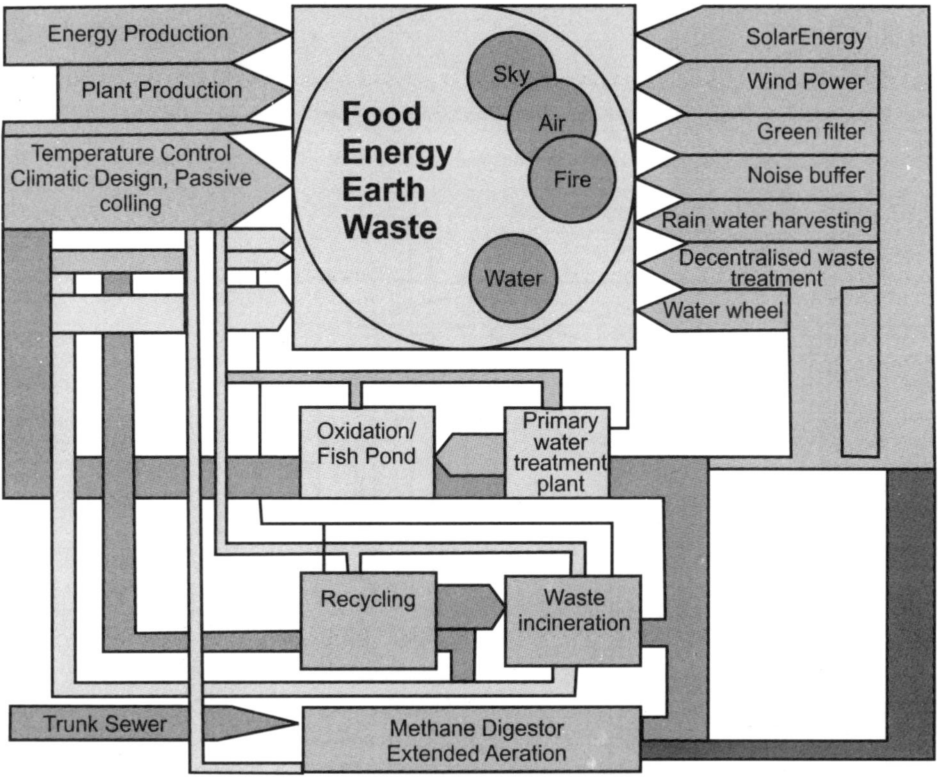


**Fig. 6.20 : The waste management process should embody the principle of circular metabolism, which means recycling wastes to produce energy, adoption of eco-technology for zero polluting energy (wind, solar and water wheel), development of green filters, noise buffers and rainwater harvesting.**

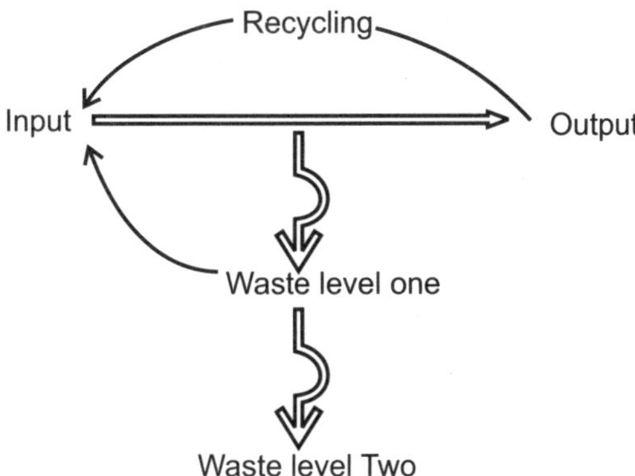


**Fig. 6.21 : Circular Metabolism**

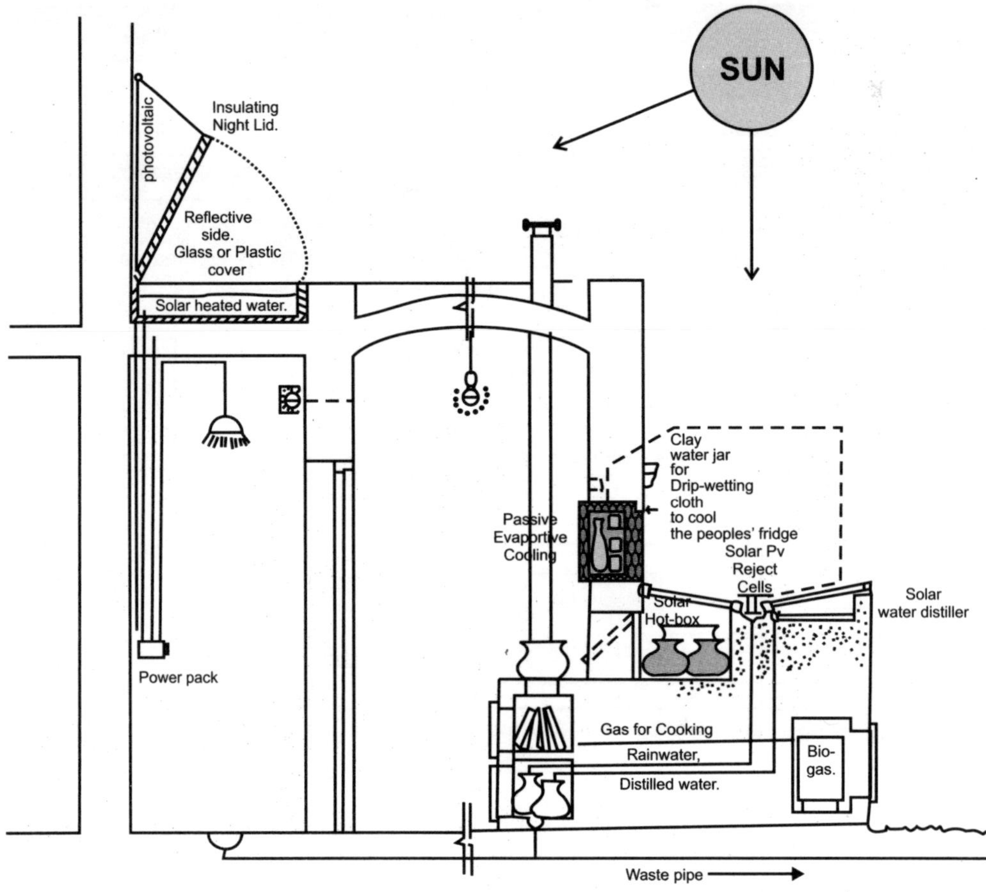


**Fig. 6.22 : Self contained Solar House using bio-gas, rainwater harvesting and waste recycling**

## Power Packs

- Can effectively replace small generators based on kerosene and petrol that cause pollution and noise.
- Installed in shops, clinics, banks etc, could provide power for lights, fans, computers, etc.

## Street Lights/Garden Lights

- Dusk to dawn systems of 74/75 Wp SPV modules with 11W/18W CFLs could be suitable for gardens roads, boundaries of hospitals and industrial units, etc. which do not require high intensity lighting.
- Increased use of solar lights can be help conserving electricity during evening peaks.

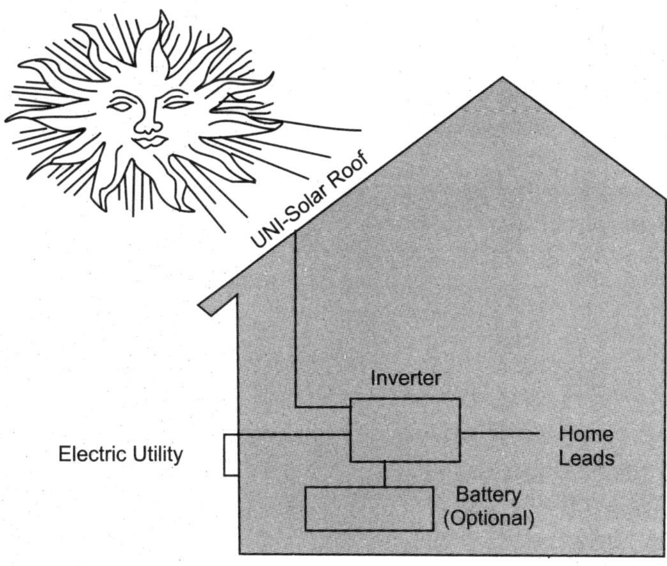


**Fig. 6.23 : Integrated Solar Photovoltaic is a new class of building products that combines Photo-voltaic technology not only to generate electricity, but also to serve as roof, walls, windows, skylights and building façade.**

# Bibliography

ADB (2001). Technical Assistance to India for conservation and Livelihoods Improvement in the Indian Sunderbans (TAR:IND 34272), Asian Development Bank, Manila.

Aggarwal, Anil & Sunita, Narain, (ed.) (1917). Dying Wisdom: Fall and Potential of India's Traditional Water Harvesting Systems. Centre for Science and Environment. New Delhi.

Axion G.H. & Nano (1997); Collaboration in International Rural Development, Sage, New Delhi.

Barton, Hugh, M. Grant and R. Guise, 2003, Shaping Neighbourhoods, Spon Press, London

Bagchi, A. (2005). 'Political and Administrative Realities of Employment Guarantee Scheme', *Economic and Political Weekly,* XL (42),c October 15, 2005.

Barrett, C., S. Holden, and D. Clay (2004). 'Can Food-for-Work Programmes Reduce Vulnerability, Discussion Paper, Agricultural University of Norway.

Behera, B. and V.R. Reddy (2002). 'Environment and Accountability Impact of Industrial Pollution on Rural Comunities', *Economic and Political Weekly,* January 19th, pp. 257-265.

Bhaduri, A., (2005). 'First Priority—Guaranteeing Employment and the Right to Information', *Economic and Political Weekly,* January 22.

Blair, W. Harry, (1996). Democracy. Equity and Common Property Resource Management in the Indian Subcontinent and Change, 17.

Bono, Edward de (1983), Atlas of Management Thinking, Penguin Books, England.

Bono, Edward de (1985), Six Thinking Hats, Viking Press, England.

Bon, E. Common Property Resources Two Case Studies, Economic and Political Weekly, 15 July.

Bodoland Territorial Council, 2010, An Achievement–2008-09, Kokrajhar, Assam.

Cairn Cross. And E.A.R. Quano, (1991) Surface Water Drainage for low income communities, WHO-UNEP, New York.

Chandrashekhar, H. (2005). 'Subsidy and Cost Sharing in Watershed Projects', *Economic and Political Weekly.* Discussion, August 27. Chattopadhyay, R. and E. Dufto (2004). 'Impact of Reservation in Panchayati Raj: Evidence from a Nationwide Ramdomised Experiment', *Economic and Political Weekly,* Vol. 39 No 9 Chambers, Robert (1192). *Rural Appraisal: Rapid, Relaxed, and Participatory.* Discussion Paper 311. Institute of Development Studies, University of Sussex, Susex.

Chand, R (1999), 'Emerging Crisis in Punjab Agriculture Severity and Options for Future', *Economic and Political Weekly,* 2, April.

Colins, (ed.) Applying Public Administration in Development: Guideposts to the Future. Chichester: Wiley.

CSE (2006). Rural Water Harvesting Case Studies, *http://www.rainwaterbarvesting.org/Rural// Community-based-initiative.btm,.*

Dreze, Jean and Sen, Amartya (1996). India-Economic Development and Social Opportunity, Oxford India paperbacks, New Delhi.

Dreze. J. (2005). 'Time to Clean Up', *Times of India,* Mumbai Edition, August 13.

Easaw, Thomas (2005), Integrated District Development Plan of Karunkaran, Govt. of Kerala (156)

Economic Times (2006). Off-farm Jobs Growing Faster than Workforce,' 13 June, New Delhi.

FSI. (1998). The State of Forests Report 1997, *Forest Survey of India.* Dehra Dun.

Godgil M. (1993). 'Biodiversity and India's Degraded Lands, *Ambio* Vol. 22 pp. 167-72.

Ghatak, Maitreesh and Maitreya Ghatak (2002). 'Recent Reforms in the Panchayat System in West Bengal; Towards Greater Participatory Governce', in Economic and Political Weekly, Vol. 39, No. 9.

Ghildiyal, S., More women opt for rural job scheme in Rajasthan', Times of India, Mumbai Edition, June 11.

Government of Assam, 2008, Economic Survey, 2007-08, Gwahati.

Government of Assam, 2008, Statistical Handbook, 2007, Gwahati.

Government of India, Ministry of Rural Development, 2006, NREGA: Objective and Salient Features of the Act, MORD, New Delhi.

Government of Kerala, State Planning Board and State Town and Country Planning Department, (2003) Integrated District Development Plan and Local Development Plan, Trivandrum.

Govt. of India, Census of India, 2001, Reports on 2001 Census. New Delhi.

GOI (2010) *Economic Survey 2009-10* Ministry of Finance, Government of India, New Delhi.

Goyal, Ashima (2006). 'Intentive Structures in the Employment Guarantee Scheme', IGIDR, Mubai.

Guha, Ramachandra and Juan Martinez-Alier (1998). *Varieties of Environmentalism: Essays North and South.* Oxford University Press, New Delhi.

Hahn, H.H (2000). 'Environmental Engineering Education in Europe, *Water 'Science and Technology,* Vol. 41, No. 2.

IDFC (2001). 'Six steps to Accelerate Privatisation of Electricity Distribution, IDFC, Mumbai.

Jain A.K. Feb. 2006, A Roadmap for Integrated Rural Development, Coordinates Journal. New Delhi.

Jain A.K., (1996). The Indian Megacity and Economic Reforms, Management Publishing Co., New Delhi.

Jain A.K., (1994), The Cities of Delhi, Management Pub. Co., Dehradun

Jain A.K. (2001): Ecology and Natural Resource, Management, Management Pub. Co., Dehradun.

Jain A.K. (2003) Actioning new partnerships for Indian Cities', Cities Journal (UK) 20, p. 353-359

Jain A.K., (1990), The Making of a Metropolis: The Planning and Growth of Delhi, National Book Organisation, New Delhi.

Jain A.K., (2007), School Buildings-Planning, Design & Management, JBA Publishers, New Delhi.

Jain A.K., (2008), Building Systems for Low Income Housing, 2$^{nd}$ Edition, JM Jaina, New Delhi.

Jain A.K., (2008), A Practical Guide to Disaster Management, Pragun, New Delhi.

Jain A.K., (2008), Low Carbon City—Policies, Planning and Practice, Discovery Publishers, New Delhi.

Jain A.K., (2009), Urban Housing and Slums, Readworthy Publications, New Delhi.

Jain A.K., (2009), Urban Land Policy & PPP, Readworthy Publishers, New Delhi.

Jain A.K. (2009), Urban Transport Planning & Management, APH Publishing, New Delhi.

Jain A.K., (2007), Water—A Manual for Engineers, Architects, Planners and Managers, Daya Publications, Delhi.

Jain A.K. (2011) Making Infrastructure Work, Discovery Publishers, New Delhi.

Jain A.K. (2011) Informal City, Readworthy Pub. New Delhi.

Johnson, Craig (2001), 'Local Democracy, Democratic Decentralization and Rural Development: Theories, Challenges and Options for Policy', *Development Policy Review,* 19(4), 521-32.

Johnson, Ronald W. and Henry P. Minis Jr. (1996). *Toward Democratic Decentralization: Approaches to Promoting Good Governance,* Discussion Paper, Research Triangle Park, Triangle Institute International.

Johnson, Kirk (2002). *Television and Social Change in Rural India,* Sage Publications, New Delhi.

Kalam, APJ Abdul, 2005, Indomitable Sprit, Rajpal & Sons, Delhi.

Kumar, Sudhir (2005). Indian Railways: A Turnaround Story', presentation made in ASSOCHAM seminar on Rail Freight Corridor, 30 June (mimeo).

Lanjouw, P. and A. Shariff (2002). Rural Non-Farm Employment in India: Access, Income and Poverty Impact', NCAER *Working Paper Series No. 81.* New Delhi.

Ledwith, Margaret, 1997, Community Development, P.P. Publishing.

Lewis, M.F., R. Lott and R. Prinseley (2003). 'The Role of Farm Forestry in Salinity Management', *National Dryland Salinity Program.*

Maria, A. (2003). The Costs of Water Pollution in India', Paper Presented at the conference on Market Development of Water & Waste Technologies through Environmental Economics, 30th-31st October 2003, New Delhi.

MOA (2006). Agricultural Statistics at a Glance 2006, Ministry of Agriculture, Government of India, New Delhi.

MoWR (1999). *National Commission for Integrated Water Resources Development Plan,* Ministry of Water Resources, New Delhi.

Menon, S. (2006). 'Village "Dole" takes Baby Steps amid Apathy, Graft' and subsequent series of articles on NREGS, Busines Standard, August 7.

MOP (2006). *Draft Hydro Power Policy* (May 2006), Ministry of Power New Delhi.

National Institute of Applied Economic Research (NCAER), 1996: The India Infrastructure Report, the Council, New Delhi.

Nauan, F, and D. Satterthwaire (2001). The Influence of Governance on the Provision of Urban Environmental Infrastructure and Service for Low-income Groups', *International Planning Studies,* Vol. 6, No. 4, pp. 409-26.

Pachauri, R.K. and P. Mehortra (2002.) Vision 2020: Sustainability of India's Material Resources, Planning Commission Working Paper New Delhi, downloaded from *http://planningcommission.nic.in/reports/generp/bkpa 2020/13_bg2020doc.*

Pandey, Suneel, Shaleen Singhal, Prgya Jaswal, and Janraj Guliani (2006). Urban Environment in 3i Network, India Infrastructure Report 2006: Urban Infrastructure, Oxford University Press, New Delhi.

Panda, M. Mishra, S. Kamdar, and M. Tondare (2005). 'Evaluation of Food-for-Work Component of Sampoorna Grameen Rozga Yojana in Selected Districts of Maharashtra', IGIDR, Mumbai: Report submitted to the Planning Commission.

Planning Commission (2005). 'Draft Report of the Expert Committee on Integrated Energy Policy', *Planning Commission,* Government of India, New Delhi.

Planning Commission (2006a). 'Towards Faster and More inclusive Growth, An Approach to the 11[th] Five Year Plan' *Planning Commission,* Government of India, New Delhi.

Planning Commission (2007). Eleventh Five Year Plan (2007-12),GOI, New Delhi.

Planning Commission (2002) India Vision 2020, New Delhi; Government of India, New Delhi.

Radhkrishna, R. (2002). 'Agricultural Growth, Employment and Poverty–A Policy Prespective', *Economic and Political Weekly,* 19 January.

Rajendran, S (2002). 'Pesticide Spraying in Kerala–Human Cost and Environmental Loss, *Economic and Political Weekly,* EPW Comentary, 8 June.

Rao, K. (2005). 'Should EGS be Universalised'. *The Economic Times,* August 23.

Rastogi, Anupam (2003). 'The Infrastructure Sector in India 2001-02' in 3iNetwork, *India Infrastructure Report 2003; Public Expenditure Allocation and Accountability,* New Delhi: Oxford University Press, New Delhi.

Ress, W. and Wackernagel, M. (1996). *Our Ecological Footprint: Reducing Human Impact on the Earth,* Gabiola Island, BC, New Society Publishers.

Ribot, Jesse C. (2002). *Democratic Decentralization of Natural Resources: Institutionalizing Popular Participation.* World Resources Institute Discussion Paper, World Resources Institute, Washington D.C.

Ribeiro, EFN, (2003), Metroplotion Vision in Context of Rapid Urbanisation AMDA, New Delhi.

Ryan, B. (2004). 'Ecological Footprint Analysis: An Irish Rural Study', *Irish Geography,* Vol. 37(2).

Sachs, Jeffery D. 2005 The End of Poverty: Economic Possibilities for Our Time, The Penguin Press, New York.

Sen Amartya, Development as Freedom, Alfred A. Knopf, Inc. New York.

Sengupta, N. (2002). 'Traditional vs. Modern Practices in Salinity control', *Economc and Political Weekly,* 37(13), March 30.

Sengupta, N. (2001), *A New Institutional Theory of Production: An Application,* New Delhi; Sage.

Terhal, P.andI., Hirway (1998). 'Rural Public Works and Food Entitlement Protection: Towards a Strategy for Preventing Hunger', in R. Radhakrishna and A. N. Shrma (eds)., *Empowering Rural Lobour in India: Markets, State and Mobilisation,* Institute for Human Development, New Delhi.

Terhal, P., I. Hirway, R. Radhakrishna, J.H. de Goede (1992). *Towards Employment Guarantee:* Report of the Indo-Dutch Fact Finding Mission, Government of the Netherlands, Rotterdam.

TRAI (2006). 'Allocation and Pricing of Spectrum for 3G Services and Broadband Wireless Access', Consultation Paper No. 9/ 2006, Telecom Regulatory Authority of India, New Delhi.

Three *i* Network, India Infrastructure Report, 2007, Oxford University Press, New Delhi.

V. Santhakumar (2006). *Understanding Social Opposition To Privatising Public Utilities,* The Centre for Development Studies, Thiruvanathapuram.

Vaidyanathan, A. (2005). 'Employment Guarantee: Need for Involvement of States', *Economic and Political Weekly,* August 13.

Virmani, A. (2005). Contribution to Economic Times debate 'Should NREGS be Universalised', Economic Times, Mumbai Edition, Tuesday, August 23.

World Bank (2004). *Country Stategy Paper for India,* The World Bank, Washington.

World Bank (2006). *'Reforming Public Services in India: Drawing Lessons From Success'.* World Bank: Washington.

Kokrajhar.gov.in.

Wikipedia.org/wiki/Kokrajhar_district

Kokrajhar.nic.in/aboutdist.htm

www.mord.nic.in

www.nrega.nic.in.

# Index

E



F



G



H



I



J



K



M



N



P